# Making Distance Education Work:
# Understanding Learning and Learners
# At a Distance

# Making Distance Education Work: Understanding Learning and Learners At a Distance

Edited by
S. Joseph Levine

LearnerAssociates.net

PRINTED IN THE UNITED STATES OF AMERICA

Visit our website at http://www.LearnerAssociates.net

First edition published 2005
by
LearnerAssociates.net LLC
1962 Pawnee Trail
Okemos, Michigan 48864 USA

ISBN 1-4116-5355-6

*To Keith Stein, a wonderful musician and talented educator who not only taught me how to play the clarinet but demonstrated over and over again the power of being concerned about me – the learner. His genuineness as an educator had profound impact on so many.*

*To Ted Ward, my colleague, friend and mentor who challenged me to understand technology, to look to the learners beyond it, and to understand the power of reflection. His wisdom has helped me navigate so many things in my career as an educator.*

*To my students, who have provided an unending source of understanding, insight and inspiration. I value the opportunity that each has allowed me for assisting their journey in some small way as they have moved to become my colleagues.*

# Table of Contents

## Part Three: Implementing Distance Education  139

*Distance education was invented for me!*

That may sound like a rather arrogant statement. However, for many years I really felt that way. My interests in life seem to have evolved around the joining of communication technology and education – distance education. Let me try and explain.

I have always been fascinated with communication technology. I still have a very clear vision of the old Philco radio in the living room when I was a child. The circular dial was marked with call letters and locations of stations all over the world. And when I really push my memory I can still remember sitting around the radio, blackout shades pulled, with my parents listening for the latest news from the war in Europe.

Not content with the old Philco, in Junior High School I built my own radio receiver and began listening to foreign short wave stations, sending reports to them, and waiting to receive their cards confirming my report. By the time I got to high school I had received my amateur radio license, was busy talking via Morse code with "hams" across the globe and my mother quickly got into the habit of asking me every morning before I left for school, "Is everything in your bedroom unplugged? The house won't blow up, will it?"

It was also at this time that I began to realize that my years of clarinet lessons could become a source of revenue for the purchase of new electronics. I began helping other kids in the neighborhood learn how to play the clarinet. I started to learn how to teach.

As I marched forward in life, the areas of communication technology and education have always been there. In the mid 1960s, as a new graduate student majoring in education, I was able to fund my studies with a contract I received from the Library of Congress to create an extensive set of recorded materials that could assist a blind person to learn how to play a musical instrument. I was excited by the idea that it was possible to use technology to extend educational opportunity to learners via the mail and recordings.

By the 1970s things were really moving along quite well. My doctoral dissertation in Curriculum Research incorporated the use of a speech compressor to better understand the rate at which school children preferred to listen to recorded stories. (They do have a preference. And, it's for a speed faster than we typically speak.). At about the same time my next door neighbor, an accountant, dragged over his new 15 pound programmable calculator (it was a portable!) and we spent most of the night learning how to program it to do routine mathematical equations. We were so pleased with ourselves at being able to learn how to use this new marvel.

Then, in the early 80s I bought my first computer. I had arrived. I had my own computer! Nothing like computers we see today, this small 12 ounce box with it's membrane keyboard sat there doing absolutely nothing until you programmed it to do something. I was able to create a handful of nonsensical interactive routines that the computer displayed on our television. And, when I was fortunate, I would convince one of our young daughters to be my test pilot, playing a simple little game or two that would mysteriously disappear if you accidentally bumped the case.

My early technological beginnings soon became a point of strength for me. I was comfortable with most communication technologies and busy exploring their potential. It wasn't long before I was creating small group training materials using audio recordings, designing what I called "Local Learning Seminars" that were a combination of video-taped recordings and two-way telephone conference calls, and linking my graduate seminars across the state using a CODEC two-way interactive television system. Satellite uplinks were expensive but certainly had potential. And, of course, when the Internet arrived the excitement then grew for linking learners via interactive discussion boards to share ideas.

But by this time I had grown comfortable with the technology and the real excitement for me was the content of all of this technology-based activity. My content was adult learning – how to understand and effectively teach learners who were self-directing and responsible for their own learning.

Yes, distance education was invented for me. Almost by design I had invested my energies, for a number of years, in the two areas that I now understood were the essential elements in effective distance education – a command of the technology and an understanding of the learner. By being comfortable in both I realized it was possible to be effective as a distance educator. One without the other was an unbalanced situation that could not fulfill the learning potential offered by distance education.

As I have worked with educators to help them learn the power of distance education I have become aware that the technology of distance education can be blinding. Educators are challenged to immerse themselves in new technology, create programs that draw on the very latest devices, and look for ways to bridge large distances quickly and efficiently. No sooner have we mastered one piece of software then we are faced with a newer, bigger and better one. Simple graphics on a website yield to PowerPoint slide presentations and then give way to streaming video. Every corner we turn seems to point us toward new technology.

I have been concerned that the learner has become a secondary focus for many educators involved with distance education. I worry that the technology is the driving force for the creation of many new distance education programs.

This book is an attempt to help bring the learner back into balance as a key factor in distance education. Without a strong concern for the learner, even the best communication technology in the world has little potential for helping bring about change at a distance.

The original impetus for this book which encourages a learner view of distance education was from a group of learners I know well – participants in one of my graduate seminars. This group of students, who I now look to as colleagues, all shared a similar concern for learner-focused pedagogy in distance education. Their voice was strong and could not be ignored.

On these pages are assembled the ideas and experiences of an unbelievably talented group of friends, colleagues and former students – each one a powerful contributor in his or her own right to the furtherance of distance education that is drawn from a concern for the learner. As I have worked with each one of these authors I have had my own views challenged, enhanced and reinforced. It has been an exciting journey that has further strengthened my commitment to the furtherance of learner-focused distance education. My wish is that it may have the same affect on you as it has on me.

S. Joseph Levine

# Acknowledgements

As with all projects of this nature, there are a number of people who need to be acknowledged.

- Susan Crane was the first to take the many different files and create a single manuscript that flowed from section to section.

- Noorie helped create a readable format for the book and got the various graphics to behave.

- Alicia Burnell brought her expert graphic art abilities to bear on the creation of the cover design.

- Falinda Geerling spent numerous hours fixing what I thought was good English so that the ideas and concepts on the page would be understood by the reader.

- Participants in my online workshops used the different drafts of the book as the basis for spirited discussions on many of the topics.

- And, my wife Robbie deserves a medal for her patience in listening to my endless reading of confusing paragraphs to her so she could help steer me toward what really needed to be said.

A big *Thank You* to each of you for your help.

# Part One:
# Foundations for Distance Education

**Key concepts and ideas which are basic to the success of distance education as an instructional tool to empower learners.**

Distance Education: A Shared Understanding
*S. Joseph Levine*

Glossary of Key Terms and Concepts in Distance Education
*Diane Sams*

Creating a Foundation for Learning Relationships
*S. Joseph Levine*

Mobilizing Needed Resources for Distance Education
*Kathleen E. Guy*

Instructional Design Considerations For Distance Education Programs
*S. Joseph Levine*

Evaluation in Distance Education
*S. Joseph Levine*

# Chapter 1

# Distance Education:
# A Shared Understanding

## S. Joseph Levine

*Side by side with the development of radio and television, human ingenuity is evolving another method of aerial correspondence. I refer to the immediate transfer by radio of facsimile documents through the ether. Man writes a letter and - presto! - its exact image appears somewhere 3,000 miles away...Ether delivery will one day be developed so that I will be able to write a letter at my desk and have that letter transmitted in facsimile almost instantly to Australia. My correspondent in Australia should be able to reply within a few minutes. Then it would not take more time to transmit his reply than to dictate the letter...We have not reached this point as yet, but it is a development that will come within our lifetime.*

**After Television - What?**
David Sarnoff
October 10, 1936

What a tremendous vision, and the vision was occurring in 1936! David Sarnoff, the president of RCA, was clearly captivated by the idea that the "ether" could be used to carry an exact image of the printed word back and forth between people living at considerable distance from each other. And clearly the feature that most excited Sarnoff was the idea that it could be done instantaneously. There would be no need to wait for days – even weeks or months – to gain feedback on one's ideas. It could happen almost immediately.

And so was established yet another marker in the journey to establish new tools to speed our ability to communicate with one another via technology. Starting slowly at first, that journey today has taken on such tremendous speed that we get dizzy thinking about what our communication technology looked like only a few short months ago.

Thinking back in history for a minute, only 35 years before Sarnoff's vision Marconi had successfully broadcast the first wireless signal across the Atlantic Ocean. And at that time Marconi was happy with his success at transmitting just the code for the letter "S" – not a facsimile of an entire page of information as General Sarnoff would dream. Furthermore, if we were to push the clock back an additional 25 years before Marconi's accomplishment, we would find Alexander Graham Bell still tinkering with the design of what would eventually be his invention of the telephone.

And to think that today we get frustrated when a worldwide web page takes more than a second or two to load onto our computer!

So here we are bursting at the seams with more communication technology than even Bell, Marconi or Sarnoff could ever imagine. We are not only able to send a facsimile copy of something to Australia and back in a fraction of a second, but the technology guarantees the communication will be free of errors, in vivid color, and our computer will even play a small tune when it arrives. Today, we enjoy an unbelievable array of technology to fulfill just about any dream that we could have when it comes to communication.

As we know, however, communication that is truly effective is only partly a function of the technology that is used or its speed. The larger part of good communication is the design of the message that is being sent. Although it is exciting to be able to transmit messages at lightning speed around the world, unless the design of the message fulfills its function it doesn't matter how quickly it can be delivered! The key to effective communication is the use to which we put the technology.

## The Learner in Distance Education

Distance education is an area of practice that draws significantly on the power of technology. Yet it must focus more heavily on the instructional aspects of the communication process in order to facilitate learning. The challenge is to keep the many parts of a distance education teaching and learning system in balance. For most of us, however, the brightness of the technology can often blind our view of the variety of essential considerations that are foundational in distance education. And first among these considerations is the learner. Reid (1995) suggests that "…managing learning support will bring many challenges, but its success in any institution will be underpinned by the sharing of a common vision and model of support which places the learner firmly at the centre of *everyone's* efforts" (p. 274).

Tait (1995) supports Reid with his concern that the development of open and distance learning (ODL) systems must begin with an understanding of who the students are rather than starting with the production of the course materials. "Who are your students? This central question lies at the heart of the issue, and yet is often ignored. The question, though short and to the point, is one of considerable depth and complexity. It is not an original observation to say that education has represented a provider-led rather than a client- or consumer-led activity. ODL systems that start with the production of course materials in whatever medium can also ignore in important ways the consideration as to who their students are" (p. 233).

Probably the most essential characteristic of the successful learner in a distance education teaching and learning environment is that the learner must be willing and able to be **self-directing**. Such a self-directing learner is one who is able to take responsibility for his or her own learning agenda. Deciding what to learn, how to learn it, when to learn it, and when the learning goal has been achieved are all important aspects that a self-directing learner must consider. For distance education to make a serious and constructive impact on an individual demands that the individual be a full and active participant in the learning environment. In other words, **a learner who is accepting and exercising responsibility for his or her own learning**.

Why is self-direction such an important consideration in distance education? Any time there is an instructional system that is removed from the learner because of location, the teacher loses a significant amount of control over the learner. And, of course, control by the teacher often plays a major role in the teaching and learning environment. Without a lot of teacher control, the situation we most often find in distance education, the assumption is that the learner will step in and exercise the needed control to make learning successful.

This student-directed learning can be very exciting when it happens. As a teacher, it's a wonderful feeling to be involved with a group of learners who are willing to accept responsibility for learning. However, in many cases the very opposite can be true. The learner can be acting in very dependent ways and working hard to avoid accepting responsibility. This situation can be disastrous in a distance education setting and can often leave the teacher without the power to facilitate or direct much learning.

One of the many challenges for the distance education teacher then is to recognize this need for self-directedness on the part of the learner and to begin to build it from the very beginning of the program. Evans and Nation (1989) push this idea even further when they suggest that the foundation to self-directedness is critical reflection and must be practiced by both the teachers and the students. "The process of critical reflection is continuous and leads to a set of transformatory practices through which students (and teachers) become competent, self-directed learners. The process of critical reflection is not just about distance teachers reflecting on their practices but is also about critical reflections in distance education. In this sense both distance teachers and students are engaged in a reciprocal teaching-learning/action-reflection process which leads to each other's understanding of themselves and the social conditions of their existence" (p. 252).

In later chapters specific strategies will be described for assisting students in distance education to assume a meaningful and responsible role as self-directing learners. This is truly a challenge for distance educators – to be concerned not only about the content of the instruction, but also the instructional strategies that clearly foster the emergence of self-directed learners and the growth of learner responsibility. When both agenda are working; that is, content is being delivered well and learner responsibility is being strengthened, then the power of teaching at a distance can be fully realized.


## Who controls the learning environment in distance education?

As we focus our attention on learning and the learner we must also explore the wider framework of distance education and consider the issue of exactly who exercises control in the learning environment. Distance education, more than many other educational initiatives, provides the potential for a distribution of the power of control in the educational setting.

Writing from a perspective of higher education, Dirr (1990) describes four barriers of access and equity that can prevent a learner from controlling his or her education and deriving full value in higher education.

> "The first barrier is one of distance (i.e. for many people educational sites are too distant to encourage them to take advantage of the programs offered). The second barrier is time (i.e. available courses are not offered at times convenient to the busy schedules of many of today's adults). Study after study has shown that most college students today juggle schedules that include responsibilities to family, job and community, and often conflict with college schedules. The third barrier is access to rich resources (e.g. library and laboratory materials) needed to get the most out of college courses. Finally, there is the barrier of cost." (p. 398)

Distance education offers significant potential for reducing these barriers and putting more control in the hands of the learner.

Starting with the advent of the printed page, there has been a continuing development of media. This development has made receiving information a more efficient and effective process, which can be controlled by the receiver or the learner. This ability for the learner to control his or her own learning has made a tremendous leap ahead in recent years with the development of the worldwide web and is certain to continue in unforeseen ways in the future. This equity of control between the learner and the teacher is sure to be an ongoing strength of distance education as it blends both formal and nonformal education in a balanced and dynamic learning environment.

## Why call it distance "education" and not distance "learning"?

Although the field seems to be split between the use of "distance education" and "distance learning", we will consistently use the term "distance education" throughout. This distinction might seem strange in light of the concern for learning that forms the foundation for these writings. However, using Maslow's humanistic view of psychology as a base, we began with the assumption that learning is something that is a very personal phenomenon that goes on within the learner. Maslow (1962) states, "We can no longer think of the person as "fully determined" where this phrase implies "determined only by forces external to the person." The person, insofar as he *is* a real person, is his own main determinant" (p.36).

In other words, the learner is in control of his or her own learning. And in the best of all possible worlds, the educator is able to contribute to the individual's learning agenda through meaningful and appropriate instruction.

Within this view then to suggest that there can be "distance learning"; that is, implying that learning can go on away from the learner makes little sense. Certainly, however, it is possible and correct to use a phrase such as "learning that is stimulated by instruction from a distance." The key is that the instruction is that which is at a distance and not the learning.

Moore (1990) adds further clarity to the use of the phrase "distance education" when he reflects on the historical roots of the phrase.

> "After nearly half a century of practice a group of mostly American and Canadian correspondence educators, most but not all from university extension divisions, met in Vancouver, Canada, in 1938 to form an organization which they called the International Council for Correspondence Education (ICCE). Conferences of these correspondence educators were held about every four years, and it was at the conference in Warrenton, Virginia, in 1972 that the use of the term "distance education" in English, and the concept of distance as a dimension of teaching and learning, was introduced. The use of the term was proposed after a search for a name that would describe not only correspondence instruction, but a whole family of teaching-learning arrangements that had emerged in the 1960s. These arrangements had the common characteristic that the learner and teacher were normally separated, geographically and often in time, and the communication that normally in education occurred by word of mouth in a classroom was carried by correspondence, and, increasingly, by electronic media. These media came to include not only radio and television broadcasting, but audio and video recording, and teleconferencing through computer modems, telephone, satellite and microwave systems" (p. xiv).

## So what exactly is distance education?

Distance education is the process of helping people learn when they are separated by time or location from the more typical "live" face-to-face learning environments that most of us have grown up with. According to Moore (1990), "Distance education consists of all arrangements for providing instruction through print or electronic communications media to persons engaged in planned learning in a place or time different from that of the instructor or instructors" (pg. xv).

Distance education that is designed well empowers the learner through an increased ability to exercise control over the sequence and pace of the instruction, along with the opportunity to be able to have such control at a time and location that is most convenient to the learner. A helpful way to conceptualize distance education and when it is most appropriately used is through a 2 x 2 matrix that compares time with location. Table 1 presents such a matrix and identifies the types of learning environments that can be created in each of the four quadrants when time and location variables are viewed in their extreme.

In Table 1 the factors of Time and Location are only presented as extremes. Certainly there are numerous learning environments that are designed at a variety of points along the continuum from "same time" to "times that are convenient" and the continuum from "same location" to "locations that are convenient." However, Table 1 serves as a guide when considering the variables that help define whether a learning environment can be considered distance education. But does this mean that all distance education courses must emanate from only Quadrant 3 and Quadrant 4?

## Must an entire course be technologically mediated in order for it to be considered distance education?

We are now beginning to get a sense of when a learning environment is rather typical – Quadrant 1 and Quadrant 2 – and when it begins to have characteristics that make it clearly viable as a distance education candidate – Quadrant 3 and Quadrant 4. However, it is not necessary for an entire sequence of instruction to be delivered in a mediated form in order for the instruction to be considered distance education. A course does not have to be exclusively in a single quadrant. A course can be made up of a variety of different strategies or components that effectively move the course in and out of different quadrants. In other words, it is very possible to take a rather traditional looking course, class, or program and to effectively integrate the use of distance education to support and enhance learning by varying the learning environment.

**Table 1**
**Learning Environments as a Function of Time and Location**

| | | | Time | |
| --- | --- | --- | --- | --- |
| | | | ⟷ | |
| | | | Instructional activities are designed with the assumption that all learners will be together at the **SAME TIME.** | Instructional activities are designed with the assumption that learners will be available for instruction at **TIMES THAT ARE CONVENIENT** to each individual. |
| Location | ↑↓ | Instructional activities are designed with the assumption that all learners will be together at the **SAME LOCATION.** | *Quadrant 1* In-person learning environments that bring learners and teachers together. | *Quadrant 2* Replicable learning environments that allow learners to learn independently at a single defined location. |
| | | Instructional activities are designed with the assumption that learners will be available for instruction at **LOCATIONS THAT ARE CONVENIENT** to each individual. | *Quadrant 3* Synchronous learning environments that are enhanced by using technology to allow learners and teacher to meet together at the same time though at a distance from each other. | *Quadrant 4* Asynchronous learning environments that are enhanced by using technology to allow learners and teacher to exchange ideas at times convenient to each and at a distance from each other. |

For instance, considering a situation where a course operates at one time or another in all four of the quadrants may sound rather ambitious, but it is now occurring much more frequently. The course begins in Quadrant 1 in a face-to-face situation, using a traditional classroom. Course objectives are clarified, teacher and learners get to know each other, and dialogue begins. In other words the Quadrant 1 aspect of the course becomes the foundation of the course. To help everyone in the class gain access to needed readings, the instructor can add a Quadrant 2 component whereby a special reading shelf of "reserved" publications are placed in the library and made available to the students. Periodically Quadrant 4 asynchronous activities are added to the instruction by using the worldwide web to put the learners in touch with content posted by the instructor on the course website and to move the learners to additional content at distant websites. A web-based course bulletin board can also allow for asynchronous threaded discussions on a variety of topics. Moreover, as the semester progresses there will most likely be times when instructor and learners will want to "get together" outside of the scheduled class times to discuss key ideas and concepts. These meetings could easily be accomplished by adding a Quadrant 3 synchronous learning component through the use of a chatroom. In short, the use of multiple quadrants in a teaching situation can tremendously enhance the learning environment.

By using a broad and encompassing view of distance education, it is possible to begin to understand the complexity of what can go on in a teaching and learning environment. A multitude of arrangements can be created to capitalize on the best learning opportunities from all four quadrants in Table 1. The challenge in distance education is not to attempt to remove all aspects of face-to-face learning. The challenge in distance education is to enrich the learning environment through appropriate selection and use of instructional strategies that are drawn from all four quadrants.

## Must you have a teacher to have distance education?

Using premises upon which the study of adult learning is founded, we have adopted the view that learning and education do not necessarily require a teacher. Merriam and Caffarella (1991) state,

> Learning on one's own, being self-directed in one's learning is itself a context in which learning takes place. The key to placing a learning experience within this context is that the learner has the primary responsibility for planning, carrying out, and evaluating his or her own learning. Participation in self-directed learning seems almost universal – in fact, an estimated 90 percent of the population is involved with at least one self-directed learning activity a year. (p. 54)

This broader view of adult learning allows us to consider a greater spectrum of designed learning experiences that are both formal and nonformal in nature and include one or more distance education learning segments. Ward (1984) has provided a very helpful set of definitions of formal and nonformal education. He describes formal education as very school-like and having characteristics that are "...deliberate, planned, staffed, financially supported, using time-and-space fixed procedures" (p. 2) Nonformal education is also described by Ward (1984) as deliberate, planned, staffed and financially supported. However, he goes on to say that nonformal education, "is also functional, unrestricted as to time and place and, in general, responsive to need" (p. 5).

More importantly, however, Ward (1984) makes a strong point in saying that nonformal education must not be seen merely as a methodology: "Nonformal education borrows its methodologies widely. Although some instructional methods are more appropriate, others less, defining nonformal education as a particular methodology blurs the important distinctions" (p. 5).

He further states, with similar caution, that nonformal education should not be considered as a new term created especially for adult learners since it has often been used with children. And likewise it should not be considered as a new way of describing continuing education since continuing education is almost always concerned with the furthering of an educational experience that has its roots in formal education.

Similarly, distance education must not be restricted to a single and simplistic view of a learning environment, limited only to a certain set of instructional technologies, focused on one set of outcomes or responding to only a particular type of learner. Distance education must be seen in its broadest and most inclusive manner. It cannot be seen exclusively as a teacher-or-institution-designed-and-controlled, formal education phenomena. Distance education must be viewed in the context of facilitating learning for a vast array of learners, unique to each learner due to the conditions of his or her environment and the learning agenda each is attempting to fulfill. To be successful, distance education must be seen as powerful both to the institution and the learner in fulfilling their goals of teaching and learning.

## References

Dirr, P. J. (1990). Distance education: policy considerations for the year 2000. In M. Moore (Ed.), *Contemporary issues in American distance education* (pp. 397-405). Oxford: Pergamon Press.

Evans, T., & Nation, D. (1989). Critical reflections in distance education. In T. Evans & D. Nation (Eds.), *Critical reflections on distance education* (pp. 237-252). London: The Falmer Press.

Reid, J. (1995). Managing learning support. In F. Lockwood (Ed.), *Open and distance learning today*. London: Routledge.

Sarnoff, D. (1936). After television - what?". *Liberty Magazine*, 13(41), p. 49.

Maslow, A. H. (1962) Some basic propositions of a growth and self-actualization psychology. In *Perceiving, behaving, becoming: a new focus for education*. Washington: Association for Supervision and Curriculum Development.

Merriam, S. B. and Caffarella, R. S. (1991) *Learning in Adulthood*. San Francisco: Jossey-Bass.

Moore, M. (1990). Introduction: Background and overview of contemporary American distance education. In M. Moore (Ed.), *Contemporary issues in American distance education*. Oxford: Pergamon Press.

Tait, A. (1995). Student support in open and distance learning. In F. Lockwood (Ed.), *Open and distance learning today* (pp. 232-241). London: Routledge.

Ward, T. (1984). Nonformal education -- what is it?." In Ward, T., Levine, S.J., Joesting, L. and Crespo, D (Eds.), *Nonformal education: reflections on the first dozen years*. East Lansing, MI: Institute for International Studies in Education.

# Chapter 2

# Glossary of Key Terms and Concepts in Distance Education

## Diane Sams

**Andragogy:**

Approach to education promoted by Knowles and premised on at least four crucial assumptions about the characteristics of adult learners that are different from the assumptions about child learners on which traditional pedagogy is premised. A fifth was added later. (1) Self-concept: As a person matures his self concept moves from one of being a dependent personality toward one of being a self-directed human being. (2) Experience: As a person matures he accumulates a growing reservoir of experience that becomes an increasing resource for learning. (3) Readiness to learn. As a person matures his readiness to learn becomes oriented increasingly to the developmental tasks of his social roles. (4) Orientation to learning. As a person matures his time perspective changes from one of postponed application of knowledge to immediacy of application, and accordingly his orientation toward learning shifts from one of subject-centeredness to one of problem centeredness. (5) Motivation to learn: As a person matures the motivation to learn is internal (Smith, 2002).

**Asynchronous:**

Not occurring at the same time. Asynchronous communication does not require that the participants be connected to the communication device at the same time (The CMC Resource Site, 2002).

**Behaviorism/Behavioristic Psychology:**

Belief that learning results in an observable change in the learner's behavior. Learning involves controlling the environment to obtain a desired response. (Robinson, 1995)

**Chat:**

Two or more individuals connected to the Internet have real-time text-based conversations by typing messages into their computer. Groups gather to chat about various subjects. As you type, everything you type is displayed to the others of the chat group (Texas A&M, n.d.).

**Collaborative learning:**

A learning environment in which individual learners support and add to an emerging pool of knowledge of a group; emphasizes peer relationships as learners work together creating learning communities (Moore & Shattuck, 2001).

**Constructivism:**

School of human learning which believes in the need to identify current learning prior to constructing new meaning. Knowledge is seen as a mental construct that is built on and added to. Learners create an image of what the world is like and how it operates and they adapt and transform their understanding of new experiences in light of what they already "know." This theory of learning has consequences for teaching and learning strategies. Educators must recognize how a learner already sees the world, and how that learner believes it to operate.

New information presented to the learner will be modified by what the learner already knows and believes. By starting 'where the learner is at,' that is, engaging prior knowledge with present learning, the educator assists the students to build on her understanding of the world and its workings (NEIU, n.d.)

**Correspondence education**:
First generation in the evolution of distance education: with the advent of postal delivery in the mid 1880s, interaction between learners and teachers at a distance was possible for the first time. In the United States, correspondence became known later as "independent study" and "home study" before becoming recognized as part of the expanding field of "distance education." Interaction by surface mail is still widely used, especially in less developed countries (Moore & Kearsley, 1996, pp. 20, 36, 199).

**Curriculum model**:
The structure in which a program of study is offered. Distance education courses of study are divided into either a subject-matter-oriented curriculum model or a competency-oriented model. The distinction is an important consideration for design, delivery, and assessment (Moore & Shattuck, 2001).

**Delivery medium**:
The physical means of providing a distance education program. The delivery medium could include audio, video, computer, print, and combinations of all (Schlosser & Simonson, 2003).

**Distance education**:
Education in which the student and instructor are physically separated from each other and use technology—such as TV or the Internet—to complete the instruction. (PBS Advice Center, n.d.).

**Distance education consortium**:
Two or more distance education institutions or units who share in designing distance education courses, teaching them, or both (Moore & Shattuck, 2001).

**Distance education institution**:
College, university or school system organized exclusively for distance education (Moore & Shattuck, 2001). A "unimodal" distance education institution as compared to a dual mode conventional institution which adopts distance education courses and programs. (Cookson, 2000)

**Distance education program**:
"Distance education activities carried out in a conventional college, university, school system, or training department whose primary responsibilities include traditional classroom instruction" (Moore & Kearsley, 1996, p. 2).

**Distance education system**:
All the component processes that result in distance education, including learning, teaching, communication, design, management, and evaluation (Moore & Shattuck, 2001).

**Distance learning**:
What happens as a result of distance education (PBS Advice Center, n.d.).

**Dialog/Dialogue:**

>Interplay of words, actions, ideas, and any other interactions between teacher and learner; determined by the educational philosophy underlying the course; influenced by size of learning group and the learners' language (Moore & Kearsley, 1996, p. 201).

**Emoticons:**

>Also known as Smileys. These are symbols used to add emotional expression to a text-based statement (Schlosser & Simonson, 2003). (See also Smiley)

**F2F:**

>Initials for "face-to-face." Traditional classroom instruction where teacher and learners are together in the same room. (Schlosser & Simonson, 2003).

**Facilitation:**

>Assisting/guiding approach ("guide-on-the-side") to a learning situation; can be contrasted to the directive teacher-instructor ("sage-on-the-stage") approach. Heavily influenced by humanistic psychology (Moore & Shattuck, 2001).

**Flaming:**

>An asocial behavior whose sole purpose of communication is to provoke a negative emotional response in another member of an online community (The CMC Resource Site, 2002). An angry response to a written statement over the Internet (Schlosser & Simonson, 2003).

**HTML:**

>"The *lingua franca* for publishing hypertext on the World Wide Web. HTML uses tags such as <h1> and </h1> to structure text into headings, paragraphs, lists, hypertext links, etc." (W3C, 2003)

**Humanism/Humanistic Psychology:**

>A view of learning as having a quality of personal involvement, being self-initiated, pervasive, evaluated by the learner, and the essence of which is meaning. (Rogers, 1969)

**Hyperlink/Hotlink:**

>An image or portion of text on a Web page that is linked to another Web page, either on the same site or at another Web site. Clicking on the link takes the user to another Web page, or to another place on the same page. Words or phrases which serve as links are underlined, or appear in a different color, or both. Images that serve as links have a border around them, or they change the cursor to a little hand as it passes over them (GetNetWise, 2003).

**Hypermedia:**

>A hypermedia document may contain text, graphics, photography, animation, sound, music and video, interrelated, in a non-sequential fashion, via hypertext links (hyperlinks/hotlinks). World Wide Web publications are commonly referred to as hypermedia (Academic Computer Center, 1995).

**Learner autonomy:**

>"Concept that learners have different capacities for making decisions regarding their own learning." Relates to the structure and interactive expectations of a distance education course. A key element in adult learning (Moore & Kearsley, 1996, pp. 24-25, 204-205).

**Learner-centered education**:

An educational philosophy in which the needs of the individual are primary; therefore, the teaching and learning process provides flexible sequences of study, negotiated objectives and content, negotiated learning methods, negotiated methods of assessment and a choice of support mechanisms (PBS, n.d.).

**Learning platform**:

A generic term for types of software that support all kinds of asynchronous group communication. Its main feature is the threaded discussion. The more advanced learning platforms include the option to constitute study groups for collaboration, and folders for students to post assignments to the instructor. (Hülsmann, 2003).

**Listserv**:

An e-mail program that allows multiple computer users to send and receive messages on a single system. Listserv software is frequently used to administer electronic bulletin boards (Schlosser & Simonson, 2003).

**LOL**:

Initials for "laughing out loud" (Schlosser & Simonson, 2003).

**Netiquette**:

Contraction of "Internet etiquette", the etiquette guidelines for posting messages to online services, and particularly Internet newsgroups. Netiquette covers not only rules to maintain civility in discussions (i.e., avoiding flames), but also special guidelines unique to the electronic nature of forum messages. For example, netiquette advises users to use simple formats because complex formatting may not appear correctly for all readers. In most cases, netiquette is enforced by fellow users who will vociferously object if you break a rule of netiquette (Webopedia, 2003).

**Open learning**:

An educational philosophy that emphasizes providing learners with choices about media, place of study, pace of study, support mechanisms and entry and exit points (PBS, n.d.).

**Pedagogy**:

Literally means the art and science of teaching children. Pedagogy is often used as a synonym for teaching. Pedagogy embodies teacher-focused education as opposed to learner-focused education (andragogy). (NEIU, n.d.).

**Self-directed learning**:

The ability to exercise "learner autonomy." No one is autonomous at all times or able to be fully self-directed as a learner at all times, but the development of these capacities is the aim of many educational philosophies. The teacher aims to transfer to the learner the skills associated with teaching, i.e., to decide what ought to be learned, the most effective means of learning it, and to know realistically and correctly when the learning has been achieved (Moore & Kearsley, 1996, p. 119-120).

**Shouting**:

Sending email or discussion messages in all UPPER CASE LETTERS is known as "shouting." It is usually considered rude to shout in online communication, but can be used in moderation for emphasis (The CMC Resource Site, 2002).

**Smiley:**

These are also known as emoticons. They are graphic symbols used in place of the voice to add emotion to words (Schlosser & Simonson, 2003).

**Synchronous:**

Occurring at the same time. Synchronous communication requires that participants be connected to the communication device at the same time (The CMC Resource Site, 2002).

**Systems approach:**

Application of industrial principles including recognition of the division of labor and of specializations where teams of specialists work together to provide quality education. Includes carefully planned integration of the full range of technology and human resources so that each operates to maximum efficiency and effectiveness (Moore & Shattuck, 2001).

**Threaded discussion:**

A type of discussion forum in which each original message and all of its replies are linked together. The "thread" is analogous to a conversational thread. The benefit of threaded discussion is that it is easier to follow the conversation (The CMC Resource Site, 2002).

**Transactional distance:**

Theory developed by Michael Moore which emphasizes that distance is a pedagogical/andragogical phenomenon which must be addressed by design curriculum, forms of communication and interactions, and management of distance education programs (Moore & Kearsley, 1996).

**Uploading:**

The transfer of copies of a file from the user's own computer to a database or other computer. The reverse of downloading (Texas A&M, n.d.).

**Virtual university:**

A higher education institution that has no physical classrooms. Instruction at a virtual university is delivered to students at-a-distance (PBS, n.d.).

# References

Academic Computer Center. (1995). *Glossary.* University of Illinois at Chicago. Retrieved March 6, 2005, from http://www.uic.edu/depts/adn/webclass/glossary.html

Cookson, P. S. (2000). Transformation of the academy, institutional coevolution, and expansion of higher distance education: Steering through the rapids. Retrieved March 6, 2005, from http://ccism.pc.athabascau.ca/html/ccism/deresrce/taiwan_paper.html

GetNetWise. (2003). *Guide to internet terms: A glossary.* Retrieved March 6, 2005, from http://www.getnetwise.org/glossary

Hülsmann, T. (2003). Texts that talk back – asynchronous conferencing: A possible form of academic discourse?. In U. Bernath and E. Rubin (Eds.), *Reflections on teaching and learning in an online master program* (pp. 79-120). Germany: Bibliotheks- und Informationssystem der Carl von Ossietzky Universität Oldenburg

Moore, M. G., & Kearsley, G. (1996). *Distance education: A systems view.* Belmont, CA: Wadsworth Publishing Co.

Moore, M. G., & Shattuck, K. (2001). *Glossary of Distance Education Terms.* Retrieved March 6, 2005, from https://courses.worldcampus.psu.edu/public/faculty/DEGlossary.shtml

Northeastern Illinois University (NEIU). (n.d.). *HRD 408: Glossary of Terms.* Retrieved March 6, 2005, from http://www.neiu.edu/~dbehrlic/hrd408/glossary.htm

PBS Advice Center (n.d.). *Glossary.* Retrieved March 6, 2005, from http://www.pbs.org/campus/003_Advice/003-08.html

Robinson, R. D. (1995). *An introduction to helping adults learn and change.* Omnibook Co.: West Bend, WI.

Rogers, C. R. (1969). *Freedom to learn.* Charles E. Merrill Publishing Company: Columbus, OH.

Schlosser, L. A., & Simonson, M. (2003). *Distance education: Definition and glossary of terms.* Association for Educational Communications and Technology: Bloomington, IN.

Smith, M. (2002). *andragogy: The history and current use of the term plus an annotated bibliography.* Retrieved March 6, 2005, from http://www.infed.org/lifelonglearning/b-andra.htm

Texas A&M University. (n.d.). *Glossary of Distance Education Terms.* Office of Distance Education. Retrieved March 6, 2005, from http://www.tamu.edu/ode/glossary.html

The CMC Resource Site. (2002). *Glossary of CMC Terminology.* Retrieved October 10, 2003, from http://cde.athabascau.ca/cmc/glossary.html

W3C. (2003). *HyperText Markup Language (HTML) Home Page.* Retrieved March 6, 2005, from http://www.w3.org/MarkUp/

Wĕbopēdia. (2003). Retrieved March 6, 2005, from http://www.pcwebopaedia.com/TERM/N/netiquette.htm

# Chapter 3

# Creating a Foundation for Learning Relationships

S. Joseph Levine

## Overview

The most essential aspect of any teaching-learning situation must be the *learner*. However, in distance education this concern for the learner is often moved to a secondary level, and the primary focus of attention is captured by the challenge of the media – the actual delivery of the instruction via some form of distance-bridging technology. The concern for the learner is overshadowed by a focus that has been shifted to computer programs, TV monitor resolution, type of telephone cable, broadcast quality, or some other technology-based issue. The shifting of attention away from the learner and toward the media is often done by default without any real examination of the central role that the learner must have in any teaching-learning relationship.

Gibson (2003) writes, "It goes without saying that learners and learning are at the heart of the distance education enterprise. Thus, it comes as a bit of a surprise that Koble and Bunker (1997) determined that only 17% of the 117 articles published in the *American Journal of Distance Education* in its first 8 years of publication had a focus on learners, learning, and learner support" (p. 147).

In this chapter, the focus on the learner, the most complex aspect of any teaching situation, will be established and strengthened through an examination of the variety of learner relationships that are foundational to a strong distance education setting.

## Key Questions for this Chapter

Why is it important to begin considering distance education with a concern for the learner and then move on to other concerns?

What is it about the media of distance education that makes it so attractive that the media, and not the learner, become the key basis for planning for so many educators?

What are the different learner relationships that must exist in a distance education setting?

Why do we as educators often assume that the creation of a distance education learning environment is basically the same as establishing a face-to-face teaching-learning relationship? How are they different?

## Building the Learning Relationships

The very thought of framing this chapter in terms of a *relationship* runs counter to many popular views of what teaching is all about. A relationship is an intimate concept that assumes there is a meaningful linkage between the learner and the things that make up the instructional environment – other learners, the media, the content, and the educator. And, it is through the development of such a relationship that the learner develops the trust that is needed to allow new learning to occur.

The contrary view of the teaching-learning relationship is built around the effective and efficient *delivery of information*. The challenge in a *delivery of information* view is to create replicable procedures by which information can be organized, packaged, and delivered. Then, once created, the delivery part of the process can be replicated as many times as is needed for successive groups of students. The key to such a view is to gain a sufficient enough understanding of the student's knowledge or skill needs to allow the educator to do the selection of appropriate content and then to package it in such a manner that it will be deliverable to a group of learners with minimal loss of information. Instructional objectives are defined, curriculum is organized, procedures are identified, lessons are developed, and when ready the information is delivered to the learners. This view then goes on to assume that, once packaged, the information can be marketed through a variety of sources for continued delivery in the future. The delivery of information view appears to be very similar to a supermarket approach to instruction – stock the shelves with well advertised products that are guaranteed to fulfill a need and then wait for the customers to come to purchase the products.

So why is a relationship view of teaching and learning often avoided? A relationship view of teaching and learning holds that learning is a very personal phenomena and care must be taken to reduce the impersonal aspects that often accompany the teaching and learning situation. Such a view can present a very complex picture and leave the educator with much less control over the learner – the control moves to the learner. Adhering to an exclusive concern for information delivery, can be comforting to the teacher because of the opportunity for strong teacher control. A relationship view holds that it is not possible nor desirable to create packaged approaches to teaching without first taking into serious consideration the uniqueness of each individual learner. In fact, the relationship view begins with the assumption that each learner is so unique and different that it is impossible to treat any learner in the exact same manner as another. If prepared instructional materials are used in the relationship approach, it is imperative that the distance education system be developed to accommodate the uniqueness of each learner.

The idea of building teaching and learning opportunities around relationships is seen by some as a serious roadblock that stands in the way of distance education – a mediated form of education that is usually delivered to large groups of students without a concern for personalization. The challenge for the distance educator is to look for ways to develop relationships and personalization, even when the tendency is to do, however, otherwise.

The remainder of this chapter will examine the four sets of relationships that must be accommodated within the distance education environment to create the basis for meaningful learning – learner-instructor relationships, learner-learner relationships, learner-instructional content relationships, and learner-technology relationships.

## Building the Learner-Instructor Relationship in Distance Education

Interestingly, distance education has a greater potential for viable learner-instructor relationships than a typical face-to-face teaching environment. In a face-to-face situation the learner and the instructor are just a matter of a few feet from each other. We assume that, due to the lack of any distance barriers, the learner-instructor relationship will have no problems and operate in wonderful ways. Yet that is seldom the case.  Let me share something that happened to me.

> *I remember a rather large class I was teaching one evening a number of years ago. It was the very first class of the semester and I had my usual jitters that accompany the beginning of a new course. I made sure to begin the class with an activity and before I knew it things seemed to be moving along quite well. Students were organized into small groups and discussing the topic I had written on the chalkboard. We then moved to a large group discussion and I was able to summarize key ideas. Appropriate questions were being asked. People were taking notes. I was starting to learn the names of the students. I was beginning to relax as the class momentum was picking up!*

> *Finally it was time for a break and I suddenly remembered that in my nervousness to get started I had forgotten to do introductions. So, following the break I began the class by writing the course name and number on the chalkboard along with my name, office address and phone number. Immediately three students got up out of their chairs, grabbed their paper and pencils, and darted out the door. They had been in the wrong class! Wow, what if I had not mentioned the course name until the third week!*

In face-to-face instruction it is easy to assume that there is a sense of relationship between the instructor and the students. It is easy to assume that since we are together in the same room, there is a high level of personal relationship. Wrong. If the learner-instructor relationship in a face-to-face setting is not made a point of concern, it will not exist. Regardless of how physically close instructors may be to the learners, unless they work to facilitate relationships they won't happen by themselves.

In a distance education situation, however, the prerequisites for establishing learner-instructor relationships are built in. The course is advertised by name and number, the instructor's name is posted, and contact information is prominently displayed. The basis for a relationship with each student is already in place as an instructor begins the course. Then it is up to the instructor to build on that beginning with each student. Let me try to clarify this further with something from my own experience.

> *As an amateur radio operator I have always been familiar with what is referred to as a "net." This is the situation where a number of different amateur radio operators, each operating their radio station from a distant location, join together for a roundtable discussion. If the number of operators is small enough there is no need for a moderator – each person remembers the order in which they joined the net and the discussion continues around the group with each person talking for a few minutes and then turning the conversation over to the next person. The net continues around and around until the topic is exhausted or everyone leaves. It usually works well because everyone is familiar with the protocol of how a net works.*

> *When there are a large number of amateur radio stations on the net it requires a moderator, a net control station, to keep things organized and flowing well. The net control station keeps track of all participants, the order in which they will each share their comments, and also maintains order. As each radio operator finishes speaking he turns the control back to the net control station who, in turn, moves it to the next contributor. The net control station accepts the responsibility for keeping things organized so that everyone can make their contribution. The best nets have net control stations that are able to artfully balance between too much and too little control.*

It is essential for the distance education instructor to accept responsibility not only for the content of the instruction, but also for the process that is used. A viable distance education program has as its foundation a strong sense of relationship between the learner and the instructor. Acting as a moderator, the instructor must be aware of all learners who are participating, the interests and motivations of each, and work to provide appropriate opportunities for everyone to make his or her contribution. Acting much like a gracious host, the distance education instructor at times will work to either encourage or challenge each learner. Moving from one learner to the next and not forgetting any of the learners, the distance education instructor helps each learner understand that his or her desire to learn can be achieved and the instructor is willing to assist. The instructor must be able to use his or her own relationship with each learner as a key to involving the learners in the course and establishing the culture for the course. The instructor must be able to move his or her own ego to the side to allow such relationships to forge the basis for learning. Without the instructor serving to welcome each learner to the interaction, there is a high probability that the course will turn into a one-way exercise in information delivery, something that is probably better accomplished by reading a textbook.

## Building the Learner-Learner Relationship in Distance Education

When we are one of the key players, the work of developing relationships that will enhance learning is certainly easier. This is clearly seen in the learner-instructor relationship. In the learner-learner relationship, however, instructors might seem to be key players; the key players are then the learners. However, in much the same way that the instructor can be a significant helper to developing the learner-instructor relationship, the instructor can also significantly help learner-learner relationships.

*The "hit meter" on my website was indicating that traffic was starting to pick up. Though it had taken nearly 4 months for this to occur it was now apparent that more and more people each week were stopping at the website for information. Occasionally I would receive an email from a visitor inquiring about one thing or another. Now it was time to see if I could stimulate a bit of interaction among those who were visiting the site. Certainly it was fun to see the numbers begin to rise and to receive an occasional email, but I was really interested in finding out what sorts of things the visitors were interested in.*

*I found a free Bulletin Board on the worldwide web and I linked to it from my website. I created a link to the Bulletin Board, invited visitors to enter their comments, and then I sat back and waited to see the sorts of messages the visitors would start leaving. The first day went by, as did the second, third, fourth and fifth. No messages were being left on the Bulletin Board! Why not? The Bulletin Board was there and ready for people to use. Certainly they had things they would like to share with each other.*

*After waiting for nearly three weeks with no messages on the Bulletin Board I finally began to understand that there might be an important role for me play. I needed to leave some sort of message that would stimulate others to share their ideas. I first considered leaving a "guilt" message but quickly dismissed it as inappropriate and probably ineffective (You know the type – – "This is your Bulletin Board and you have to contribute to make it work – or else!"). I realized that such a message might stimulate reaction to me but I really wanted interaction rather then reaction. And, I wanted the interaction to occur between the visitors to the website – not between a visitor and me.*

*I needed to better understand the visitors and to find ways to encourage them to share their thinking. If I could get a few to begin to do some sharing, others were certain to follow. I got on the phone and called one of my friends who had previously checked into the Bulletin Board. I challenged her to leave a message on the Bulletin Board that would allow others to get insight into what she was thinking. She did it and things immediately began to pick up!*

As an instructor it is important to understand the difference between true interaction and merely reacting to his or her comments. To establish a basis for interaction demands that the instructor adopt a set of assumptions that places value on the learners and their experiences, knowledge, and ability to help each other to learn. Then, to actually energize the interaction, the instructor must search out ways to unobtrusively encourage the learners to share their experience, knowledge, and willingness to help each other. When the instructor is able to accomplish this form of learner encouragement, learner-learner relationships will develop and form a powerful foundation for the instruction.

## Building the Learner-Instructional Content Relationship in Distance Education

The learner-instructional content relationship is often beyond the direct control of the instructor. Such a relationship is usually built around a teachable moment for the learner whereby certain content becomes interesting or essential to the learner. When this connection occurs, the learner recognizes the importance of the content and works to become involved with it. The instructor can assume much more of a "consultant to the learner" role in such a situation and work to bring important content to the learner. Yet, the learner's role is significant in helping to define the instructional content.

Of course, instructors often face the very opposite situation — one that can be quite disastrous — when the learner sees no need for the content. In such a situation the instructor fights an unending battle to try to get the learner involved. But since this situation often appears to be a waste of everyone's time, the typical outcome is extremely frustrating.

> *It was my first semester for teaching this course and I spent a number of weeks reading articles, books and anything else that seemed to be related to my topic. When I felt I had enough "stuff" to make a meaningful course I sat down to the task of organizing the content. What started out as a seemingly easy task soon turned difficult. Each time I went about organizing the content I could only go so far before I decided that there was a better way to do it, an alternative strategy for the organization. I would then start all over again trying to organize the content in this new alternative way. After a number of these false starts I began to realize that, though I knew the content, I really wasn't very sure of the best way to organize it for presentation for this particular group of learners.*
>
> *What to do?*
>
> *I selected what seemed to be the most logical organizational plan and used it as the basis for my syllabus. I decided, though, that this would only be a decoy, a way to get the learners to relax at the beginning of the first class. With a bit of luck I would be able to enlist their help in building a syllabus that truly represented their interest in the content. They would enter the class assuming I would have a syllabus for them and they would be right – I would have one. The thing they would not know is that I didn't plan to really use this organization plan. And the reason was because I didn't know the learners and their need for the content.*
>
> *Once the class began and things settled down a bit I was able to start drawing from the learners bits and pieces of their own concern for the content. Carefully writing down their ideas on the chalkboard, I tried to document what they were saying. At a key point I suggested to the class that it might make sense if we reorganized the course around specific content*

*concerns and questions they had. (Aha, there it was, I was trying to link the learners directly to the instructional content.) We broke into small groups and within an hour we had a number of recommendations for how to best organize the semester's content. The learner-instructional content relationship was off to a good start!*

The instructor desiring to help build the learner-instructional content relationship is confronted with helping to empower the learners. The challenge is to create a situation where the learners are given the freedom to express their interests and to define content that is meaningful to them. Rather than having the instructor play the lead role in this process and risk creating a sense of learner dependence, the instructor helps the learners assume the lead role. The instructor's role is to facilitate the learners' direct interaction with the content. If it works well the learners will be able to move forward and explore content that is defined by prior experience, knowledge and interest.

Building this link between the learner and the instructional content is not nearly as easy to accomplish in a distance education setting as it is in a face-to-face situation. Searching out creative and functional ways to help learners identify their content needs and then linking them directly to the course content to gain needed information is a considerable challenge. A few ideas:

Have learners post short resumes on a website that describe their background and experience in relation to the content of the distance education program. Have them identify particular questions, issues, and content that they would like to search out.

Ask learners to individually identify ways in which they will be able to make a contribution to the instruction. What specific questions is each learner prepared to help his or her classmates answer?

Develop a listing of content resources that are suggested by members of the class. Post the listing and the name of the class member who contributed each item to a website for all to access.

Have learners individually prepare an outline of specific areas within the course content that they plan to explore in depth. Enter into a contract with each learner that is based upon his or her outline and identifies specific output during the course.

Hold part of one class session at the library and invite one of the reference librarians to help the class members understand how to best search out relevant information at the library. For a distance education course, invite the librarian to join the group online or on the air to share ideas on how the learners can be more successful at getting in touch with relevant content.

As you have success in helping one student get closer to the content that he or she is looking for, share a description of how it happened with others in the class. Encourage others to follow a similar path.

## Building the Learner-Technology Relationship in Distance Education

If instructors can remember the first time they tried to use a friend's cellular phone, or the time the copy machine jammed and the mess they made as they tried to fix it quickly before anyone saw that they had broken it, then they may have some idea of the potential apprehension that the learners may face in a technology-based learning environment. Adding technology to the learning environment, though potentially offering all kinds of wonderful advantages to the educator, may be very threatening to the learner. Helping to establish a meaningful learner-technology relationship in a distance education program is an essential activity for the educator. When the learner gains a sense of control over the technology, when the learner-technology relationship has been well established, instructors can then expect viable learning to take place. The fit between the technology used for distance education and the learner can greatly determine the eventual success of the distance education program. The fit must be a good one.

*My friend's voice sounded a bit tired and very weary. He had just returned from Detroit where he had witnessed one of his staff member's attempt to link four groups of local citizens at locations around the state via two-way interactive television. Even forgetting the 20 minutes at the beginning of the event that were lost when problems of compatibility of equipment had to be solved, he felt that the entire ordeal had been an expensive lesson in failing to communicate. A half hour panel discussion had droned on for almost 50 minutes; a couple of prepared questions had been asked; there had been little interaction, and the guest expert turned out to be a lot less expert than they had planned. It appeared that the only smart thing he had done was not to distribute the evaluation or feedback form that had been prepared. He already knew what the reactions would be.*

*His call to me was in desperation. They had another similar four-way hookup scheduled in another month, and he feared that it would again lead to less than wonderful results. And, of course, the real fear was that they might lose the learners. Those people who had showed up for today's session may not want to try it again! Their time was valuable, and it seemed there was not a lot to be gained from sitting in a room watching a television screen for two and a half hours. I asked him to describe the learners' reactions to what went on, and, as can be expected, he described a scene where people sat in neat rows, rather uninterested in what was going on, and non-communicative.*

*My suggestions -*

1) Don't try the two-way interactive television the next time. The technology seemed to be extremely more powerful than was needed. The learners were probably intimidated by such a powerful medium to the point where they were afraid to enter into dialogue.

*2) Use a facilitator at each of the four sites who would be able to start interacting with the group before going "on the air." Use this first segment of time to help people become involved with each other and to identify questions that they would like to ask of both the other groups and of the guest expert.*

*3) Use a simple speaker phone at each site and hook them all together via a telephone conferencing system. Everyone involved is familiar with the telephone and how it works. The technology was not formidable.*

*4) Have each facilitator help identify a group spokesperson who would relay comments from his or her group to the others on the conference call. Make sure this person felt comfortable with the technology.*

*5) Periodically stop the conference call and go "off line" to allow each group to react to what was being said and to compose their next round of questions and concerns.*

*6) Instruct the facilitators in how to use the "mute" button on the speaker phone, so each group could periodically break away from the conference call to poll its members, decide on a group response, or share a thought or two without disturbing the others who were on line.*

*7) Finally, after a couple of sessions and the groups had mastered the speaker phone technology so it is working well, then consider once again trying two-way interactive television. The learner-technology relationship would then probably be strong enough for it to work well.*

*My friend was excited. He had felt he had to use the latest and best technology, even though it was apparent that it wouldn't be easy to establish a relationship between such technology and the learners. By altering the technology, however, the learner-technology relationship was improved to the point where the technology would not interfere with the learning.*

Selection of technology to support distance education can be made for a variety of reasons. But all of the reasons that are used for selecting distance education technology are made with the learner clearly in mind. For instance, some of the more typical reasons for choosing particular distance-bridging technology include:

**Cost** - The new technology is affordable to purchase and inexpensive to use.
**Newness** - The new technology is the latest thing available.
**Flexibility** - The new technology can be used to respond to a variety of different needs.
**Transportability** - The new technology can be easily moved about and used at different locations.
**Transparency** - The new technology is not obtrusive and will not get in the way of teaching and learning.
**Compatibility** - The new technology can be used in conjunction with existing technology.

Although these criteria can all be very meaningful in their own way, when considering specific technology to be used in support of distance education, one additional criteria is essential:

**Embracability** - The new technology will be welcomed and embraced by the learners.

If the distance education technology is embraced by the learners, it will most certainly provide for learner comfort, trust, and most importantly, relationship.

### References

Gibson, C. (2003). Learners and Learning: The Need for Theory. In M. G. Moore & W. G. Anderson (Eds.), *Handbook of distance education* (pp. 147-160). Mahwah, NJ: Lawrence Erlbaum Associates, Publishers.

Koble, M. A. and Bunker, E. L. (1997). Trends in research and practice: An examination of the American Journal of Distance Education 1987 to 1995. *The American Journal of Distance Education* 11(2): 19-37.

# Chapter 4

# Mobilizing Needed Resources for Distance Education

### Kathleen E. Guy

## Overview

In this chapter we begin with the assumption that teaching at a distance can be successful and it is something we are committed to doing. Our attention can then turn to the question of how do we secure resources to support such an initiative? Recognizing the commitment of existing resources to "traditional" methods of educational delivery, the investment in distance education requires either a reallocation of funds or a significant new effort to secure external funding - or both.

When seeking resources it is important to begin with an assessment of institutional need. When presenting the case for resources, either new or reallocated, it is essential to translate institutional needs into benefits that will be realized by investing in this system of distance education. Our attention gets focused on a) what are we going to look for, b) where are we going to look, and c) what are the strategies that will be successful for securing financial support?

In almost every case, it is not what the institution needs, it is how the realization of these institutional needs will benefit students, employers and citizens. In order to be successful, distance education must be perceived as providing distinct benefits and added value to the overall instructional repertoire - rather than merely seeking a "trophy" for the sake of keeping pace with the competition or with technology.

## Key Questions for this Chapter

Prior to seeking funding for the implementation of a distance education program, it is important to have both considered and developed an institutional consensus regarding the following:

What are the most powerful arguments in support of distance education?

What are the challenges surrounding the full implementation of distance education? Which of these challenges can be met through the allocation of new resources?

What are the benefits to students and employers of a dynamic distance education program?

What resources are available for distance education funding?

What strategies must be implemented to successfully acquire funds?

What resources are necessary to insure a viable and demonstrably effective distance education program?

# Needs Assessment

When seeking external investment in a program of distance education it is not what the college *needs* but rather the *benefits* or results of distance education that are important. Maintaining this perspective is a continuing challenge for those who seek external resources. Too often there is a strong tendency to focus on institutional needs for survival/development and give too little attention to the results that will accrue to students and the community. The need can not be founded on an institutionally self-serving emphasis. The need must be systematically connected to the institution's capacity to deliver on promised benefits to students and the community.

Institutions must be clear about the reasons for embarking on distance education. Creating a distance education program because it is a trend or it is assumed that it will provide a more economical means of educational delivery are the least compelling reasons. More important in the long run and for sustainability are the likely benefits to participants. From a resource development perspective, it is also useful to have the distance education effort supported by and involving faculty and the full range of student support services.

The most compelling basis for introducing this alternative method of teaching and learning is *learner needs*. Determining whether distance education will meet the needs of students not currently being served or provide a new option for an existing student population on campus is essential in developing the overall rationale for investing in distance education.

"Universities are feeling the pressure to control costs, improve quality, focus directly on customer needs, and respond to competitive pressures. Information technology (IT) has the potential to solve many of these problems. It can change the roles of students and faculty, facilitate more learner-centered, personalized education, save money through improved business processes and distance education, and expand the scope and content of the curriculum." (Horgan, 1998, p.1)

In a recent study of benchmarks for quality distance education, National Education Association president Bob Chase indicated that, "Many of the benchmarks will sound like common sense" (Carnevale, 2000, p. A45). The results of the study point out "that distance learning can be quality learning only if colleges and universities recognize the needs of the students" (Carnevale, 2000, p. A45). Among the 24 benchmarks: a documented technology plan; minimum standards for course development, design and delivery; and student access to library resources. (Carnevale, 2000).

The evidence of inadequately researched student needs makes headlines. Consider the much-ballyhooed Western Governor's University, a multi-million dollar investment involving 40 colleges and universities from 22 states that has failed to meet any of its enrollment goals and still lacks accreditation. Likewise, the California Virtual University never launched more than a website.

A **needs assessment** - preferably conducted by an agency not affiliated with the college or university considering the distance education program - should be undertaken to determine the target market in terms of:
- student demographics and geography,
- course and program interests,
- education and employment goals,
- desire for prior learning credit,
- service and support needs and
- propensity to enroll.

A comprehensive needs assessment study of this nature will cost time and money up front but be well worth the investment in providing evidence for the need to commit college or university resources - and to offer an appropriate rationale to prospective external funding sources. Needs assessments can also help to determine the level of technical sophistication of the audience and provide guidance in selecting the most appropriate technologies to serve them. The regional capacity for connectivity to the "backbone" that will make Internet connections possible must also be investigated.

An added benefit of such a comprehensive study of needs is the use of this information in developing highly targeted promotion and recruiting efforts to an audience that will be most receptive to the offering of distance education.

A **comprehensive marketing survey** will examine current distance education student profiles in comparable institutions, survey employers to determine their interest in promoting distance education among employees as well as their attitudes toward hiring those who have earned credit through distance education, determine the subjects (courses, programs) in which potential students are interested, the preferred scheduling of courses, and the types of information that will help students to make the enrollment decision.

The profile of distance education learners will be essential in developing programs, schedules, support services and promotional appeals to prospective enrollees. The value of needs assessments provides ample justification for the resources required to conduct them. Once completed and the survey data are analyzed, the report must be shared with faculty and administrators - anyone responsible for assisting in implementing distance education programs. As noted earlier, this information will be valuable in making the case for distance education among internal and external funding sources. Additionally, the earlier this information is shared with all interested parties the more likely there will be the needed "buy in" to develop institutional ownership for the program at all levels.

Fund raising professionals will attest that donors and funding agencies are more receptive when the case for support is based upon the *benefits that will accrue to individuals, the labor force, and communities* rather than a proposal that states a *financial need* and is otherwise void of the results - outcomes - of the proposed development of distance education programs.

For example benefits/outcomes of a distance education program that could impact the community might include:

  . enhanced potential for community members to solve local problems
  . general quality of life improvement through increased educational opportunity
  . a better educated work force to better serve local employers
  . the ability to draw new enterprises to the community

The list of benefits can be tailored to each community, region and funding source.

**The Costs of Distance Education**

The cost to create and maintain distance education programs is significant, as is the continuing investment to maintain currency in technology. Entering into distance education for the purpose of saving money on instruction will prove a disappointing premise. There are costs for infrastructure (computer lines, email and Internet capacity, video conference classrooms, cable, T1 lines,), equipment (CODEC units, cameras, monitors, microphones, computers and continuous equipment replacement), teacher training and support (instructional design, faculty training, faculty stipends and/or release time) and ongoing operational expenses (outsourced services, cable and long distance charges, equipment maintenance, licensing of courseware, software, firmware, promotion and advertising materials).

While costs will vary by geographic region and system complexity, representative infrastructure and equipment costs for three typical distance education systems are outlined in Table 1 - Description, Cost and Advantages/Disadvantages of Distance Education Technologies.

The most successful distance education programs provide extensive teacher training components that include designing courses and providing support services for distance education. Some colleges and universities employ instructional designers who serve as resource experts on distance education teaching methodologies. Additionally, technicians and support staff are required to keep equipment running, troubleshoot the inevitable technological glitches, develop course schedules and support materials, and ensure that students at distance sites have all necessary student services.

Beyond the obvious hardware and course development issues are some institutional support benchmarks that have resource implications as well. "Quality On the Line," is a March 2000 publication listing benchmarks for success in Internet-based distance education programs prepared by The Institute for Higher Education Policy and sponsored by Blackboard Inc. and the National Education Association. In the study, they attempted to validate benchmarks that have been published by various organizations and to specifically focus on Internet-based distance education.

**Table 1**

**Description, Cost and Advantages/Disadvantages
of Distance Education Technologies** [1]

|  | Voice Teleconferencing | PC-Based On-Line Internet | Compressed Video |
|---|---|---|---|
| **Description** | Multiple sites connected via telephone/speaker phone, print material via mail/FAX | Multiple sites connected via computer/modem Synchronous or asynchronous | 2-5 sites connected via 2 way interactive television, instructor and students able to see each other, multiple cameras to allow for selective transmitting of graphics/instructor image/class image |
| **Equipment** | Telephones/speaker phones Digital conference bridge | Multimedia PCS, modems, peripheral hardware as needed, software as needed | CODEC units, monitors, TV cameras, FAX availability, directional microphones, high quality communication line (fiber, T1, T3, ISDN, etc.) |
| **Costs** | Digital bridge: $4000/port Conferencing system: $1500 long distance charges | $1500-$3000/unit depending on hardware/software configurations, salary of part-time support person | $60-80,000 per classroom site, rental of communication lines (+/- $1000/month), salary of part time technician |
| **Advantages** | Real-time voice communication Low-tech approach Equipment readily available capital investment Multiple locations are possible | Ease of use, general availability, cost effective - cost is shared by institution and students, general knowledge of how to use | Similar to real television transmission of classroom interaction, everyone is able to see/hear/interact with everyone, high quality communication |
| **Disadvantages** | No visual component | Potential incompatibility of PCs, need for on-call support system | High initial costs, expensive support system, may be intrusive to learning climate |

[1] Based on "Table 3.2: Open and Distance Learning Technologies" (Williams, Paprock and Covington, 1999).

Among the top institutional support benchmarks cited by the study of six exemplary Internet-based distance education programs in the U.S. was the existence and implementation of a documented technology plan. Student support benchmarks included adequate "virtual library" access to information through electronic databases, interlibrary loans, and other sources.
The costs of distance education must be fully considered and understood - including the costs to provide traditional services like library resources, academic advising, and faculty office hours - to students at a distance.

The opportunity to enlist resource partners in the distance education venture - K-12 schools, other colleges and universities, businesses/employers, compatible non-profit organizations and the like - offers the potential to optimize the use of distance education infrastructure while sharing its costs among organizations.

Armed with documentation supporting the creation of a distance education program from a qualified needs assessment and a reliable projection of infrastructure, equipment and operational budget needs, a goal for the level of service and the funding required to provide it can be established. This up-front process can take 12-24 months of diligent effort and research and it must be led philosophically by the president of the college or university and endorsed by the governing body. Table 2 presents the variety of steps needed in developing a viable fund raising initiative to support a new distance education program.

The president must state the vision for and support of distance education publicly and consistently - and commit resources to the effort. This commitment of resources includes the appointment of a distance education project team - including a distance education resource person, a writer, a fund raiser, a faculty member - to develop a program, facilities, equipment and operational (business) plan for the distance education venture. If educational or business partners are to be considered in the funding equation, the strategy team can benefit from the input of partner representatives.

Distance education will ultimately face the same pressures as other forms of higher education It will require the full range of funding strategies including endowments, third party payments and at least some level of government support.


## Systematic Acquisition of Distance Education Financial Resources

Although a case statement is usually associated with a fund raising campaign, it is a good way to get everyone "on board" and bring together the results of the needs assessment in a commonly agreed upon document. (See Fund Raising Campaign section for a more complete discussion of the case statement.) In the area of grants, the case statement must be adapted to conform to the requirements of the funding agency.

**Table 2**

**Distance Education Fund Raising Time Line**

| Year | Month | Activity |
|---|---|---|
| 1 | 1 | College/university conducts needs assessment to determine feasibility of DE delivery systems |
| | 2 | |
| | 4 | |
| | 6 | Feasibility affirmed; trustees adopt goal to expand degree options via DE in response to community need |
| | 8 | Internal DE Team formed to design the program |
| | 10 | DE Team reports findings to president |
| | 12 | President assigns work teams to pursue equipment, facilities and financial needs |
| 2 | 2 | |
| | 4 | |
| | 6 | Work teams report to president. Facility and equipment needs and operational costs are determined |
| | 8 | Fund raising feasibility study conducted |
| | 10 | Decision to proceed with fund raising; goal established |
| | 12 | |
| 3 | 2 | |
| | 4 | Fund raising campaign begins; requests for proposals sent to equipment suppliers |
| | 6 | DE system work designed and bid |
| | 8 | DE system work begins; program planning continues |
| | 10 | |
| | 12 | |
| 4 | 2 | |
| | 4 | |
| | 6 | |
| | 8 | Fund raising goal achieved; program marketing begins |
| | 10 | DE system completed; equipment tested |
| | 12 | |
| 5 | 1 | DE program begins |

Identifying the financial resources for distance education is not for the faint of heart. It requires passion for the cause and persistence in the field, knowing where to look for funding, the ability to articulate the *benefits* of distance education, the organizational commitment to be accountable for results and a team approach.

When the distance education project team completes its strategy formulation and the financial needs for the distance education system are known, the organization should conduct a feasibility study to determine how much could be raised from private sources. The answer to this question will help determine the overall strategy for seeking funds from all possible sources: government, project partners, foundations, corporations and individuals.

Assuming a positive outcome from the fund raising feasibility study, the college or university must move swiftly to establish a fund raising goal from private sources and organize a fund raising team.

**Table 3**

**The Fund Raising Team**

> President - provides the vision, serves as chief spokesperson and fund raiser for the cause

> Fund raising staff - provide the strategy, coordination, training and support for fund raising; participate in fund raising

> Faculty - provide pedagogical expertise and testimony to the benefits of distance education, suggest donor prospects, participate strategically in fund raising,

> Distance education resource expert - provide technical expertise in the program design and with technically-literate donor prospects, suggest donor prospects

> Partner representatives - represent the interests of their organizations in the project, suggest donor prospects, participate strategically in fund raising,

> Volunteers - serve as community and constituent "champions" for the distance education campaign, suggest donor prospects, participate strategically in fund raising, host cultivation events, assist with donor recognition

The team should be led by and composed primarily of community or alumni volunteers along with the college/university president, fund raising staff, faculty and staff connected to the distance education program and partners. Regular meetings of the team and clearly identifying milestones to be achieved will be effective in moving the initiative along in a timely fashion.

**Table 4**

**Sample Meeting Agendas for Fund Raising Team**

| Sample Meeting Agenda for Fund Raising Team<br>Meeting #1 |
|---|
| 1. Welcome and introductions - Campaign Chair<br>2. Campaign goal and theme - Campaign Chair<br>3. Case statement review - Development Officer<br>4. Discussion of plan of campaign - Development Officer<br>5. Prospect suggestion forms - Campaign Chair<br>6. Date for volunteer training - Development Officer<br>7. Campaign video viewing<br>8. Questions/Answers - All<br>9. Next steps - campaign chair |

| Sample Meeting Agenda for Fund Raising Team<br>Meeting #2 |
|---|
| 1. Welcome - Campaign Chair<br>2. Prospect lists and date for prospect review session - Development Officer<br>3. Subcommittee reports<br>    Foundation gifts<br>    Corporate gifts<br>    Individual gifts--cultivation events<br>    Donor recognition<br>    Publicity/PR<br>4. Review of campaign timeline - Campaign Chair<br>5. Questions/Answers - All<br>6. Next steps - Campaign Chair |

| Sample Meeting Agenda for Fund Raising Team<br>Meeting #3 |
|---|
| 1. Welcome – Campaign Chair<br>2. Report of donations to date - All<br>3. Subcommittee reports - All<br>    Foundation gifts<br>    Corporate gifts<br>    Individual gifts--cultivation events<br>    Donor recognition<br>    Publicity/PR<br>4. Upcoming cultivation events - Development Officer<br>5. Campaign PR report - Publicity Committee Chair<br>6. Questions/Answers - All<br>7. Next steps – Campaign Chair |

## Pursuing Grant Funds

Resources for distance education programs must be creatively pursued from public sources (grants, partnerships) and private sources (individual, corporate and foundation donors). As is shown in Table 5, the rule of thumb among grant seekers says that if a successful quest for funds equaled 100 points, 70 of them would be focused on formulating a well-conceived project idea. Twenty points represent the researching of the prospects and 10 points represent the actual writing of the proposal. Much work has to be accomplished up front before beginning to seek the actual external funding. Once completed, however, finding and securing the resources becomes much more do-able and the effort potentially much more successful.

**Table 5**

**Grant Project Planning, Prospect Research and Proposal Writing:
Percentage of Time Allocated to Each Task**

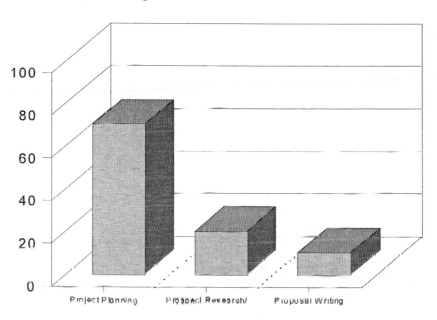

Helpful resources are available to those seeking government, corporation or foundation grants. Knowing where to look for the best match between your proposal and their dollars is important. Excellent resources are **Grants for Technology** (Mudd, 2001) and **The Distance Learning Funding $ourcebook** (Krebs, 1999). They contain a wealth of information about funding sources and approaches to seeking funding, including extensive listings of foundation and corporate giving programs and government grant programs and the types of distance education initiatives they support. Every issue of the **Chronicle of Higher Education** contains a section on distance education projects that have received funding and a listing of upcoming grant possibilities. An on-line foundation resource is the **Foundation Center.**

Unless there is a dramatic reversal in trends, it is clear that governmental sources will not be sufficient to underwrite the investments needed to produce flexible, adaptable, up-to-date distance education programming. In order to be successful, those responsible for distance education programs must attract private individual investment. Distance education programs will need to attract endowments. It will be important to be able to attract unrestricted resources that permit timely acquisition of new technology and new courseware.

Raising money from individuals means capturing the attention of a population embedded in the larger society - visionaries who see beyond libraries and laboratories to the frontier of nontraditional educational delivery systems of what might be considered traditional content - at the right time and the right place.

## The Fund Raising Campaign

Armed with the results of a bonafide needs assessment and a carefully designed distance education program, fund raising can begin. Elements of a fund raising campaign that taps government, foundation, corporate and individual sources include the case statement, the plan of campaign, donor prospects, cultivation and solicitation, and donor recognition.

**Case Statement** The case statement is a reasonably brief, 3-6 page, document that explains to prospective donors why you are asking for their support. Experienced fund raiser Henry Rosso describes the language of fund raising as "the gentle art of persuasion" (in Greenfield, 1999, p. 56) The case statement is an opportunity to persuade the donor audience of your organization's worthiness, urgent and compelling plans for the future, and the benefits that will accrue to students, employers and communities as a result.

According to Greenfield (1999) the case should include the following elements:

1. The problem (or opportunity) to be addressed
2. Trends affecting the problem (or opportunity)
3. Your response to the problem (or opportunity)
4. Role of the prospective donor
5. Your mission
6. Your history, track record, and marketplace position
7. Goals, strategies and objectives
8. Organizational resources
9. Accountability and evaluation
10. Future organization plans
   (Greenfield, 1999, p. 57)

The case statement provides the basis for all future fund raising campaign communications - speeches, grant proposals, videos, brochures. Once the case is written, usually by the development officer or a consultant, and approved by the president, then all future uses of it, or elements thereof, do not require additional approvals.

**Plan of Campaign** The plan of campaign is a step-by-step outline and time-line for the fund raising campaign. It includes a description of the dollar goal and theme of the campaign, the volunteer structure and job descriptions, the types of collateral materials that will be needed (brochures, videos, pledge cards, etc.), the anticipated number and amount of gifts necessary to achieve the goal, a description of the cultivation-solicitation process, a list of named gift or donor recognition opportunities and a master campaign calendar.

The plan of campaign should be prepared by the development officer or a consultant and reviewed, understood and endorsed by staff and volunteers.

**Donor Prospects**  A comprehensive list of donor prospects should be compiled by the development office based upon suggestions and input from everyone involved in the development of the distance education program as well as from the roster of current donors to the organization.  Donor prospects should include vendors, foundations and corporations, individuals, government sources, individuals, alumni, faculty and staff.

Once the donor prospect lists are compiled, each name on the list should be ranked by anticipated level of interest and capacity to give.  Also helpful in the ranking process is determining who the best person(s) is to call on the prospective donor.  An axiom of fund raising is that people give to people, not to causes, so identifying the right person to do the asking often spells the difference between getting a gift or walking away empty-handed.

**Cultivation and Solicitation**  This is the deliberate and methodical process of story telling, relationship building and asking for contributions.  Cultivating means developing a relationship with the donor prospect through information sharing, visits to the college or university, and meetings with people who have a passion for the distance education project.  Sometimes this takes just one meeting but more typically the time it takes to move a prospect from the initial meeting through completion of a gift can span weeks or even months.

Through this relationship building, the donor prospect gains an understanding for and appreciation of the benefits of the proposed project and the people who are connected to it (faculty, administrators, the development officer, volunteers, etc.).  Cultivation can be done one-on-one or in groups.  Cultivation events are typical in major fund raising campaigns, often hosted by members of the volunteer fund raising committee.  Events range from meetings over breakfast, lunch or dinner, to evening receptions.  They can be conducted in private homes, at restaurants or at the project site.

The list of prospects to invite to cultivation events begins with the largest potential donors first.  Invitation lists to these events are typically small by design and usually include no more than 20 people.  More individual attention can be paid when the number of guests is limited, and the follow-up that is necessary afterward by staff and volunteers is more manageable.

It is a good rule of thumb to follow up with donor prospects in one week or less after they have attended a cultivation event.  The follow up, in person or by telephone, is to answer any questions the prospect may have about the project and to ask for the gift.  If the solicitor senses that the donor prospect is not yet ready to give, then an appropriate set of follow-up measures should be noted between the solicitor and campaign organizers and assigned.

The cultivation and solicitation process continues until all prospects have been contacted.  Maintaining the momentum and energy of a capital campaign is challenging, and, depending on the goal, should not last more than two years.  That is why campaigns of this nature should be undertaken only with the full support and participation of the president, adequate development staff or consultants and volunteer commitment.

**Donor Recognition**  Prior to starting the campaign, a process should be in place to recognize donors.  Timely individual acknowledgement letters and personal notes from the president, the development staff and the volunteer should be standard operating procedure. Usually two business days is ideal. Other forms of recognition will depend on donor preference and the college or university's policy on donor recognition. Typical forms of recognition include news releases, signage on rooms and buildings and celebration events - dedications, grand opening ceremonies, campaign galas. Every "thank-you" is accompanied by an implied "please," and it is important to recognize that the acknowledgement and recognition process are the beginning of cultivation for future gifts. Timeliness and sensitivity to donor wishes (including confidentiality, if requested) is essential.

## Conclusion

Seeking resources for distance education is a process that requires documentation of need and benefits, a well-planned program to create and sustain the distance education effort, and president and board commitment. Partnerships with other education providers or organizations can optimize the use of the distance education infrastructure while sharing its costs.

Raising money for distance education requires capturing the attention of a population embedded in the larger society - visionaries - who see beyond libraries and laboratories to the frontier of nontraditional delivery systems.

The real challenge facing the future success of distance education will be to employ strategies that bring the significant resources from individual donors to the effort - endowments, major gifts, planned/estate gifts. People who become passionate about the benefits of distance education for the sake of learners and educational innovation can do for distance education what previous generations have done for bricks and mortar.

**References**

Carnevale, D. (2000). A study produces a list of 24 benchmarks for quality distance education. *The Chronicle of Higher Education*, 46(31), A45.

Mudd, M. (Ed.). (2001). *Grants for technology*. New York: Aspen.

Greenfield, J.M. (1999). *Fundraising* (2nd ed.). New York: John Wiley & Sons.

Horgan, B. (1998). Transforming higher education using information technology: first steps. *The Horizon*, Spring 1998.

Krebs, A. (1999). *The distance learning funding $ourcebook*. (4th ed.). Dubuque, IA: Kendall/Hunt

Phipps, R. & Merisotis, J. (2000). *Quality on the line*. The Institute for Higher Education Policy, Washington, D.C.

The Chronicle of Higher Education. http://www.chronicle.com

The Foundation Directory On-line. http://www.fconline.fdncenter.org/

Williams, M.L., Paprock, K. & Covington, B. (1999). *Distance learning: The essential guide*. Thousand Oaks, CA: Sage.

# Chapter 5

---

# Instructional Design Considerations
# For Distance Education Programs

## S. Joseph Levine

## Introduction

As I became involved in the design of distance education programs, I was challenged with the idea that development of a listing of the many variables that should be considered for the effective design of a distance education program might be possible. My vision was of a "menu" that had a couple of columns that listed a variety of sets of alternative instructional options. And, of course, I assumed that once such a listing was developed, it would then be an easy matter to merely make a decision for each set of options on the list and – *zoom* – you would have a fully designed and well operating distance education program. On a few occasions I even went about creating such a list, adding more and more items as I would contemplate a specific distance education design I was working on. Each time, however, I found that as the listing progressed and more items were added to it, the list became more and more complex. And as the complexity became great, I would set aside the list, deciding that I had not yet happened upon the correct set of options for it.

At some point I began to realize that my thinking was extremely naive. I was misguided by a vision that I could control the technology of distance education, so every conceivable learner and instructional situation could be accommodated. I began to realize that although the technology had a limited number of options to consider and could be categorized and organized, the learner variables were boundless. In order for such lists to be effective, I would have to be able to identify all possible learner variables that could ever be encountered in a distance education program and then match them to instructional options for each. *Whoa!* That large an effort would border on insanity. Thus, I gave up my attempts at creating such a list. I moved away from any attempt that would be seen as reductionistic.

Once I admitted to myself that the task of creating a comprehensive menu of distance education options was impossible because of the complexity of the learner, I was able to settle on a much more reasonable approach. I identified a set of five major design considerations that must be considered during the development of a distance education program. I viewed these as guideposts rather than neatly defined specific instructions. These five design considerations are all under the control of the teacher or instructional designer and can be manipulated in one way or another – hopefully to better accommodate both the focus of the instruction and the uniqueness of each learner. I limited myself to broadly defining each design consideration rather than once again getting caught in the trap of attempting to identify all of the possible learner variations that could affect each consideration.

### Design Consideration 1
### Assumptions About the Learner

Probably the most significant of the five design considerations are the assumptions we hold about the learners who are involved with our distance education program – the feelings we hold about the people we are teaching. Demonstrated in so many different ways, the assumptions that we have about the learners color everything we do. Our selection of language, the immediacy of our responses, our willingness to accept answers that are different from our own, and our responsiveness to the requests of the learners send very clear and strong messages to the learners. We must clearly think through what our assumptions are and make sure we operate in a manner consistent with them. And, if we feel that our assumptions don't support the sort of distance education learning environment that we would like, we must then go about changing how we feel about the learners: change our assumptions.

## Andragogy-Pedagogy Continuum

| Program Is Based On Andragogical Assumptions About The Learners | Program Is Based On Pedagogical Assumptions About The Learners |
| --- | --- |

Chapter Seven presents the concept of "andragogy" as established and clarified by both Eduard Lindeman (1926) and Malcolm Knowles (1984). This idea, a continuum of views that goes from seeing learners as very self-directing to seeing learners as being very dependent, helps identify the types of assumptions that we hold about our learners, and our assumptions dictate how we operate as distance educators. And, of course, our assumptions come through so clearly to our learners. If we assume that our program is focused on highly self-directed learners, rather than dependent learners, we are leaning more toward an andragogical set of learner assumptions and away from pedagogical learner assumptions. Other indications of having andragogical assumptions are when we assume that the learner is self-motivated from within (rather than externally controlled), has rich experiences in life that form the basis for further learning (rather than having no important experiences to build upon), has an orientation toward learning that is life-centered (rather than subject-centered), and the uniqueness among learners increases as learners age (rather than assuming all learners continue through life with the same needs and aspirations).

The first design consideration then is to decide where our distance education program will be located on the andragogy-pedagogy continuum. *What are the assumptions we hold about the learners and how will our distance education program demonstrate those assumptions in a consistent and clear manner?*

### Design Consideration 2
### Cognitive Domain

Assuming that our distance education program is focused primarily on the teaching of cognitive material, rather than affective or psychomotor material, the next concern we must have is the level of the cognitive domain at which we would like our program to be anchored.

### Bloom's (1956) Taxonomy of the Cognitive Domain

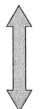

Level 6 – Evaluation (Value Judgment)
Level 5 – Synthesis
Level 4 – Analysis
Level 3 – Application
Level 2 – Comprehension
Level 1 – Knowledge

A program at Level 1, the knowledge level, would be focused primarily on the presentation of information, whereas a program at Level 3 would be concerned with helping the learner apply the information that is presented. Programs at the highest three levels would make significant use of dialogue between and among learners as well as between the instructor and the learners. At the highest three levels the distance education teacher is the one responsible for encouraging that dialogue. And it's important to remember that each level of the cognitive domain is hierarchical, so that in order to operate at Level 4 the learners must have already mastered the three lower levels.

Establishing an appropriate cognitive level for the design of the distance education program, that is, one that meets both the needs of the learners and the instructor, is the second design consideration. *At what cognitive level will our program operate?*

## Design Consideration 3
## Learner Interaction

The third design consideration is concerned with the type and level of interaction that is present in the distance education program. Viable interaction among the learners and between the instructor and the learners is an essential element in ameliorating the vacuum that is often created because of the inability to operate in a face-to-face manner. Without interaction the distance education program runs the risk of becoming nothing more than a set of one-way lectures that may or may not have meaning for the learners.

As teachers or designers, therefore, we must clarify, both to ourselves and the learners, the level of interaction that we are expecting within the distance education program and some of the strategies we will be using to help promote and encourage this interaction. By openly sharing this concern with the learners, there is a much greater chance that we will be able to achieve the level of interaction that we desire.

Some ways to promote learner interaction include:

- Provide meaningful feedback, both public (directed to all learners) and private (directed to only a single learner), that encourages response. This response might be in the form of emails, mailed letters, recorded comments, or telephone calls.
- Use open-ended questions that encourage a variety of answers from the different perspectives of different learners.
- Acknowledge and encourage views from learners that are different from your own views.
- Use an online discussion board or bulletin board.
- Share responsibility with learners for some aspects of the distance education course.
- Use a collaborative approach to teaching that encourages learners to work together in small groups.
- Develop a set of written signs or signals that you and the learners can use to denote emotions (HI = laugh, LOL = laughing out loud, etc.).
- Respond in short sentences (and encourage learners to do the same) so many people can easily join an online discussion.
- Allow ample time for everyone to reflect on their ideas before (and after) sharing them.

- When operating in synchronous mode, establish a rotation (and stick to it), so everyone has a chance to share.
- Allow learners to share the leadership role (i.e. take turns) in guiding discussion or dialogue.
- Encourage learners to ask questions, so you aren't the only one asking.
- Redirect questions to others in the group. Although you may have good answers to the questions, establish a model that values the redirecting of questions, so others have a chance to have input.

Establishing interaction and then maintaining that interaction is the third design consideration for an effective distance education program. *What will we include in the design of our distance education program that will encourage learner interaction?*

## Design Consideration 4
## Location and/or Time of Instruction

The advent of the worldwide web has created a strong foundation for asynchronous distance education. Learners and teacher need not be located at the same place or available at the same time to evolve into an effective learning community. Similarly, the use of pre-recorded audio CDs and/or video DVDs can further support an asynchronous mode of operation.

Synchronous learning opportunities, however, can still be a powerful format for distance education. In synchronous distance education formats learners can be challenged with real-time demands for immediate responses, problem solving, and reflection.

|  | Same Time | Convenient Time |
|---|---|---|
| **Same Location** | *Face-to-Face* | *Replicable Learning Environments* |
| **Convenient Location** | *Synchronous Distance Education* | *Asynchronous Distance Education* |

Strong distance education programs can be built upon the creative combination of both synchronous and asynchronous learning environments. And, of course, an occasional face-to-face opportunity, if available, can help bridge any problems that may arise because of the distance that separates the learners. *How will we integrate a concern for synchronous, asynchronous, and face-to-face education to make our distance education program a success?*

## Design Consideration 5
## Technology/Media

And finally, the fifth design consideration for a viable distance education program is the meaningful selection and use of appropriate technology or media. Although many distance educators begin their design with decisions about the technology or media that will be used, I have saved this consideration for last. The reason that technology or media is often the very first design consideration is that it is very often a given. It is the technology or media that is available, and we are expected to use it.

If you find yourself in such a situation, don't dismay. One very obvious way to compensate is to bring together a number of different technologies or media, instead of just using a single one. Be sure to use the one that you are expected to use, but in addition add other media to enrich the learning. So, if a web-based distance education program is where you are heading, try including a conference telephone call at the beginning to help each learner establish his or her identity with the group. Or, send out a short DVD of yourself, introducing the program, so each learner gets to know a bit more about who you are, what you look like, and some of your ideas. In addition to a discussion board, be sure to send frequent emails to each of the learners, encouraging his or her continued participation.

Here are a number of technologies or media that you may want to consider as part of your distance education program:

- Correspondence – emailed or mailed materials and communications.
- Audio CDs or Cassette Tapes – recorded presentations, lectures, or guided visits.
- DVDs, Video Tapes – PowerPoint presentations, demonstrations, lectures.
- Computer-Delivered Instruction – compact disk-based information and resource materials, programmed instruction.
- Telephone – interactive conference calls, one-on-one reinforcement or feedback.
- Radio Broadcast – local listening groups, individually delivered instruction.
- Television Broadcast – one-way communication, two-way interactive TV (CODEC).
- Internet – email, listserv, or discussion board.
- Web-Available Resources – websites and web pages with relevant content.
- Educational/Instructional Web page – programmed instruction, topically focused material, units or lessons from other sources.

Be careful in your selection of technology for the delivery of your distance education program. Make sure that both you and the learners will be able to easily master the technology, so it moves to the background, thereby allowing the content of the instruction to be the primary focus. Help ensure the success of your program by using a variety of media that can effectively reinforce content and also serve to back-up systems that may not function well when needed. ***What technology or media will we select for our distance education program?***

# References

Bloom, B. S. (ed). (1956). *Taxonomy of educational objectives, Handbook 1: Cognitive domain.* New York: Longman.

Knowles, M. S. (1984). *The adult learner: a neglected species.* Houston: Gulf Publishing Company.

Lindeman, E. C. (1926). *The meaning of adult education.* New York: New Republic. Republished in a new edition in 1989 by The Oklahoma Research Center for Continuing Professional and Higher Education.

# Chapter 6

---

# Evaluation in Distance Education

## S. Joseph Levine

## Introduction

The challenge of evaluation in distance education is both a complex and confusing enterprise. Most of us would like to merely get on with it, do an evaluation of our distance education program, and not spend an inordinate amount of time defining evaluation terms, clarifying evaluation concepts, and being confused with semantic differences that are apparent whenever the topic of evaluation is presented. However, the truth is that we must work our way through all of the terms, concepts, and semantic differences if we are ever to move to the point of being able to construct and implement meaningful evaluation in distance education. The good news is that once we understand the "playing field", our evaluation practice can become a rather simple task, instead of a daunting challenge.

A major challenge of evaluation in distance education emanates from the very distance that exists between the learner and the teacher. This distance creates a situation whereby the control of the teacher is reduced and the control of the learner is increased. And, of course, as the teacher's control is reduced so is the teacher's ability to completely control the design and implementation of evaluation strategies. It is imperative, therefore, that the educator in distance education explore evaluation strategies that provide for increased ways in which the learner can exercise control for the purpose of individual growth and development. Without such recognition of the enhanced role played by the learner in distance education, evaluation runs the risk of becoming a meaningless exercise that yields little valuable information. Involvement of the learner in the evaluative process is essential in a well designed distance education program.

This chapter has been organized around a set of three discrete and powerful concepts that could form the basis for the successful selection, design, and implementation of evaluation strategies in distance education, especially evaluation strategies that accommodate a concern for significant learner involvement.

## At the conclusion of this chapter you will:

1. Be able to differentiate between **measurement, assessment,** and **evaluation** and know when each level is most appropriate in distance education.

2. Understand that evaluation strategy changes in relation to the recipient of the evaluation results. The intended audience for the evaluation results directly influences the type of evaluation that is used. For instance, an evaluation that is to be presented in a report to a **sponsoring agency or group** is inherently different from one that a **teacher or instructional designer** might use to get better insight into the teaching process used in the distance education program or from an evaluation that would help the **learners** assess their own learning at a distance.

3. Appreciate that evaluation can be used at different times during and after a distance education program in order to allow the examination of different program elements. Key elements that could be examined include the **inputs** that were selected, the **processes** that were used, the **products** and **outputs** that were achieved, and the **outcomes or impacts** that affected the lives of the learners, their community, or their organizations. Evaluation differs in purpose and in difficulty, depending on which element is to be evaluated.

4. Be able to identify actual evaluation instruments in terms of the above characteristics.

## Differentiating Between Measurement, Assessment, and Evaluation

Evaluation consists of the merging of three very powerful ideas – the collection of information, the comparing of that information against another set of information, and the placement of value on the comparison. If we are going to truly conduct evaluation, we have to accommodate all three ideas.

Major errors that are made in the practice of evaluation frequently occur because the evaluator assumes that once the first step has been conducted, the information has been collected, an evaluation has been conducted. Or, going a step further but still being short of a true evaluation, the evaluator assumes that once the collected information has been compared to another set of information, the evaluation has been accomplished. Evaluation can be fulfilled only when all three steps in the process have been fulfilled – collection of information, comparison of information with another set of information, and making a value judgment on the comparison. "Both description and judgment are essential – in fact, they are the two basic acts of evaluation. Any *individual evaluator* may attempt to refrain from judging or from collecting the judgments of others. Any individual evaluator may seek only to bring to light the worth of the program. But their evaluations are incomplete. To be fully understood, the educational program must be fully described and fully judged" ( Stake, 1967, p. 3).

The first level or step toward a full educational evaluation of a distance education program can be considered an educational measurement. Measurement consists of a single set of information regarding some aspect of the distance education program. It is presented as fact with no attempt to compare it with anything else or to assign any value to the information.

A measurement is the clear presentation of a set of scores, outcomes, or information that has been drawn from an instructional program. It is like a snapshot or a single picture taken of a program with no attempt to compare the picture to another picture, that is, another program, criteria, expectation, or different point in time.

**Educational Measurement**

(A snapshot/single picture of an educational program.)

Measurement statements:

*The distance education learners scored a combined 87% on the final examination.*

*The concept of a t-test was learned by all learners at the 3 downlink locations.*
*Clarity of materials, flexibility of learning times, and prompt feedback were rated 4.8 by*
*the learners on a 5.0 scale.*

The second step toward an educational evaluation is that of assessment. Two different measures or sets of information are brought together to allow comparison. However, no attempt is made to assign any value to the similarity or difference between the two sets of information.

Educational assessment is the comparison of two measurements.

| Measurement I (Pre-Test, Program A, Time A, Criteria, Expected Outcomes, etc.) | Compared With | Measurement II (Post-Test, Program B, Time B, Actual Outcomes, etc.) | = | Assessment |
| --- | --- | --- | --- | --- |

Assessment statements:

*The distance education learners scored a combined 87% on the final examination, **which was**
***4% higher than the same class taught in a face-to-face situation.***
*The concept of a t-test was learned by all learners at the 3 downlink locations **of which only**
***10% knew the concept at the beginning of the course.***
*Clarity of materials, flexibility of learning times, and prompt feedback were rated 4.8 by the
learners on a 5.0 scale. **A rating of 4.0 was identified in the funding proposal as the**
***minimum acceptable mean rating.***

And finally we can move on to educational evaluation or the comparing of two sets of information and the placement of value on this comparison.

Evaluation statements:

*The distance education class **surpassed our prediction** when they scored a combined
87%, which was 4% higher than the same class taught in a face-to-face situation.*
***Great improvement was shown** when the concept of a t-test was learned by all learners
at the 3 downlink locations of which only 10% knew the concept at the beginning
of the course.*
*The computer-based correspondence program **exceeded expectations** when clarity of
materials, flexibility of learning times, and prompt feedback were rated 4.8 by the
learners on a 5.0 scale. A rating of 4.0 was identified in the funding proposal as
the minimum acceptable mean rating.*

For instance, we may have data that describe the learning outcomes of a face-to-face instructional program (a measurement). When these data are compared with similar data drawn from a distance education program (another measurement), we are on the road toward evaluation. First, though, we are faced with an assessment or comparing the two sets of information.

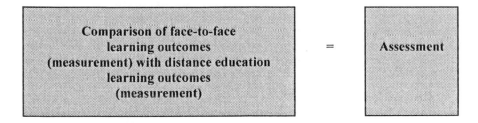

Next, when we assign a value to this assessment, we have arrived at evaluation.

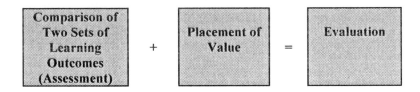

But why in the world would someone want to stop at assessment, the comparing of two sets of information, when turning it into an evaluation could easily be achieved by just adding a statement of value to the comparison? The answer, of course, is politics and risk. The minute we place a value on the comparison, we are opening ourselves to risk. What if the learning outcomes of a distance education instructional program are not greater than those of a face-to-face program? We might want to merely state those facts (assessment) or go on to say that the face-to-face program was **better** (evaluation). The decision is ours! However, we must remember that assessment and evaluation are not the same thing. To move to the level of an evaluation demands that a value be placed on the outcomes of an assessment.

| Words that can indicate an assessment | Words that can indicate an evaluation |
|---|---|
| More (Less) | Better (Worse) |
| Greater (Lesser) | Benefit |
| Larger (Smaller) | Stronger (Weaker) |
| Higher (Lower) | Improved |
| Farther (Closer) | Significant |
| Louder (Softer) | Enhanced |
| Increased (Reduced) | Enriched |
|  | Good (Bad) |

For some, even the use of assessment, the comparing of two sets of information, can be perceived as a high risk. These educators fear that the mere presentation of information in the form of an educational assessment is just waiting for someone to assign it a value and then turn it into an evaluation.

## Considering the Purpose or Use of an Evaluation

A large trap that many evaluators (assessors or measurers) fall into is assuming that one type of evaluation can successfully respond to the unique questions of a variety of different interested parties.

> One influence on the direction of evaluation is its potential audience. During the formative evaluation the project writers and policy makers are the prime, although not sole, audience for the evaluation efforts. During both formative and summative evaluations, the funders are generally concerned with progress. The schools participating in the experimental use of materials are interested and deserve reports of the efforts in which they are involved. For publicly funded projects, the public has a right to be kept informed on the use of its funds, and provisions for such information should be considered an obligation even where the funding agency does not require it. (Grobman, 1968, p. 15.)

An evaluation conducted to specifically answer questions of the teacher might be inappropriately sent on to the agency that is funding the program. Clearly, the sorts of answers that the teacher had planned to get from the evaluation would be quite different from the sorts of questions the funding agency would like to have answered. Or, an exercise to help distant learners better understand how to improve their own self-discipline for learning via a satellite-delivered program is inappropriately used by the producer of the satellite program to find segments that need to be replaced with new content. An evaluation designed to provide insights to the distance learners would be very different from one designed to help the producer identify content that needs to be changed. Both of these examples describe the inappropriate use of an evaluation to fulfill a secondary purpose.

**Three Major Recipients of Evaluation Results**

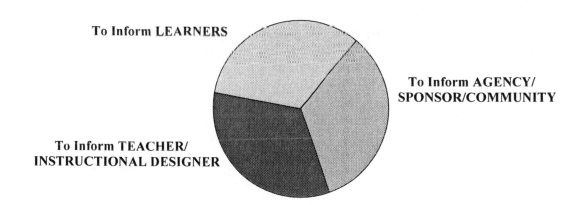

To Inform LEARNERS

To Inform AGENCY/ SPONSOR/COMMUNITY

To Inform TEACHER/ INSTRUCTIONAL DESIGNER

**Purpose - Evaluation Intended to Inform the Agency/Sponsor/Community.** Clearly the use that is most often the basis for an evaluation is a concern for accountability by the group that has sponsored the program. Tyler (1991) refers to this as program evaluation that is used to "provide estimates of effects and costs"(p. 4). It is a most appropriate expectation for a sponsoring group to want to find out to what extent its assistance has "paid off." Has the program focused on the purpose that was intended? Have the program objectives been achieved? Have the observable outcomes been in line with what was originally planned? Was the program a good investment? These questions and other similar ones form the basis for what Michael Scriven (1967) originally referred to as **summative**

**evaluation** or evaluation that occurs at the conclusion of a program and is intended to look at effects in a conclusive manner.[1]

Evaluation that intends to inform the agency, sponsor, or community could be truly evaluation, but often it stops just short of being an evaluation and takes the form of assessment whereby two sets of information are compared and no defined value is placed on the comparison. One set of information for the assessment is that which is collected at the conclusion of the program. These data may be drawn from participant observations, cognitive testing, instructor reactions, or other ex post facto forms of data. The second set of information, that which allows an assessment to be made, is often taken from the preliminary plan for the program. According to Stake (1967), these are the "intended student outcomes" that are part of the original vision for the program.

Statements of expected or intended outcomes, as presented in the initial program plan, are compared with the data collected at the end of the program and a comparison is made. It is then possible to make a clear comparison between what was intended and what was achieved, that is, an assessment of the program. Such assessments are very common and are often referred to as an evaluation, but typically they omit the drawing of judgments regarding the comparison. They are therefore really summative assessments.

**Summative Assessment:**
**Intended to Inform the Agency/Sponsor/Community**

| A. Information Drawn from Program Plan Regarding Expected Outcomes | Assessment (Comparing A & B) ◄—► | B. Information Drawn at Conclusion of Program Regarding Actual Outcomes |
|---|---|---|

**Purpose - Evaluation Intended to Inform the Teacher/Instructional Designer.** A second popular use for evaluation, though not as frequently employed as the above, is to inform those responsible for providing the instructional program. Data are collected that help the instructor and others involved with the design and delivery of the distance education program get a sense of how they are doing and what might be changed if the program were to be repeated. This type of focus for an evaluation is seen as developmental in nature, one that builds and changes over time, and the evaluation is called **formative** since it is designed to help *form* the program in new ways or to make improvements in the program. Collection of data is not reserved exclusively for the conclusion of the program. Data are collected throughout the program and continually compared with the planned or expected data. Value is assigned to these comparisons, and judgments are made regarding how "good" the program is and what aspects might need "improvement" or "refinement." Changes and improvements in the program are able to be made "on the run" to take full advantage of the information that is being collected as it is collected.

---

[1] On the other hand, formative evaluation refers to that form of evaluation that is done to make improvements in a program. Summative evaluation, when compared to formative evaluation, was expressed well by Robert Stake when he described the difference as the difference between when the cook tastes the soup (formative evaluation) and when the guest tastes it (summative evaluation).

**Formative Evaluation:
Intended to Inform the Teacher/Instructional Designer**

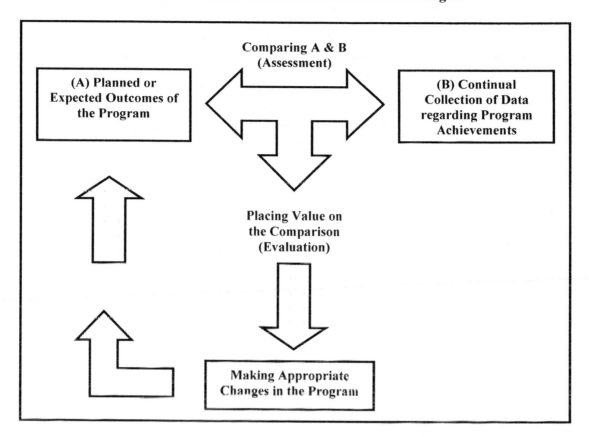

**Purpose - Evaluation Intended to Inform the Learners.** The evaluation use that is least often implemented is that which is created to inform the learners, that is, to let the learners self-reflect in order to let them know whether they are being successful, whether their goals and objectives are being attained, and if they have made a good investment of their time and energy in the distance education program. Such learner-focused evaluation is often an instinctive part of the learning process and goes on unobtrusively and rather automatically. Seldom is evaluation that is intended to inform the learners made explicit through a strategy implemented by a teacher or learning facilitator in a distance education setting. Instead it often occurs haphazardly as a function of the learner's own desire to evaluate. However, since distance education demands a high degree of self-direction on the part of the learner, it follows that evaluation that is intended to inform the learner should be made a significant focus for evaluation in distance education.

Evaluation that is implemented with the intention of informing the learners is very different from evaluation that is designed to inform the teacher, who, in turn, informs the learner. Evaluation that is truly designed to inform the learner and remove the teacher from a "middle person" role, could be viewed as **empowering evaluation**. Such evaluation often is based on reflective opportunities, times when learners are encouraged to reflect on their learning. These times are built into the instructional program. Garrison (2003) writes, "Transactional elements within a critical community of inquiry will have to be articulated for distance education to be relevant and flourish in this communication age" (p. 166).

49

To encourage reflective opportunities in support of empowering evaluation, it is important to provide enhanced opportunities for dialogue and for learners to interact directly with each other. Such opportunities may be as simple as the distance instructor providing time and structure that allow learners to give written feedback to each other via a bulletin board or the use of small group discussions that are conducted by learners via email without the intervention of the instructor. These reflective or evaluative activities can have a significant empowering effect on the learners.

It is often hard to differentiate evaluation that is intended to inform the learners from a highly learner-interactive distance education program. A hallmark of such a highly interactive program is the considerable amount of responsibility that the teachers share with the learners.

**Empowering Evaluation:
Intended to Inform the Learners**

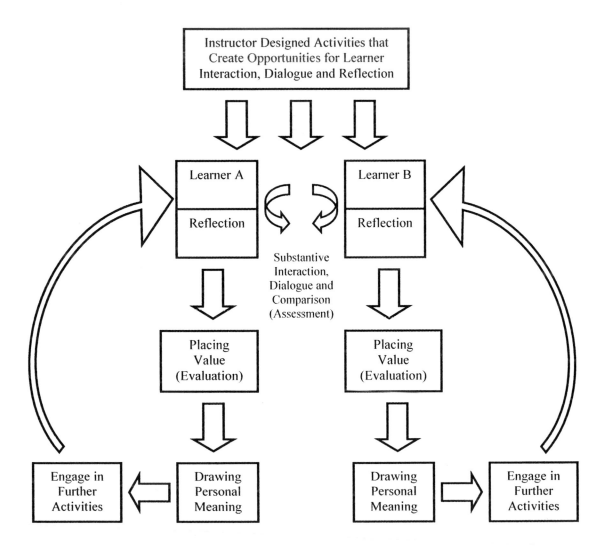

A comprehensive approach to evaluation in distance education should include some aspect of each of the three uses for evaluation: to inform the agency, sponsor, or community; to inform the teacher or instructional designer; and to inform the learners.

**Comparing the Three Purposes of Evaluation**

| *Evaluation that is intended to:* | *Can be labeled:* | *And is usually described as:* |
|---|---|---|
| **Inform the Agency/ Sponsor/Community** | **Summative Assessment** | **Most frequently used**<br>**Expected by the funding agency**<br>**Reflects back on original intentions**<br>**Occurs at the conclusion of the program**<br>**Only an assessment** |
| **Inform the Teacher/Instructional Designer** | **Formative Evaluation** | **Often used**<br>**Helps the designer make changes**<br>**Occurs in an ongoing manner**<br>**Developmental in nature**<br>**Immediately useful** |
| **Inform the Learners** | **Empowering Evaluation** | **Least frequently used**<br>**Controlled by the learners**<br>**Self-reflective in nature**<br>**An instinctive part of the learning process**<br>**Helpful when the educator makes it explicit**<br>**Builds on learner-learner interaction** |

# Considering Which Aspect of the Distance Education Program Will Be Evaluated

With distance education, more so than other less technologically based forms of education, the question of which aspect of the program will be evaluated becomes a major focus. This question occurs because there seems to be so many more aspects to consider! Will we be evaluating the array of equipment and technology that has been brought together to facilitate teaching at a distance (e.g. computer software, telephone lines, CODEC units, interactive classrooms)? Or, will we be evaluating learning to gain a sense of exactly what changes have taken place in the learners? And, if we are evaluating change as a result of learning, will we be looking at recall immediately following the distance education program or will we be considering the application of the learning months after the conclusion of the program? These and other similar questions become the basis for considering the specific aspects of the program that will be evaluated.

Kaufman (1983), in a chapter focusing on needs assessment, presents the Organizational Elements Model (OEM), which provides a very helpful perspective on five separate elements or aspects that can be the basis for evaluation. Kaufman (1983) presents his elements in a sequential manner based upon their occurrence within an educational program.

**The Organizational Elements Model (OEM)**
**Roger A. Kaufman (1983)**

| *Organizational Efforts* | | *Organizational Results* | | *Societal Impact* |
|---|---|---|---|---|
| **Inputs** | **Processes** | **Products** | **Outputs** | **Outcomes** |

**Organizational Efforts (Inputs and Processes).** The first two elements are referred to as Organizational Efforts and describe the array of resources and teaching-learning methods that are orchestrated by the educator and educational organization. The Organizational Efforts – – inputs and processes – – are those aspects of a distance education program that are under the complete control of the educator and are designed and delivered by the educator in such a manner to facilitate learning.

| Organizational Efforts | |
| --- | --- |
| **Element** | **Examples in Distance Education** |
| **Inputs** | Interactive Classroom<br>Computers<br>Broadcast Studio<br>Instructional Objectives<br>Community Access Locations<br>Resource People<br>Computer Bulletin Board<br>Video Lectures |
| **Processes** | Sequence of Topics<br>Learner Feedback from Instructor<br>Organization of Curriculum<br>Informal Discussion Groups<br>Virtual Field Trip<br>Scheduled Contact Hours |

Organizational Efforts are those efforts that are most controlled by the educator or organization. And, it logically follows that the organizational efforts are also those parts of the educational program that are the easiest to evaluate. As a result, it is the organizational efforts that are most often the focus for evaluation.

Questions that can be answered through an evaluation of Organizational Efforts might include:

> *Was the selected technology appropriate for the learners? content? (Inputs)*
> *Was the selected technology appropriate for the content? (Inputs)*
> *Did the instructor provide sufficient structure to allow an appropriate comfort level for*
> *the learners? (Processes)*
> *Were appropriate educational resources available to the learners in a convenient and*
> *timely manner? (Inputs)*
> *Did the technical systems operate as expected? Did breakdowns occur? (Inputs)*
> *Were the learners able to maintain the pace that was established for the program?*
> *(Processes)*

It becomes clear that an examination of *learning* is not a function of an evaluation of Organizational Efforts. Learning evaluation, evaluation which examines the degree to which change has taken place, is a function of an examination of Organizational *Results*.

**Organizational Results (Products and Outputs).** Products and outputs, what Kaufman (1983) labels as Organizational Results, moves evaluation away from those aspects that the organization is responsible for putting into place and focuses on the results that accrue from their efforts. Organizational Results are often seen as countable phenomena that allow the organization to suggest with some assuredness that certain specific outcomes have been achieved as a result of its efforts. These achievements, directly related to the distance education program, can be as diverse as the completion of certificates and degrees or the acquisition of specific knowledge, attitudes, skills, and aspirations (Bennett, 1975). The examination of Organizational Results is often what most distance educators have in mind when they go about the challenge of evaluation. It is understood that to achieve meaningful Organizational Results demands the appropriate implementation of meaningful Organizational Efforts. The two are clearly linked and the way to insure their viability is through evaluation.

| Organizational Results | |
|---|---|
| Element | Examples in Distance Education |
| Products | Number of Students Completing a Program<br>Number of Certificates Issued<br>Number of Degrees Awarded<br>Specific Knowledge, Attitudes, Skills and Aspirations Acquired<br>Number of Learners Who Have Passed an Examination<br>Validation of a Specific Program<br>Documentation of the Use of an Instructional Technology |
| Outputs | Public Awareness of the Distance Education Program<br>Increased Use of Local Learning Resources<br>Learner Application of Skills<br>Increased Participation by Distance Education Learners in Various Programs |

Kaufman (1983) cautions that our understanding of the words "Products," "Outputs," and "Outcomes" is important and that unfortunately "common language usage intermix these three words" (p. 55). His own defining of the terms is precise and provides a very helpful guideline for considering the two types of Organizational Results and also the difference between Organizational Results and Societal Impact, which, according to Kaufman (1983), is the essence of Outcomes.

Questions that can be answered through an evaluation of Organizational Results might include:

> *How have the graduates of this program impacted the local community? (Outputs)*
> *In what way have the learners involved with the distance education program been able to make meaningful use of the skills that have been taught? (Outputs)*
> *How many learners that began the distance education program were able to successfully complete the program? (Products)*

**Societal Impact (Outcomes).** Kaufman's (1983) view of evaluation is very expansive. The focus moves beyond the individual learner and clearly brings into focus the greater community and the potential that education has for affecting change at that level. In Kaufman's (1983) words, a major role of education is as a "means to societal ends" (p. 56). Outcomes are seen as the impact that Outputs have in and for society. "These are the external or outside-of-school results (or indicators of results) that determine the utility of organizational efforts and organizational results in and for society" (Kaufman, 1983, p. 56).

Within the context of distance education, a concern for Societal Impact allows us to go beyond the mere concern for elaboration of technology or self-indulging learning and, instead, develop a sense of the value of learning at a distance within the greater context of society. It significantly strengthens our position and stretches our thinking to look past considering only the learner and his or her own immediate learning needs and creates a greater sense of community as the basis for ultimate change.

Distance education evaluation that encompasses a concern for Societal Impact looks to the contribution that learning and learners make and the contribution that the program has made to the self-sufficiency of learners and society.

| Societal Impact | |
|---|---|
| **Element** | **Examples in Distance Education** |
| **Outcomes** | New Legislation by Government Agencies<br>Greater Community Participation in Local Decisions<br>Change in the Local Job Market<br>New Initiatives in the Community<br>Resolution of Community Problems |

Questions that can be answered through an evaluation of Societal Impact might include:

> *In what ways is the community now better able to accommodate new voices in decision making since the distance education program was offered? (Outcomes)*
> *What have been the long term effects of the program on the responsiveness of the organization in dealing with issues? (Outcomes)*
> *How have the lives of the learners been enriched in unexpected ways since the conclusion of the program? (Outcomes)*

## The Challenge of Evaluation in Distance Education

All forms of education evaluation play a major role in justifying programs, improving practice, and projecting into the future. However, in distance education, where the learner has the potential to move away from the control of the teacher and operate in very autonomous ways, it is essential that the practice of evaluation be moved closer to the learner. Moving evaluation closer to the learner demands that evaluation be appropriately influenced by the learner's needs of growth and development. Through appropriate learner-focused evaluation practice in distance education, it is possible to recognize the learner as a major partner in the teaching-learning environment, which is something that can be too easily overlooked in face-to-face learning situations. Evaluation in distance education must be carefully balanced between a traditional view that allows for program justification or development and a new view that has the potential for empowering learners.

**References**

Bennett, C. (1975). Up the hierarchy. *Journal of Extension*, 13(2).

Garrison, D. R. (2003). Self-directed learning and distance education. In M. G. Moore & W. G. Anderson (Eds.), *Handbook of distance education* (pp. 161-168). Mahwah, NJ: Lawrence Erlbaum Associates, Publishers.

Grobman, H. (1968). *Evaluation activities of curriculum projects: a starting point.* (AERA Monograph Series on Curriculum Evaluation). Chicago: Rand McNally & Co.

Kaufman, R. (1983). Needs Assessment. In W. E. English (Ed.), *Fundamental curriculum decisions: prepared by the ASCD 1983 yearbook committee.* Alexandria, VA: Association for Supervision and Curriculum.

Scriven, M. S. (1967). The methodology of evaluation. In R. Tyler, R. Gagne, & M. Scriven (Eds.), *Perspectives of curriculum evaluation* (AERA Monograph Series on Curriculum Evaluation). Chicago: Rand McNally & Co.

Stake, R. E. (1967). The countenance of educational evaluation. *Teachers College Record*, 68(7).

Tyler R. W. (1991). General statement on program evaluation. In M W McLaughlin & D C Philips (Eds.) *Evaluation and education: At quarter century.* Chicago: National Society for the Study of Education.

# Examples of Evaluation Instruments and Their Application in Distance Education

**Example 1**

| Evaluation Level | | Recipient of Evaluation Results | | Program Element to be Evaluated | |
|---|---|---|---|---|---|
| X | Measurement | | Agency/Sponsor/Community (Summative Assessment) | X | Inputs (Organizational Efforts |
| | Assessment | X | Instructor/Developer (Formative Evaluation) | X | Processes (Organizational Efforts) |
| | Evaluation | | Learners (Empowering Evaluation) | | Products (Organizational Results) |
| | | | | | Outputs (Organizational Results) |
| | | | | | Outcomes (Societal Impact) |

**How will data be used?**

To establish some baseline information and identify possible aspects of the project that should be considered in the future for improvement/change.

**Johnson County Extension Service
At-Home Video Learning Program
*Feedback Form***

To improve the **Basic Family Economics** at-home video learning program we would appreciate if you would complete the following items.

The strengths of **Basic Family Economics** were:

_____

_____

The weaknesses of **Basic Family Economics** were:

_____

_____

If another video learning program was to be developed for at-home use, it should include:

_____

_____

General Comments about the video learning program:

_____

_____

Please return your completed feedback form when you return the DVD.
**Thank You!**

**Example 2**

| Evaluation Level | | Recipient of Evaluation Results | | Program Element to be Evaluated | |
|---|---|---|---|---|---|
| X | Measurement | X | Agency/Sponsor/Community (Summative Assessment) | | Inputs (Organizational Efforts |
| | Assessment | | Instructor/Developer (Formative Evaluation) | | Processes (Organizational Efforts) |
| | Evaluation | | Learners (Empowering Evaluation) | X | Products (Organizational Results) |
| | | | | | Outputs (Organizational Results) |
| | | | | | Outcomes (Societal Impact) |

**How will data be used?**

To provide an immediate check of learning that is taking place as a basis for possible justification of the program.

## Basic Family Economics
## Web-Based Learning Module

### Unit 2 Test

1. The major obstacles to good family economic planning are:

    _____ Lack of ability
    _____ Poor time management
    _____ Inability to communicate with each other in family
    _____ Lack of sufficient funds
    _____ Misunderstanding


2. Most families, when faced with a major economic problem, turn to:

    _____ Friends and family
    _____ Financial agencies (bank, credit union, etc.)
    _____ Financial planners
    _____ No one


3. Economics is a concept:

    _____ unknown to most people
    _____ familiar to everyone
    _____ only understood by a few
    _____ that only applies to people with a lot of money

## Example 3

| Evaluation Level | | Recipient of Evaluation Results | | Program Element to be Evaluated | |
|---|---|---|---|---|---|
| | Measurement | | Agency/Sponsor/Community (Summative Assessment) | | Inputs (Organizational Efforts |
| X | Assessment | | Instructor/Developer (Formative Evaluation) | | Processes (Organizational Efforts) |
| X | Evaluation | X | Learners (Empowering Evaluation) | | Products (Organizational Results) |
| | | | | | Outputs (Organizational Results) |
| | | | | X | Outcomes (Societal Impact) |

**How will data be used?**

For independent reflection and personal development by individual learners without the supervision of the teacher.

From: "Joe Levine" <instructor@msu.edu>
To: "Online Learners" <aee801@msu.edu>
Subject: Special Assignment
Date: Mon, 4 Mar 200X 20:18:06 -0500
X-MSMail-Priority: Normal
X-Mailer: Microsoft Outlook Express 5.00.2919.6600
X-MimeOLE: Produced by Microsoft MimeOLE V5.00.2919.6600

It appears that all of the Learning Groups are now functioning very well. Congratulations!

The following is an individual task that I would like to ask each of you to do. There will be no grade for this task and you are not required to send copies of your emails to me. I hope you will find this task valuable for your own learning.

Here is the task –

1) Prepare an email in response to the following assignment. Send your email to each member of your Learning Group.

Assignment:
Rate (and discuss) your ability to be a self-directing learner who is capable of establishing your own learning objectives and learning on your own. What materials and activities do you find to be very helpful in assisting you as a self-directing learner?

2) Read and respond to emails that you receive from other members of your Learning Group. Using your response, try and help the other members of your group better understand how they are approaching their own self-directed learning.

3) Reflect on this activity – especially the feedback you receive from the members of your Learning Group. Prepare an entry for your Online Journal that captures some of the important aspects of your reflection.

**Example 4**

| Evaluation Level | | Recipient of Evaluation Results | | Program Element to be Evaluated | |
|---|---|---|---|---|---|
| | Measurement | X | Agency/Sponsor/Community (Summative Assessment) | X | Inputs (Organizational Efforts |
| X | Assessment | | Instructor/Developer (Formative Evaluation) | X | Processes (Organizational Efforts) |
| X | Evaluation | | Learners (Empowering Evaluation) | | Products (Organizational Results) |
| | | | | | Outputs (Organizational Results) |
| | | | | | Outcomes (Societal Impact) |

| How will data be used? |
|---|
| To decide if the Local Learning Program should be changed to include the regular use of the ***Question & Answer Conference Call.*** The Conference Call will be adopted if all statements receive a mean score of 3.8 or greater. |

Local Learning Program
Evaluation

Thank you for participating in last week's *Question & Answer Conference Call* for Unit 2 of our Local Learning Program. Please take a few minutes and indicate how much you agree/disagree with each of the following statements. Your responses will help us understand whether a *Question & Answer Conference Call* should become a regular feature of future programs.

1) The *Question & Answer Conference Call* was a good use of my time.

   Strongly Agree  5  4  3  2  1  Strongly Disagree

2) My questions/concerns were answered during the *Question & Answer Conference Call.*

   Strongly Agree  5  4  3  2  1  Strongly Disagree

3) Everyone had a chance to participate during the *Question & Answer Conference Call.*

   Strongly Agree  5  4  3  2  1  Strongly Disagree

4) It was important to have a good facilitator during the *Question & Answer Conference Call.*

   Strongly Agree  5  4  3  2  1  Strongly Disagree

5) Comments:

# Part Two:
# The Learner in Distance Education

---

**Focusing attention on learners and their uniqueness as they attempt to learn when separated by time and/or location from the instructor.**

# Chapter 7

# The Learner in Distance Education

**Gary Teja**
and
**S. Joseph Levine**

As we begin to understand the motivations and characteristics of the learner in a distance education environment, clearly a comparison to an "adult learner" is not only meaningful, but also very helpful. This vision of the distance learner as an adult learner is drawn from one of the most essential demands that distance education environments place on the learner – being able to effectively work and learn in a **self-directed** learning situation. Garrison (2003) says, "The concept of self-directed learning has considerable potential to help distance educators understand student learning" (p. 167). As we move ahead in this chapter, dealing with the learner in distance education, we will be using the terms "adult learner," "distance learner," and "self-directed learner" in interchangeable ways. To be an effective distance learner demands a high degree of self-discipline and structure, which is the same as that demanded in self-directed learning and is the basis for effective adult learning.

In this chapter we will be looking at key concepts and ideas that are the foundation of understanding distance education or self-directed learning. How do we describe a self-directed learner? What are the meaningful assumptions that the educator should make about this learner? How and why are these learners motivated? And how does learners' life stage affect their readiness to be effective distance learners? These and other similar questions will be the foundation on which this chapter will be built for discussing the learner in distance education.

## Setting the Stage

Let's begin by looking at three different learners.

> *Jim Johnson, a middle-management employee of an accounting firm, finds himself at a dead-end in his job. To climb the "ladder of success," Jim decides to earn an MBA. His travel schedule prevents him from enrolling in a regular on-campus program of study. On his many flights across country, he reads about "MBA degrees at a distance" and decides to enroll in one of these programs.*

> *Marcos Garcia is a single parent of two children living in a large metropolitan city. Marcos would like to learn more about his three and five year olds. He has decided to participate in a six – week, not-for-credit, online offering in child development that is being offered by the Cooperative Extension Service.*

> *Samantha Vanderkamp is a retired postal worker. With time on her hands, Sam decides to learn something about her Dutch roots. Sam now has the time to "surf" the worldwide web for sites on Dutch art and history.*

In all three of these scenarios an adult is about to embark on a period of learning. Two of the learners will be participating in organized educational programs – one formal and the other nonformal. The third learner has chosen to learn in a non-structured manner. All three will be required to be self-directed as they go about their learning projects. In all three cases, electronic technology will be a major part of the learning experience, that is, using a computer in some form. All three are embarking on a form of distance education. All three are typical adult learners.

## The Assumptions the Distance Educator Holds About the Learner

Malcolm Knowles (1970, 1980), building on the foundational ideas of Eduard Lindeman (1926), has done a tremendous service to distance educators by focusing attention on the assumptions that educators hold about their learners, that is, the feelings and biases that we have when we consider the people who are trying to learn from us. Knowles (1984) would suggest that our assumptions about our learners – our understanding of who and what they are – define our potential for being successful in helping them learn. The teaching methods and techniques we use as distance educators are merely reflections of the assumptions that we hold about our learners. We can make frequent changes in our teaching methods, but unless we set about to change the assumptions we have about our learners, we will probably see little difference in our effectiveness as educators!

Knowles (1984) uses the term "andragogy" as a keystone to the understanding of adult learners, the assumptions we hold about them, and how we relate to them. The term "andragogy," originally used in Western Europe, was brought into adult education literature in the United States by Lindeman (1926) and later popularized by Knowles (1970, 1980). The term draws its meaning from a set of comparisons between andragogy and the more familiar word that it is compared with – "pedagogy." As Knowles (1970, 1980) points out, pedagogy is drawn from the Latin that means "to lead children." He felt that using a term such as "pedagogy" to define interactions with an adult learner was rather inconsistent and inappropriate. He felt there needed to be a term that better defined the adult as a learner and how we interact most effectively with such a learner. He consequently worked to define operationally the concept of andragogy, to clearly differentiate between it and pedagogy, and to popularize the term as a meaningful way to describe a set of assumptions best held by an adult educator – assumptions that respected the learner as someone who was approaching the challenge of learning in a self-directing manner.

Knowles (1970, 1980) began by providing simplistic definitions of the two terms. He defined pedagogy as "the art and science of *teaching* children." Carefully selecting his words, he then went on to define andragogy as "the art and science of *helping* adults learn." He was careful not to refer to andragogy as "teaching adults" since he was concerned that the role of the educator be that of a "helper" rather than someone in control who merely wanted to "teach." Being a helper created a very different view of an adult educator and one that was significantly more difficult to operationalize than an educator who has set about the business of "delivering" education to learners. An educator of adults, according to Knowles (1984), would not be able to fulfill his or her educator functions without developing a strong relationship with the learner. The role of the adult educator was dependent upon this learner-educator relationship, which was a significant departure from earlier practice. Knowles (1970, 1980), in defining the concept of andragogy, drew heavily on a humanistic rather than a behavioristic view of the learner. It was to become an important differentiation between the two terms and reinforced the concept of self-directed learning as a major differentiation between the way in which an adult approaches learning as compared to how a child approaches learning.

# The Assumptions of Andragogy

To provide clarification of how significant the differences are between one who practices andragogy and one who practices pedagogy, Knowles (1984) defined a set of assumptions about learners that should most appropriately be held by the adult educator or the "andragog." This same set of assumptions holds significant promise as the assumptions that should be held about learners in a distance education environment.

**Table 1**

**Knowles' Andragogical Assumptions**

1. Adults are motivated to learn as they experience needs and interests that learning will satisfy.

2. Adults' orientation to learning is life-centered.

3. Experience is the richest resource for adults' learning.

4. Adults have a deep need to be self-directing.

5. Individual differences among people increase with age.

Knowles, M. S. (1984). *The adult learner: a neglected species.* Houston: Gulf Publishing Company. p. 31.

As we examine these four basic assumptions about the adult as a learner, a number of understandings gain further clarity. For instance, as the needs and interests of the adults become understood and clarified by the educator, their motivation for learning becomes stronger and they are more likely to invest the needed time and resources for a successful learning experience. Such a readiness to learn is often referred to as a "teachable moment" and forms the basis for very significant learning events. Learning that is based on the needs of the learner is often self-motivated and internally directed and is most easily seen in out-of-school settings such as conferences, community forums, web browsing, or independent reading. The large number of self-improvement books found in local bookstores often attempt to respond to adults' motivation to learn that is based on their experiences and interests.

Focusing learning on life that we are encountering, not life as it may appear in a year or two, seems to be such an obvious link as we reflect on our own day-to-day lives. Yet, as educators, we often forget this as we are trying to help others learn. The challenge of helping others learn is most typically organized around a set of views and recommendations that are brought by the educator and imposed on the learner. The more powerful approach is one whereby the concerns that form the basis for learning are drawn from the very problems that are being faced by the learner. The astute distance educator builds the curriculum in such a way to allow a problem-centered focus that is able to respond with a sense of immediacy to the real problems being faced by the learner.

This idea is built on the premise that the learner does, in fact, have significant experience that can form the basis for further learning. Knowles (1984) reminds us that the adult learner does not come to the classroom as a blank book. Instead, the learner brings a richness of experience that can and should be used by the educator as the basis for further learning. Of course, to take full advantage of the adult's experiences as the basis for learning also suggests that the learner must be empowered to be self-directing as he or she goes about the learning. To establish learning agendas that are dependent upon the educator as a *middle person* who is needed for learning to occur is counter to the principles of andragogy. The adult can best bring his or her own experiences forward as the basis for learning when the adult feels that he or she has the power to be self-directing in his or her own learning activities.

Knowles (1984) does not suggest, however, that the adult or self-directing learner always appears, as if by magic, at the doorstep of the educator with all of these characteristics or assumptions fully functioning. No, that would certainly be a bit too idealistic. What Knowles (1984) does suggest, though, is that it is possible for the educator to hold these assumptions as strong beliefs, to use them as the basis for creating a safe and powerful instructional environment in which the learner is able to accept them as appropriate behaviors, and then to help the learner in a variety of ways to demonstrate and adopt these behaviors. Within the distance education setting these assumptions help establish the foundation on which specific instructional strategies and delivery technologies should be selected and implemented.

> *Considering the cases presented at the beginning of this chapter, it is easy to make assumptions about all three of the learners that are consistent with Knowles' view. We can view Jim Johnson, with his desire to earn an MBA to help him move ahead in his job, as someone who is ready to learn, has a strong need to know, and is ready and willing to display that need. Marcos Garcia's desire to learn child development, on the other hand, can be assumed to be clearly problem focused with Marcos having a significant experiential base that can be built upon for further learning. And it is easy to see Samantha Vanderkamp as someone who is clearly self-motivated and inner-directed in her desire to surf the worldwide web as she goes about learning about her Dutch roots.*

## Motivation for Learning

Adult motivation to learn is often considered in light of two categories:

> **Learning for instrumental motives** – where learning activities are clearly engaged in based upon what specific outcomes (skills, knowledge, abilities) will accrue to the learner. The learning of new job skills fits in this category.

> **Learning for intrinsic motives** – where learning is not nearly as utilitarian and is engaged in for a host of reasons that appeal to the inner motivations of the learner. Learning how to play a musical instrument, surfing the worldwide web for information on a hobby, or asking a neighbor to explain how to fix one's lawn mower are examples of intrinsic-focused learning.

This simplistic set of two categories of motivators for learning is drawn from the early research of Cyril Houle (1961). Houle (1961) conducted a study of adults attending a formal adult education program. Based upon the adult's motivation to participate in a formal adult learning program, Houle was able to identify three distinctly different types of learners.

> **Goal-oriented learners** – where the learners are motivated by the accomplishment of a particular end. Their motives were clearly instrumental in nature. They wanted to learn skills that could be transferred to specific areas of their lives (e.g., work, family, community).

**Activity-oriented learners** - where the learners are motivated by their social and interactive needs. Investment of time in a learning activity would be deemed successful by the learner if ample and meaningful opportunities to interact with other learners were available.

**Learning-oriented learners** – where the learners are motivated by the excitement and joy that comes from the act of studying and learning. The content of the learning activity, though important, is secondary to the very act of learning itself.

Within Houle's (1961) framework, the challenge for the distance educator becomes very clear. Understanding the reasons why a learner has chosen to participate in a particular distance education program can help define the manner in which the program is promoted, designed, implemented, and evaluated. For instance, clarifying specific skills that will be learned through the distance education program is essential information for the goal-oriented learner – one who is learning for instrumental motives. However, such a specification of skills to be learned may be of little help to the activity-oriented learner who is trying to make the decision about whether to participate in the program based upon the type and depth of learner interaction that will be available. In fact, distance education programs are often avoided by activity-oriented learners, those who are trying to learn for a specific set of intrinsic reasons, since it may be assumed that most of the learning time will be spent in isolated and non-interactive ways.

> *Returning to the three cases presented earlier, it would seem that Jim Johnson's pursuit of the MBA is clearly guided by a goal orientation. He wants to develop specific skills that will allow him to move on in his job. Similarly, Marcos Garcia's need as a single parent is also guided by a goal orientation with his desire to learn more about his children. However, it can also be assumed that for Marcos another important avenue for his learning, as a part of the online program is the opportunity to interact and share information with other parents facing similar concerns. This goal would be seen as characteristic of an activity-oriented learner and would help Marcos better understand that he is not alone in facing the problems of raising his two children. And finally, Samantha Vanderkamp, with lots of time available for her to surf the worldwide web, would appear to be most like a learning-oriented learner. She is most apt to take many "side trips" of discovery as she moves ahead with her learning agenda.*

A more recent addition to Houle's (1961) trilogy of adult motivations to learn is that of emancipatory learning (Freire, 1973; Horton, 1990; Mezirow, 1991). The learner who is motivated to pursue emancipatory learning will have some of the same social-interaction needs that are seen in the activity-oriented learner. However, the key motivation will be the opportunity to learn, especially about self, through significant reflective opportunities. Emancipatory-oriented learners are more likely to participate in face-to-face learning situations where immediate feedback is available, ideas can be challenged and built upon, and new courses of action can be planned. Those forms of distance education that can support emancipatory learning are typically synchronous forms that minimize the technological interface and promote as much person-to-person interaction as possible.

## The Relationship of Adult Development to an Understanding of the Adult Learner

Although the old adage, "You can't teach an old dog new tricks," would have us believe that as an adult moves through life his or her readiness, willingness, and ability to learn becomes less and less flexible, it really is not so. And, the easiest way to understand this view of continuing lifelong learning for the adult is to understand the basic concepts and ideas behind adult growth and development. A number of adult developmentalists (Erikson, 1950, Neugarten, 1968, Gould, 1978, Atchley, 1983, Sheehy, 1995) have documented the variety of stages and phases through which adults proceed as they progress through life. Though each developmentalist tends to take a somewhat different perspective on how the stages and phases are described, he or she does share certain notions, ideas, or concepts in common. They can be summarized as follows:

> Adult development, the way we progress through our life, is *definable and made up of certain predictable events* that provide markers along our path of life. Labels such as "mid-life crisis," "generativity," "settling down," "re-evaluation," and "middle age" are some of the many words chosen to describe these markers.

> The concept of adult development implies a *positive or a forward movement.* Adult development doesn't move backwards. At worst an adult may fail to develop and maintain a static position, but he or she will never move backward. In much the same way that we don't unlearn how to walk, the adult does not unlearn the growth that has been achieved.

> As we progress through life there is not only a difference in how a particular event is labeled but there is also a *qualitative difference* in the event itself. Each successive event in life is dependent in some measure on a preceding event and, as such, each successive event, as it builds on earlier events, becomes more and more complex – in the same way that life itself becomes more and more complex.

> As we move forward in our development our *ability to reflect back on earlier stages or phases is improved.* Through such reflection it is possible to meet later stages of life with a keener awareness of how to be successful in our own development.

Now with all of that as prologue, exactly how does an understanding of adult development assist the distance educator in better knowing the learner? And, of course, how can such a developmental understanding of the learner be translated by the distance educator into the more effective design and implementation of a distance education program.

The obvious first answer is that a developmental perspective of the adult learner helps to define the subject matter or area of focus for the learner. The younger adult learner, in such a view, would be more interested in degree-completion activities, whereas the thirty-year-old learner might be interested in learning that helps provide a sense of job security that would insure the safety of a young family, and the mid-age learner would be more interested in learning that assists in gaining work-related promotions that could help fulfill a sense of personal accomplishment and worth.

However, it is important that adult learners be cautious in their assumptions here, as adult development also teaches us that *as learners mature they become more and more complex,* and our ability to simplistically define them in terms of subject-matter interests becomes less and less viable. It would seem most appropriate, therefore, for the distance educator only to begin with an initial view of the content the learner's developmental stage suggests, but then to be willing to alter that view based upon further understanding of the learner, his or her complexity, and the actual involvement of the learner in the modifying of the instruction based upon his or her developmental needs.

When adult development is viewed as successive periods of transition and stability, another insight for the distance educator becomes apparent. *A prime time for learning is during periods of transition rather than periods of stability.* This is due in large part because it is at transition times in life that the adult is more apt to turn to learning as a way to assist in the resolution of the instability of the transition. After all, learning is traditionally defined as "change in behavior" (Gagne and Driscoll, 1988). Stable times in life tend to be those times when everything seems to be working well, change isn't needed, and our learning agenda becomes rather minimal. Assuming that the learners involved in a distance education program are in a transitional period of their lives suggests the need for a variety of program supports that can assist the learner in effectively dealing with change. The distance education program must be ready to make needed adjustments and changes based upon the transitions being dealt with by the learners. This idea, programmatic change based upon the transitional needs of the learner, is very contrary to the popular view of distance education that assumes that successive uses of a program are easy since the program has been "field tested" and can now be run over and over again with minimal change. A "canned" distance education program, one that is merely played over and over again for different sets of learners, risks failure because of its inability to effectively accommodate the changes that the learners may be encountering.

Although the perspective of the learner has the potential to improve with each successive developmental stage, the learner does not necessarily have the inherent ability to make effective use of such a perspective during a transition. Therefore another very valuable role for the distance educator is to assist the learner in reflecting on the changes that he or she is encountering so the learner can successfully deal with the change and transition that is being experienced.

Using a developmental view of the adult learner encourages the distance educator to provide the technology and teaching strategies that allow for personal reflection, to allow the flexibility that provides opportunities for defining and redefining specific content foci, and to create opportunities for learners to gain insight from others who are experiencing or have experienced similar development-initiated agendas. Regardless of whether an asynchronous or synchronous teaching and learning environment is being used, the technological aspects of distance education must be carefully examined to assure that they are not repressing or overpowering those aspects of adult development that are the basis for defining one's own learning agenda.

A final concern that an understanding of adult development helps to bring into focus is the reality that the lives of learners and teachers can be very similar. Both learners and teachers can be experiencing a transitional period in their lives, can hold insight for each other, have a need for flexibility, and can make qualitative changes in their perspectives, even while the distance education program is underway. Such a thought serves to "even the playing field" and brings both teacher and learner to a position of mutual respect for what each has to offer. Gone is the more traditional view that the teacher is empowered to be the deliverer of knowledge and the learner is only empowered to be the receiver of such knowledge.

> *Thinking back to our three hypothetical cases, Jim Johnson might be at what Daniel Levinson(1978) refers to as a "mid-life crisis" or Gail Sheehy (1995) a "second adulthood" whereby his pursuing of an MBA will help him resolve a potential crisis of purpose and propel him on the "ladder of success." Hopefully the involvement in an MBA program at a distance will help to bring a new sense of quality to the life he is leading.*

> *Meanwhile Marco Garcia appears to be at an earlier developmental stage, one that Erik Erikson (1950) refers to as Young Adulthood, where the key developmental focus is on establishing a sense of intimacy through a relationship of love. In Marco's case the loving relationship may be the one between his children and him. He would hope that the six-week online offering will help build and strengthen the relationship that he has established with his children.*

> *Samantha Vanderkamp, when viewed as an adult going through a developmental transition*

*period, finally has the needed time to pursue a learning agenda previously out of reach because of the other demands of her life. Developing a sense of historical relationship by learning about one's ancestors creates a strong qualitative approach to life in retirement. Samantha is clearly at a time where she is in charge of her learning agenda and not about to yield it for unneeded structure. The help that Samantha might best benefit from is what Allen Tough (1979) describes as an essential role of the educator of adults – helping the learner become a more effective and efficient planner of their own learning projects.*

## Conclusion

The task of designing and providing a meaningful distance education program for a group of self-directed learners may sound exceedingly daunting. After all, it demands that we not only think through the content of what will be delivered in the program but also be able to accommodate an andragogical set of assumptions about the learner, be sensitive to the learner's motivation and whether his or her participation is based upon instrumental or intrinsic motives, and to be able to respond to the developmental stage and corresponding needs that the learner may be experiencing. Not an easy challenge in a face-to-face learning situation and an even more difficult challenge in distance education. However, it is through the meeting of these challenges in distance education that the potential for a meaningful learning opportunity is achieved.

### References

Atchley, R. C. (1983). *Aging, continuity and change.* Belmont, CA: Wadsworth Publishers.

Erikson, E. (1950). *Childhood and society.* New York: Norton.

Freire, P. (1973). *Pedagogy of the oppressed.* New York: Seabury Press.

Gagne, R. & Driscoll, M. (1988). *Essentials of learning for instruction, 2nd Edition.* Englewood Cliffs, New Jersey: Prentice Hall.

Garrison, D. R. (2003). Self-directed learning and distance education. In M. G. Moore & W. G. Anderson (Eds.), *Handbook of distance education* (pp. 161-168). Mahwah, NJ: Lawrence Erlbaum Associates, Publishers.

Gould, R. L. (1978). *Transformations: Growth and change in adult life.* New York: Simon and Schuster.

Horton, M. (1990). *The long haul.* New York: Doubleday.

Houle, C. (1961). *The inquiring mind.* Madison: University of Wisconsin Press.

Knowles, M. S. (1970). *The modern practice of adult education: Andragogy versus pedagogy.* New York: Association Press.

Knowles, M. S. (1980). *The modern practice of adult education: From andragogy to pedagogy.* New York: Association Press.

Knowles, M. S. (1984). *The adult learner: A neglected species*. Houston: Gulf Publishing Company.

Levinson, D. (1978). *Seasons of a man's life*. New York: Alfred A. Knopf.

Lindeman, E. C. (1926). *The meaning of adult education*. New York: New Republic. Republished in a new edition in 1989 by The Oklahoma Research Center for Continuing Professional and Higher Education.

Mezirow, J. (1991). *Transformative dimensions of adult learning*. San Francisco: Jossey-Bass Publishers.

Neugarten, B. L. (Ed.). (1968). *Middle age and aging: A reader in social psychology*. Chicago: University of Chicago Press

Sheehy, G. (1995). *New passages*. New York: Ballantine Books.

Tough, A. (1979). *The adult's learning projects* (2nd ed.). Austin, TX: Learning Concepts.

# Chapter 8

# Responding to Learner Needs in Distance Education: Providing Academic and Relational Support (PARS)

**Stephen D. Lowe**

## Attrition in Distance Education

High attrition[1] rates in adult distance education reflect, at least in part, on the inability of distance education providers to provide students adequate relational and academic support. Of course, the problem of attrition in distance education cannot be solved by only addressing institutional responsibilities. However, the solution to the problem begins there and certainly ought to be initiated by the institution since many would argue the institution has the higher ethical obligation. While recognizing that institutions and their instructors play a vital role in addressing the persistent problem of attrition, the Providing Academic and Relational Support (PARS) model places an equally high responsibility on adult learners. Tinto (1987) makes this same point when he argues that, "To single out the institution as being solely responsible for student departure, as do many critics, is to deny an essential principle of effective education, namely that students must themselves become responsible for their own learning." (p.181) This last phrase is especially critical for adult learners at a distance, although it should be a consideration at any level. An adult student in a distance education environment is confronted with the reality of being the only one truly responsible for his/her own learning. If distance learners have not learned how to take responsibility for their own learning prior to enrollment in a distance education program, they are at a serious disadvantage and may be jeopardizing their academic success in that institution.

Attrition or retention data for distance education courses across the country do not currently exist. Carr (2000) concurs when she notes that, "No national statistics exist yet about how many students complete distance programs or courses." Although it is difficult to obtain attrition data from institutions, there is enough evidence in the literature to suggest it is a perennial problem in adult education in general, and distance education in particular.

Historically, distance education providers have experienced higher attrition rates than traditional institutions. Kerka (1995) reports attrition rates as high as 60-70% among adult basic education

---

[1] A word of clarification about terminology is in order. *Attrition* is a synonym for *dropout, student departure,* or *student leaving* and refers to those who enroll in a course or degree program but never complete it. *Persistence* is a synonym for student progress and is the opposite of attrition. It refers to student behavior whereby one continues to make *progress* through a course or degree program by remaining continuously enrolled. *Retention* refers to institutional efforts taken to keep students enrolled in a course or degree program. Retention rates refer to the number or percent of students who complete a course or degree program. Retention rates are the opposite of attrition rates that depict the number of students who withdraw, in various ways, from a course or degree program before completing the stipulated requirements.

programs as reported to the federal government. Thompson (1997) also makes the same assertion when she notes that, "The drop-out rates for distance education courses are usually higher than those for comparable on-campus courses." She goes on to report the results of studies at her own institution (Edith Cowan University) that show, "the attrition rates over the last four years for external students have been more than double those for internal students." Beck (2000) asserts that, "Attrition rates for most distance education programs are worse than for traditional college courses, with dropout rates as high as 80% at some colleges." She cites data from Piedmont Technical College in Greenwood, South Carolina to indicate that the "overall attrition rate for traditional classes average 25%, while attrition rates for online courses average 45%." Kember (1995) reports attrition data that range from 28% to 99.5% in distance education settings including correspondence courses that can have attrition rates as high as 70% (p. 23-24). The American Institute for Chartered Property Casualty Underwriters (CPCU) and the Insurance Institute of America reported attrition rates in their distance education courses as high as 50% (Zolkos, 1999).

Many studies in areas outside of distance education have demonstrated a relationship between the provision of appropriate academic and relational support and a decrease in attrition rates both in traditional and nontraditional institutions. The most significant variables identified from these studies that contribute to student persistence are orientation experiences of various sorts, level of commitment to the institution, early faculty contact, academic support (sometimes referred to as developmental programs) comprising a variety of strategies, learner self-confidence and self-perception, and affective support that takes on a variety of forms but in essence provides emotional encouragement and motivation to students encouraging them to persist in their academic endeavors (Turnbull, 1986; Tinto, 1987, 1990; Tallman, 1994; Gibson, 1996). As a result of this research, most traditional colleges now require freshman or first-year student orientation designed to alleviate some of the causes correlated with attrition and many have now hired full-time retention coordinators. The "first-year experience" is a major topic at seminars and workshops. The result of all of this attention is that most traditional institutions provide year-long interventions during the first year of study. Taylor University, a private Christian college in Indiana, has required orientation and other retention strategies to address the problem of attrition, and now reports 87 per cent of their incoming freshmen return for the second year. (xap.com, Undergraduate Student Plans section, para. 1)

Personal variables such as personality, motivation, age, sex, and income level have not been shown to influence attrition rates in distance education (Eastmond, 1995, p. 53). In fact, Kember states flatly that "entry characteristics are not good predictors of final outcomes" (p. 77). The one personal variable that has been shown to affect completion rates is academic ability. However, even this finding is found to be tenuous when more mature adult students from limited academic backgrounds are included in the sample (Kember, p. 72)

Another important variable for student progress is the impact of the part-time status of most adult students in distance education programs. Generally speaking, part-time students have higher attrition rates than full-time ones. A few years ago, the Evansville Press and Courier reported that the University of Southern Indiana had a four-year attrition rate of about 70% when the majority of their students were enrolled on a part-time basis. Now about 95% of their student body is considered full-time and their attrition rate stands at about 28% over four years. Studies conducted on student attrition have found external factors, those that are external to the institution but related to the life of the student, play a significant role in student progress. With this in mind, Kember notes that "external factors become increasingly important when study is a part-time activity" (p. 47). The most plausible explanation for this phenomenon is the lack of "collective affiliation," to borrow Kember's term, or integration of the student into the life of the institution. Tinto's model of institutional departure as well as Kember's model of student progress makes provision for the integration of students into the community of the institution. Tinto notes that, "the effect of institutions upon student leaving highlights the intricate web of reciprocal relationships which bind students to the communal life of the institution" (p. 181). Those students who feel at home, comfortable, and accepted by the institution are more likely to persist than those students who feel alienated and alone.

## The Effect of A Traditional Educational Background on Nontraditional Learners

While the issues just enumerated certainly are valid and legitimate aspects of the problem of attrition in distance education, the most critical ingredient has been ignored: the majority of students who matriculate into a nontraditional, distance education degree program come from traditional educational institutions. Given this reality, distance education providers are confronted with a subset of derivative issues. Students in traditional classroom settings are often not taught the essential skills of self-directed learning and learning-how-to-learn so critical for academic success in distance education. In addition, as Malcolm Knowles has taught us, these same students enter with learner self-concepts shaped by the realities of a classroom experience that taught them to be dependent and passive, two potentially fatal learner attributes in a distance education environment. As Knowles (1975) put it so succinctly, "most of us only know how to be taught, we haven't learned how to learn." (p. 14). Paulo Freire (1983) offers a similar critique of traditional education and its resultant negative affect on learners. Freire's famous "banking" metaphor aptly describes most traditional schooling instruction that is nothing more than "an act of depositing" (p. 58). Students passively "receive, memorize, and repeat" the "communiqués" issued by the teacher (p. 58).

Consequently, most students who enroll in distance education programs from traditional learning backgrounds are ill equipped to handle the unique demands of study at a distance. Yet, distance education providers treat them as if all of their previous educational experience has somehow magically produced in them the requisite skills of self-directedness and the concomitant abilities required for the organizing of one's learning, time management, academic self-assessment, not to mention computer and Internet skills. As part of the provision of adequate and appropriate institutional and instructional support, a distance education institution should assist new students to begin acquiring and developing the skills of self-directedness and the whole range of learning-how-to-learn skills required of those studying at a distance. Gibson (1996) made this point quite convincingly in a study on the relationship between academic self-concept and persistence in distance education. She observed that,

> "Analyses of the data provide support for continuing a number of already-suggested, although not widely used, practices. For example, a student orientation that introduces procedures for learning at a distance…should be provided. Instruction in the process of directing one's own learning and in study strategies also seems appropriate early in a student's program" (p. 32-33).

The critical phrase is "early in a student's program." The more quickly a distance education provider can begin making distance learners aware of the new learning skills they will need in distance education the more beneficial to the learner. Another study by Fjortoft (1996) found "a need for [distance] educators to help adult learners prepare for further study with self-assessment exercises and, possibly, learning-style inventories" (p. 58). One of the most comprehensive distance education retention programs was developed by Rio Salado College in Tempe, Arizona. Their three-pronged approach includes student assessment of learning needs, an orientation video, and a telephone contact program. They have seen about a 20% improvement in retention since the program started a few years ago (Case and Elliott, 1997).

## Providing Academic and Relational Support

Institutions that provide education at a distance confront a unique set of challenges. The most significant of these is to provide appropriate academic (institutional and instructional) and relational (emotional and interpersonal) support for students given the constraint of "distance" that separates learner from teacher.

**Academic Support.** Appropriate academic support must be provided to ensure the academic success of distance education students that eventually leads to course and degree completion. *Institutional academic support* includes such elements as provision of competent and credentialed faculty, competent and knowledgeable staff, quality materials, appropriate delivery technology, and other typical human and material resources. *Instructional academic support* refers to the instructional design of courses, the interaction with faculty or adjunct faculty, tutorial assistance, and so on.

**Relational Support.** Relational support describes the more affective dimension of the learning process wherein we encourage, motivate, and nurture students. The form of support being described is offered at an emotional level and attempts to strike a balance with the more intellectual/cognitive support typically provided by academic institutions of higher education. The relational aspects of learning are strongly embedded in interpersonal relationships between co-learners and between learners and instructor. These important relationships are similar in many respects to what Carl Rogers had in mind when he wrote his chapter on "The Interpersonal Relationship in the Facilitation of Learning" in *Freedom to Learn*. He argued that "the conditions that facilitate learning" are multifaceted but "that one of the most important of these conditions is the attitudinal quality of the interpersonal relationship between facilitator and learner" (p. 125). He went on to note that when such a learning climate exists it is "stimulative of self-initiated learning and growth" (p.126).

## The PARS Model

The Providing Academic and Relational Support (PARS) model is proposed as a comprehensive framework to be used by distance education providers to guide administrators and instructors in the design and delivery of academic and relational support in courses as well as entire degree programs. It is also suggested as a guide to empower adult learners who are contemplating enrollment or are already enrolled in a distance education course or degree program. In addition to the two key elements of academic support (institutional and instructional) and relational support, the PARS model also focuses on self-directed learning and learning-how-to-learn skill development. All of these elements interact with one another to create a dynamic model. The PARS model is presented graphically in Figure 1.

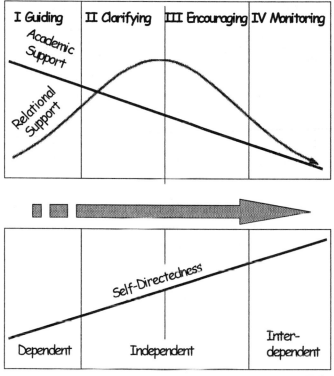

**Figure 1**

The PARS model recognizes and expects growth in learning maturity and so it also envisions a dynamic development of self-directed and learning-how-to-learn skills along a continuum from Dependent to Interdependent. The left hand side represents a *dependent* adult learner who is new to distance education and has been "domesticated" by traditional educational environments. The mid-point of the continuum represents an *independent* learner and the far right represents an *interdependent* adult learner. These levels of dependence/independence/interdependence are directly associated with the academic and relational support needed by the learner, as represented by the four columns at the top of the figure. Those learners who are moving away from a dependent stage of self-directedness are in need of less unsolicited academic support and more proactive relational support. Likewise, the learner who is gaining more independence in learning skills has similarly moderate needs for both academic and relational support. By the time a learner has essentially mastered the learning skills needed for deep learning experiences they are becoming more inter-dependent and affiliative.

The model does not lock a student, teacher, or administrator into assuming that everyone enters a distance education degree program with the same academic and learning skills. It may be that a student who enrolls with some experience and expertise in learning at a distance should be treated as a Stage 3 learner and thus by-pass many of the support scaffolding provided in columns # 1 and #2. It is probably safe to assume that most adult learners entering a distance education delivery system have had little exposure to these learning skills in a formal way. Certainly this will be the case for the foreseeable future until more and more students take advantage of distance education opportunities in higher education and other settings.

There are both informal and formal ways of assessing learning skill levels. Admissions staff, alert to verbal clues offered by prospective students, can use informal assessment. Often, students who are anxious about their ability to perform in a distance education environment may often verbalize their anxiety about lack of skills to staff members in the process of application. Informal contacts may provide information about previous distance education experience that offer some clues as to whether or not a given student had previous opportunities to acquire distance education learning skills. Institutions, instructors, and students are able to formally assess self-directed learning skill abilities by taking informal assessment instruments such as the *Competencies of Self-Directed Learning: A Self-Rating Instrument*, developed by Malcolm Knowles and included as an appendix in his book *Self-Directed Learning*. Formal learning skill assessments of this kind may be imbedded in orientation experiences or in a required orientation course.

The arrow in the PARS diagram is pointing to the right and is suggestive of the developmental nature of the figure and the model. Though there are times when a learner may need to return to an earlier stage of PARS (facing an entirely new situation, taking a new course from a new instructor, dealing with unfamiliar content, etc.) the general movement is always to the right - toward enhanced abilities as a self-directing learner.

The PARS model is both descriptive and prescriptive. It is descriptive to the extent that the model realistically portrays what often transpires when students enroll for the first time in a distance education course or degree program and then progress through the course. It is prescriptive to the extent that it suggests components an institution could put in place to enhance adult learner development and facilitate course and degree completion in distance education.

## Influences on the Development of the PARS Model

The PARS model has been informed and influenced conceptually by Hersey & Blanchard's "Situational Leadership Model" (1984); Pratt's "Relational Construct" model (1988); Smith's "Situational Instruction Model" (1989); Grow's "Staged Self-Directed Learning Model" (1991); Kasworm and Yao's "Stages of Teaching/Learning in Distance Education Model" (1993); Kember's "Model of Student Progress in Distance Education" (1995) and the theory of adult self-directedness propounded by Knowles (1975) and Tough (1979).

**Leadership Models.** Hersey and Blanchard's Situational Leadership Model, provides a useful conceptual tool for viewing and analyzing one's leadership style. The horizontal axis of the model emphasizes leader task behavior, while the vertical axis stresses leader relationships to subordinates. Four distinct leadership styles emerge from the convergence of these two variables in relationship to the maturity or skill level (from low to high) of subordinates that forms a continuum across the base of the model. Leadership style is situational in that it depends upon the maturity level of subordinates, which is presumed to grow and improve over time. As the subordinate matures (in a variety of areas), the leader's style of relating and tasking adjusts accordingly.

The Smith, Kasworm and Yao, and Pratt models are educational variations on the Hersey and Blanchard leadership style model. Although Kasworm and Yao do not use the four-quadrant approach of Hersey and Blanchard, the conceptual idea is similar. They propose a continuum of three stages from low learner autonomy and self-directedness to high learner autonomy and self-directedness.

Included in their model are task and relational roles for instructors and course designers that provide alternative ways of tasking and relating depending upon the learner's ability to become more autonomous and self-directing. Obviously, the more autonomous and self-directing the adult learner becomes, the less structure, direction, and support provided by the instructor or institution. The benefit of the Kasworm and Yao model is that it was constructed with the unique needs of distance learners in mind.

**Situational Variables.** The Pratt "Relational Construct" model is more obviously dependent upon Hersey and Blanchard's model than Kasworm and Yao. Pratt's model reflects his desire to highlight the situational variables that prevail in adult learning settings. He defines situational variables as "those conditions which prevail during learning which cannot be considered personal, psychological attributes of the learner or teacher" (Pratt, 1988, p. 162). According to Pratt, situational variables might include goals, content, time, cost, and audience size. He notes the role of external constraints from employers as a situational variable that could have drastic effects on student preferences for instructional delivery. Consequently, adult instructors and course designers must be aware of the fact that adult learners may prefer more pedagogical or more highly structured learning experiences at times rather than more andragogical or collaborative approaches. Therefore, he proposes the adjustment of instructional delivery and stratagems in response to adult learner preferences and needs. The teacher would function in the role of leader in Hersey and Blanchard's model and adjust his/her style of teaching and delivery to meet the needs of the student as the situation prevails. While this model might work well in a traditional classroom environment where such adjustments can be made relatively easily, it becomes more problematic for distance education delivery systems that already have pre-packaged courses designed with a particular instructional strategy in mind. But the model is useful in that it supports our notion that the adult learner grows and develops in his/her skills as a self-directed learner and that consequently, adjustments must be made in the way in which instruction is delivered and academic support provided.

**Student Maturity Level.** Smith's "Situational Instruction Model" has been proposed as a way to view instructional interaction in adult education. The model comprises instructional and content components conceived along a bi-polar continuum from low to high, as well as a learner component that describes the "educational maturity of the adults" involved in the learning experience (p. 7). The educational or learning maturity level of the adult student determines the appropriate teaching strategies and content level. The model recognizes the necessity of adjusting instructional delivery to the needs and abilities of the adult learner and offers, therefore, a highly dynamic view of the teaching/learning situation.

**Understanding the Non-Completer.** All voluntary educational enterprises are confronted with the problem of attendance. In some settings, the problem has more to do with identifying barriers that prevent participation in educational activities. In other circumstances, the issues are not getting people to attend but keeping them for the duration of the learning activity. Attrition rates tend to be significantly higher for nontraditional, voluntary educational activities than for other more compulsory and traditional forms of education.

David Kember has proposed a "model of student progress" designed with nontraditional or "open" educational institutions in mind. Within his model he provides a helpful taxonomy of leaving types that sharpen our ability to analyze the attrition problem. He divides students into one of several discreet persistence categories that are appropriate for distance education institutions:

1. non-starters
2. informal withdrawals

3. formal withdrawals
4. academic failure
5. transfer students
6. stop outs (students who stop attending with the intention of re-enrolling)

Kember's discussion suggests that the largest percentage of non-completers in distance education are non-starters. Non-starters are students who never submit their first lesson for grading. Here we have a student who has taken the initiative to contact a school, inquire as to its degree programs or courses, concludes that what that school has to offer he/she wants or needs, makes application and pays a fee, selects a program of study and enrolls in that program, pays all or part of the tuition, receives the course materials, and then does nothing! The really nagging question is "why?" Why did this student enroll to begin with? And, why has this student not made any obvious effort to begin what he/she clearly committed to both financially and emotionally?

The educational assumption of the PARS model is that the primary barrier to completing a course or degree program at a distance is a *skill* barrier. It is not a matter of motivation because these students enter with a high degree of motivation and expectation. An institution cannot get the materials to new students quickly enough to suit them. They are eager to begin and get on with their studies. But frequently something happens between the time course materials arrive and the time students are expected to submit their first lesson. Consequently, motivation is affected by a lack of direction and knowledge. It is at this stage that most students are confronted with the reality of distance education: "What do I do now? Where do I begin? How do I make sense out of all this? I had no idea it would be this much work!"

Typical distance education learners, who have taken all or most of their previous education at traditional institutions, are not well prepared to handle this reality. They have not been sufficiently equipped to handle the demands now being placed upon them by the distance delivery system. Most distance education providers get high marks for helping students new to distance education acquire the technical skills needed to navigate the newer delivery and learning technologies. However, most of these same institutions give little or no help to students to prepare them for the unique demands of learning at a distance. Gibson (1997) makes this point quite accurately when she observes,

> "Learners often confront the need for time management and stress management skills, increased self-directedness in goal setting, adoption of strategies to successfully assume new roles and responsibilities for teaching and learning, instigation of cognitive and metacognitive strategies etc. More often than not, these are learners who have been socialized to be passive recipients of information, competing for grades on examinations that require regurgitation of factual information. They simply are not prepared to succeed" (p. 8).

Now, possibly for the first time in their academic career, distance education students must take the initiative for their own learning, know how to do their own learning organization, plan their own schedule, pace themselves, and hold themselves accountable for whether or not a lesson is done today or tomorrow. Previously, most of these learning tasks were the primary responsibility of the faculty member. Students typically had to show up and follow directions. All of a sudden, the traits of dependency that served a student so well in a traditional setting, now become a major inhibitor to student progress in a distance education environment. Consequently, students confronted with this reality most often conclude that they are not cut out for distance education and quietly shove their course materials over in the corner or set them on a bookshelf never to be opened again! Or if they are in an online learning environment they may offer some excuse or invent some emergency that needs their immediate attention.

Students in this situation are in desperate need of institutional intervention in order to avoid becoming another statistic. Early on in a student's enrollment, the institution needs to provide direction and guidance regarding the acquisition of learning-how-to-learn and self-directed learning skills. Students who have learned how to be dependent learners can also learn how to be independent and eventually interdependent learners. It is a skill issue that has very little to do with academic ability, personal variables, or motivation.

## Assumptions of the PARS Model

The PARS model is based on the following assumptions regarding adult learners and the demands of distance education:

1. Most adult learners enter nontraditional distance education degree programs with little or no experience with the distance education delivery system.

2. Most adult learners enter a distance degree program with few if any of the essential skills of self-direction and learning-how-to-learn already in place.

3. Self-directed learning and learning-how-to-learn skills are essential if an adult learner is to succeed in a distance education environment.

4. Life circumstances beyond the control of the student and the institution often play a major role in student progress.

5. Adult students can grow and develop during the course of their degree program and this includes their skills of self-direction and learning-how-to-learn.

6. Adults who are given proper orientation and support to the unique demands imposed by the delivery of education at a distance will more likely complete their first course, first enrollment period, and eventually complete their degree program and do so at a high level of academic excellence.

7. Distance education institutions need a conceptual framework to guide their provision of academic and relational support.

## Key Components of the PARS Model

Anyone who has served in formal education will agree that the process of learning and study is not a purely intellectual endeavor. Social, emotional, psychological, and spiritual aspects also play a vital role in understanding all facets of the academic experience. The PARS model recognizes that a variety of institutional, instructional, emotional and interpersonal variables, can and do play a significant role in student persistence. When combined, these different variables provide psychological support most students need to experience success in academic endeavors.

The model assumes a whole person or whole learner perspective that appreciates the place of both intellectual and emotional aspects of the learning process. A failure to appreciate the dynamic interplay between intellect and affect, both as instructors and as institutions, will inevitably short-circuit the learning process and attenuate the developmental progress of our students. An exclusive focus on intellectual or academic matters may lead an instructor or an institution to depreciate other equally valid dimensions of the student as person. The affective or emotional aspects of a learner have just as powerful an influence on the learning process as cognitive aspects. Kember concurs when he writes, "Any view of student progress confined to a narrow academic sphere of influence will, then, ignore one of the most fundamental impacts upon the learning outcomes" (p. 219).

The PARS model is drawn from distance education experiences that suggest that most adult learners enter distance education with few skills in learning-how-to-learn and self-directed learning and with an external locus of control. An external locus of control is a psychological state in which students perceive that persons and events external to themselves have a controlling influence over the course and direction of their life. Adult learners with this perspective have been, in Freire's language, "domesticated" by the traditional educational experience to see the entire learning experience as something that happens "to" them from the outside. Since most new students entering distance degree programs have little or no experience in distance delivery systems, they are in need of guidance to assist them in maneuvering the frequently disorienting first experiences with a new delivery system. In effect, distance education providers capitalize on students' external locus of control but with the intention of moving them from this more dependent state to a developmentally mature state in which they assume greater responsibility for their own learning. As adult learners acquire greater facility in self-directedness resulting in greater learner autonomy and academic interdependence, they require less academic guidance or emotional support since the motivation for self-directedness and locus of control have been internalized.

Another way of conceptualizing the process depicted in the model is to borrow the language of "scaffolding" proposed by Vygotsky (1978). In the first column of the model the scaffolding is already in place, ready to provide academic support to the new distance education student in any way needed. As the student develops more and more facility in learning-how-to-learn and self-directed learning skills, the academic support scaffolding is gradually dismantled and the relational support scaffolding is strengthened. Eventually the student reaches the fourth column and both the academic support scaffolding and the relational support scaffolding are completely dismantled as the distance education participant becomes fully capable of being an interdependent learner with the appropriate self-directed and learning-how-to-learn skills in place and functioning well.

Adaptation to the growth experienced by adult learners as they develop more learning facility is essential. Teachers and administrators must adapt their style of relating to the learner and allow the growth of the learner to dictate the nature of the relationship between all parties involved.

## Operationalizing the PARS Model

**Column 1 - "Guiding" Academic and Relational Support.** The "guiding" style of providing academic and relational support offers the novice learner as much institutional and instructional direction as the student can handle and absorb. The relationship at this stage is more like a trail guide who is not so much concerned about establishing a relationship as he/she is in getting someone safely through rough terrain. The guide does a lot of pointing and directing but very little time is spent getting close to and emotionally engaged with those being led. Certainly institutions and instructors want to be cordial and inviting in this early stage of the learning process but the focus should be on information, direction, guidance, and counsel because that is what the student, often lacking much self-direction as a learner, typically needs at this stage of the distance education process.

It should be obvious that the most critical stage in the model is located in this first column where academic support is high but in decline and relational support is low but in ascendancy. The most critical need for adult learners at this point in a distance education experience is to receive targeted institutional and instructional support that will enable them to overcome the disorientation of a new learning experience. Assuming the traditional educational experience of most adult learners who are new to distance education, both institutions and instructors need to concentrate on providing information and skill development that will enhance an adult learner's self-directed and learning-how-to-learn skills.

The guiding stage of PARS is most essential for that large group of learners who, in Kember's language, may become "non-starters." These students enroll and receive course materials and information about how to get started in an online distance education environment. However, non-starters seem to freeze at that point not knowing what to do next or seem unsure of their ability to continue in such a demanding academic environment. For these students it is not an issue of motivation or lack of personal variables such as intelligence or ability but rather an inability to move systematically from one step to another in order to successfully complete a course. The really critical issue at the outset of a distance education experience is a need for skill intervention. Students need an infusion of academic and technical direction that can guide them through the process of assessing their own learning skills and then developing those skills that may be missing or deficient.

**Column 2 - "Clarifying" Academic and Relational Support.** The "clarifying" style is akin to the coaching relationship in which a great deal of teaching takes place along with a high level of emotional and affective support and encouragement. The focus is not so much on the providing of necessary new information but instead the focus is on how to help the learner understand and make use of the information he/she already has. As is shown in column 2, the need for academic support is continuing to decline. Relational support, on the other hand, has now become a major focus for the learner as he/she assumes a more independent and self-directing role.

As noted earlier, Kember and Tinto both indicate in their models the strategic importance of personal affiliation between the institution and the student. Students who persist feel as though they are valued members of the institution's academic community. In short, they have a sense of belonging and acceptance. The institution, which is represented by its staff and faculty, needs to continue some level of academic support and direction, but that support and direction must be coupled with greater affective and relational support. The role of faculty and course assessors not only includes the grading of assignments but must also involve the verbal and written encouragement needed by students at this stage of their academic and personal development. Kember refers to the attribute of "pastoral interest" in describing the relationship between faculty and students and advises that, "Even a few friendly words can mean that students will be prepared to contact a person at some later time as the need arises" (p. 204). Peer mentors, if they have been assigned, can provide valuable affective support and encouragement for the student's academic progress at this time. Part-time students, who are full-time professionals, may sense a feeling of being overwhelmed by work-related demands and course requirements. Middle-aged adult learners who are "sandwiched" between demands from teenage children and elderly parents often feel overwhelmed. Their need for some level of continued academic direction does not diminish their need for personal attention and the perspective of one who has gone through the process and survived to tell about it.

Relational support at this "clarifying" stage may take the form of phone calls, letters, e-mail messages, comments in chat rooms, or feedback notes on returned assignments. Staff members can play a vital role in providing this kind of support by offering a word of encouragement as they handle their institutional concerns. The institution and its staff must be attuned to the emotional needs of adult learners at this critical stage of their academic progress and be sensitive and caring while providing needed direction and guidance to help bring clarity to this new learning experience. Kember highlights this dimension of the model when he suggests that, "Warmth, interest and perceived competence will contribute towards a sense of belonging. Coolness, tardiness in responding, bureaucratic indifference and incompetence will all have a negative impact which is often not perceived by those responsible for engendering it" (p. 204). The PARS model may prove beneficial to such persons by making them more attuned to student needs and more sensitive in handling them.

The bottom line is this: the greater the contact and communication between learner and institution, the higher the rates of persistence (Kember, 1995, p. 206). At a more practical level, it seems most beneficial if a student can have regular contact with one staff or faculty member rather than have multiple contact persons. This gives distance learners the sense that they have an advocate within the institution who is watching out just for them and taking care of their needs in a personal and professional manner.

**Column 3 - "Encouraging" Academic and Relational Support.** The "encouraging" style of providing academic and relational support is much like the role of a cheerleader. Cheerleaders cavort on the sidelines offering emotional motivation to players on the field and spectators in the stands. When an instructor or institution provides relational encouragement, they recognize the student has mastered most of the skills essential to academic success in a nontraditional setting, but may need more nurturing and cultivation than direction and guidance.

At this stage of the adult's learning development, there is considerably less need for academic support since it is assumed that the adult learner has acquired a significant arsenal of academic and learning skills enabling them to function effectively as an independent, self-directed learner. Although the academic support presented in columns # 1 and # 2 is still available, it is not a major focus of attention and not offered as presumptively as might have been the case early on, when the student's learning needs were greater. At this stage adult learners need gentle nudges toward higher levels of self-directedness since the momentum has already been generated by the array of services and supports offered and accessed earlier in the program. As students mature in their development of learning skills they display greater levels of learner autonomy and increasing self-directedness.

Whereas the need for high academic attention has greatly diminished by this stage in the adult's learning development, the need for emotional involvement continues - though also at a decreasing level. What the adult needs most at this stage are words of encouragement from both faculty and administrators. An adult learner at this stage has mastered a significant array of learning abilities and should be capable at this level of functioning in an academically acceptable manner. However, there is still some level of need to be affirmed by those who are held in high esteem by the student. Approval for what a student is doing academically is needed to encourage the student to continue a course of action in which he/she has invested heavily in all aspects - intellectual, social, emotional, and spiritual. Commitment to the institution becomes a critical factor at this "encouraging" level of the adult's journey toward degree completion, as does the student's own personal commitment to the goal of degree completion. Many studies of retention in higher education and participation in voluntary organizations have demonstrated that level of commitment plays a vital role in extent and duration of participation and involvement. The consensus of the educational and sociological literature on this subject is clear: the greater the level of commitment (as measured objectively and subjectively), the higher the rates of participation (see Lowe, 1991). Tinto places a great deal of weight on institutional commitment as one of the most powerful determinants of persistence in formal education. In part he writes,

> "Institutional commitment refers to the person's commitment to the institution in which he/she is enrolled. It indicates the degree to which one is willing to work toward the attainment of

one's goals within a given higher educational institution . . . the greater one's commitments, the greater the likelihood of institutional persistence" (p. 45).

By providing high levels of affirmation and encouragement, the institution and its representatives help foster and facilitate institutional commitment. There is an increased level of loyalty toward the institution that is fostered in the student.

**Column 4 - "Monitoring" Academic and Relational Support.** The "monitoring" style is a laissez-faire approach. It is based upon the concept that mature adults who are competent and skilled at learning are no longer in need of close supervision. An institution's (instructor's) confidence in the abilities of its adult learners is demonstrated by the fact that it provides opportunities for a great deal of autonomy. At this stage both academic support and relational support are at a minimum and provided only as needed and requested by the adult learner, or as warranted by institutional constraints (graduation procedures, accreditation requirements and so on). The instructor or institution "monitors" but is not proactive. The student takes the initiative for support as it is needed. However, if institutions and instructors are not careful, the learner can misinterpret the reduction in attention. It is especially critical that learners understand the ground rules that govern the nature of the relationship at this stage of the learning process. Students need to be assured that help and guidance is available when needed but that the request for this will most often originate with the learner and not the institution or instructor. The PARS model assumes that at this final stage the student in a distance education program has acquired requisite learning skills and competencies and has received the necessary affirmations to function as an *interdependent* adult learner. Consequently, there is little need for significant amounts of either academic or relational support. This does not mean the institution withdraws and leaves the student to function alone but simply reduces the extent to which services and relationships are highlighted and aggressively offered. Developmentally maturing adult learners are capable, at this stage, of determining for themselves what help and direction they need from the educational provider. They have learned to take responsibility for their own learning. At this stage the distance education provider has created an environment in which a student can flourish academically and personally to such an extent that they require little support and direction from the institution or instructor.

## Summary

The intent of the PARS model is to guide academic and relational support activity in a coherent fashion while facilitating self-directedness and academic interdependence in adult learners unfamiliar with the demands and expectations of the nontraditional distance delivery system with the intended outcome of degree completion. Any institution can "fill-in-the-blanks" of the model and identify specific strategies and services that can be provided to match the level of appropriate academic and relational support simultaneously cognizant of the adult's level of academic and learning maturity. The model enables institutions and even individual instructors to organize and plot the variety of strategies that may already be in place organizationally but which have no guiding or coherent master plan. By adopting such a model, distance education institutions enhance their own student services as well as improve attrition rates while strengthening the academic performance and learning skills of its adult learners.

# References

Aslanian, C. & Brickell, H. M. (1988). *How Americans in transition study for college credit*. New York: College Entrance Exam Board.

Beck, E. (2000). Student attrition in on-line courses. *Adjunct Advocate*, September/October.

Carr, S. (2000). As distance education comes of age, the challenge is keeping the students. *The Chronicle of Higher Education*, 46(23), p. A39.

Case, P. S. & Elliott, B. (1997). Attrition and retention in distance learning programs: problems, strategies and solutions. In *Open Praxis* 1, pp. 30-33

Cookson, P. (1990). Persistence in distance education. In M. G. Moore et al (Eds.), *Contemporary issues in American distance education* (pp. 193-97). Oxford: Pergammon Press.

Eastmond, D. V. (1995). *Alone but together: Adult distance study through computer conferencing*. Cresskill, NJ: Hampton Press.

Fjortoft, N. F. (1996). Persistence in a distance learning program: a case in pharmaceutical education. In *The American Journal of Distance Education* 10(3), pp. 49-59.

Freire, P. (1983). *Pedagogy of the oppressed*. New York: Continuum Publishing.

Gibson, C. C. (1996). Toward an understanding of academic self-concept in distance education. In *The American Journal of Distance Education* 10(1), pp. 23-36.

_____(1997). Teaching/learning at a distance: a paradigm shift in progress. *Open Praxis*, 1, pp. 6-8.

Grow, G. O. (1991). Teaching learners to be self-directed. *Adult Education Quarterly*, 41(3), pp. 125-49.

Harasim, L. et al (1995). *Learning networks*. Cambridge: The MIT Press.

Hersey, P. & Blanchard, K. H. (1993). *Management of organizational behavior*. Englewood Cliffs, NJ: Prentice Hall.

Kasworm, C. E. and Yao, B. (1993). The development of adult learner autonomy and self-directedness in distance education. In Bruce Scriven et al (Eds.), *Distance education for the twenty-first century* (pp. 77-89). Queensland, Australia: International Council for Distance Education and Queensland University of Technology.

Kember, D. (1995). *Open learning courses for adults: A model of student progress*. Englewood Cliffs, NJ: Educational Technology Publications.

Kerka, S. (1995). Adult learner retention revisited. ERIC Digest # 166.

Knowles, M. (1975). *Self-directed learning*. New York: Association Press.

Lowe, S. D. (1991). Expanding the taxonomy of adult learner orientations: the institutional orientation. *International Journal of Lifelong Education*, 10(1), pp. 1-23.

Mezirow, J. (1991). *Transformative dimensions of adult learning*. San Francisco: Jossey-Bass.

Pratt, D. (1988). Andragogy as a relational construct. *Adult Education Quarterly*, 38(3), pp. 160-81.

Rogers, C. (1969). *Freedom to learn*. Columbus: Charles E. Merrill Publishing Company.

Smith, D. H. (1989). Situational instruction: a strategy for facilitating the learning process. In *Lifelong Learning* 12(6), pp. 5-9.

Spann, N. G. (1990). Student retention: an interview with Vincent Tinto. *Journal of Developmental Education*, 14(1), September.

Tallmann, F. D. (1994). Satisfaction and completion in correspondence study: the influence of instructional and student-support services. *The American Journal Of Distance Education*, 8(2), pp. 43-57.

Thompson, E. (1997). Distance education drop-out: what can we do? In Pospisil, R. & Willcoxson, L. (Eds.), *Learning through teaching*, pp. 324-332. Proceedings Of the 6th Annual Teaching Learning Forum, Murdoch University, February 1997. Perth: Murdoch University.

Tinto, V. (1987). *Leaving college*. Chicago: University of Chicago Press.

Tough, A. (1979). *The adult's learning projects*. Toronto: Ontario Institute for Studies in Education.

Turnbull, W. W. (1986). Involvement: the key to retention. In *Journal of Developmental Education* 10(2), pp. 6-11.

Vygotsky, L. (1978). *Mind in society: The development of higher psychological process*. Cambridge: Harvard University Press.

Xap.com. Taylor University: Student enrollment numbers (2004). Retrieved June 11, 2005, from http://www.xap.com/gotocollege/campustour/undergraduate/4956/Taylor_University/Taylor_University6.html

Zolkos, R. (1999). Online education getting good grades: despite high attrition, online courses seen as possible alternative to the classroom. *Business Insurance*, 40B.

# Chapter 9

# Online Learning:
# From the Learner's Perspective

Bernard Gwekwerere
Rory Hoipkemeier
Laura Trombley

*Editor's Note:*
*So what are the positive aspects of online learning as perceived by the learners? This chapter was created through a series of individually conducted open-ended interviews with the authors - three adult learners - who have participated in a variety of different online classes offered by different institutions. The focus of the interviews was on those qualities of online learning that they valued and should be incorporated in an online class. The following are their words. To help organize their responses, eight categories were defined after the interviews were completed. Statements were then grouped under the categories to provide an organizational framework for the chapter.*

## Having a Sense of Autonomy

An online learner is an adult who can and should take control of his/her own learning. A viable online class not only permits the learner to have this sense of control but also is structured so that the individual's personal development is allowed and nurtured. Individuality is encouraged.

> *"Distance education has lived up to the expectation I have had for it. My first distance education experience was in 1996, and done entirely via e-mail. The class had a syllabus, texts and assignments, with papers submitted electronically and grades received electronically. My experience with this class was wonderful. I loved the opportunity to sit at my desk and communicate with my instructor. I loved not having to drive somewhere to attend class."*

> *"In distance education you need to be self-motivated to persist. You need good time management skills."*

> *"Distance education classes really treat the learner as an adult. You can do it within the other aspects of your life - you can still live your life recognizing you have this responsibility but you never have to*

*forego anything in your life because of your class assignments. You can always adjust the time when you do your classwork. You can do it in the middle of the night if necessary. That is a tremendous positive aspect of online learning."*

*"Probably the most exciting aspect of distance education for me is the autonomy and freedom that I have. I like being able to find out what I wish to find out when I want to do it."*

*"In an online class I find that the intention often is focused on learning and developing throughout the course your ideas and your thinking. It isn't just focused on passing the examination at the end of the course."*

*"As I began to consider switching to an online degree program, the sense of freedom felt great! I felt much less constricted, because I could attend class at home or at work, and on my time. I knew, even before the program started, that being a distance education learner was going to be an excellent way for me to learn."*

## Being Accountable to Each Other

Taking an online course is not just a private and individual matter. There is a sense of responsibility to help each other through the course. Working together with other learners and having a strong sense of community can make the online course very powerful.

*"Getting to help somebody to solve their problem was a very powerful and positive part of the online learning experience."*

*"The idea of people dealing with each other's concerns and questions is a very exciting part of the online learning experience. It means that everyone has to commit themselves to something which then makes it possible for others in the group to respond substantively to each other. In the online learning situation each person says something and makes a contribution to the dialogue."*

*"I like online learning when I have the opportunity to explore my own interests in an environment when everyone is doing similar exploration of their interests. The class serves as the meeting place where we can each share our ideas, concerns and problems. In an asynchronous online learning situation you have the chance to think about your concern and the concerns of others in the class throughout the week as you continue to sign on to the class and share your ideas. Learning is more continuous. In online learning there is a much greater chance that learning will become integrated with your daily life."*

*"In an online class where there is a very large group of students I find that I can't be accountable to the other students - the class is too large. And, this idea of being accountable to the others in my class is so very important for learning. I really like an online class that has no more than 5 or 6 students since I feel that I can get to know the other students and be accountable to each of them. Large online classes can be overwhelming to the learner."*

*"Because not everyone is as enthusiastic about the benefits of distance education, it helps me as a learner to be surrounded by other learners who are like me. Those who remain in a distance education program seem to be self-selected learners who thrive in the environment, are positive about it, and motivated to learn."*

*"The thing that was most exciting or energizing for me was the interaction with the other students. Every student contributed a piece of their work and described the struggle they were having. And then, the next day, you would find a number of different people had responded to you with ideas from their perspective of how to deal with the problem you had identified."*

## Allowing Me To Set a Flexible Schedule

Organizing your "learning time" in your own way, to fit your own schedule and demands, is a wonderful aspect of online learning. It is a demand that is very different than what is expected in a face-to-face class. However, it does demand a degree of self-discipline to do it well. Flexible scheduling can allow learning to occur when you, the learner, are most receptive.

*"I love the idea that the course that I was in allowed me to work on course projects when I had opportunities in my own schedule, as opposed to having to be ready to learn at exactly the time that the face-to-face class meets."*

*"Flexibility is one of the biggest pluses of a distance education course. Being able to set your own time and place is really great. With three children I know I can babysit and do my class work at the same time. I can even assist them with their homework while I'm doing my own homework. For me, learning is not the highest priority. My family is my highest priority and so online learning fits me very well."*

*"I 'go to class' when it works into my schedule. Usually I have to be online at least once per day. But, that time can be early in the morning before work, during the day, or late at night. I no longer have to work my life and that of my family around a set class time in a distant city. And, if I have to miss a day online, there isn't a penalty; I just make sure I catch up the next day."*

*"In being an online learner, it is important to set up a routine for participating. I find it essential to check into the discussion board daily, in order to stay with the flow of the class. There's usually a lot of text interaction, and it can be difficult to catch up if you fall behind. I read the threaded discussions several times a day - at set times such as my lunch hour and after work - and I usually post my own thoughts either at lunch or in the evening. Threaded discussion is an important tool in the online environment, replicating the class discussion in a face-to-face classroom. It is where the dynamic give and take of ideas happens."*

## Expressing Myself in Writing

Online learning is clearly based on the ability to read and write with ease. Being able to clearly express yourself in written form allows you to fully participate in an online learning class. The sharing of ideas between and among the participants is an important and essential characteristic of an online class

*"I realize that if I wasn't so comfortable reading and writing I wouldn't be nearly as comfortable in an online situation. If I wasn't a good writer I would be terrified because everyone would quickly see that in me. I think online learning is absolutely oriented toward students who are highly literate, with excellent writing and speaking skills."*

*"Since I communicate well both verbally and in writing, this type of class discussion is easy for me. I am not afraid to put my ideas in writing or to share them. It's one of the things, I believe, that makes me well-suited to be a learner in the online classroom. Being able to express yourself in writing, and not being afraid to be involved in discussion, are important concepts for successful participation in online education. It also helps if the online learner is confident in his/her abilities. I believe these characteristics have a direct impact on the quality and rigor of the educational experience."*

*"I'm more apprehensive when I write things in an online class. Maybe it's because I'm very accountable. My ideas are there, in black and white, for others to read. So I'm much more nervous regarding how I should say something. In a face-to-face situation I can phrase things in such a way that my co-learners know that I'm not attacking them - I'm sharing some additional thoughts. However, being critical online is very different. When I am asked to critique my fellow students I am very uncomfortable."*

*"In the early part of an online course things seem to be very structured. Comments are very formal. You spend a lot of time checking and rechecking your comments before you post them. However, after awhile you begin to send your thoughts online without going over them. You become a lot more spontaneous in your communication. You don't read things over 3 or 4 times before*

*posting them. You become more relaxed. At the beginning you
assume that since your comments are always available on the online
website that your fellow students will be continually going back and
reviewing what you have said. However, because of the pressure of
the course no one ever has the time to go back and reread things that
are posted. This builds over time and you become a lot more
spontaneous once you settle down in the online course."*

## Interacting With Other Learners

The sense of "group" helps to energize the online learning experience. Interacting with other learners provides an essential form of learning feedback and helps to strengthen the crucial interpersonal aspect of online learning. The opportunity to share your ideas with other learners makes the learning experience very dynamic.

*"Writing a major paper online, where everyone - instructor and
students alike - can all see what you are doing and provide feedback
is incredibly helpful. By the time you are finished writing the paper,
with all of the feedback you have received along the way, you have
created an excellent paper. Plus, you are able to see the feedback
that other students are receiving and what they are able to do with the
feedback. You are more willing to accept the feedback from the
instructor because you see familiar feedback being given to others in
the class. The process is very public in an online learning situation
and this can be very helpful to the learner."*

*"It's very frustrating having to read twenty essays written by the
students in your online course and then having to comment on each of
them. If you have that large a class it makes more sense to group
students into small groups so each person can read and provide
substantive feedback to three or four others. Small groups in online
courses also allow you to develop a stronger relationship with some
of the students."*

*"Though I enjoy face-to-face learning, having other learners around
me for interaction is not an essential ingredient for me to learn. I am
an independent learner. I can learn successfully on my own or from
others electronically in my courses. I find that devices such as
electronic threaded discussions, e-mail interaction, and reading of
posted papers works the same for me as actually being in the same
room with fellow-learners. I'm not a person who must be able to see
my classmates to feel that I can know them or can learn from and
with them."*

*"The only thing I have found so far that I do not care for in an online
class situation is doing 'group work'. It's fairly easy to accomplish a
group task in a face-to-face classroom, to accomplish it in a timely
manner, and to make necessary adjustments if someone isn't holding
up their part. It is more difficult when the course is online and the*

*'group' may consist of learners in different parts of the world and in different time zones."*

## Learning to Live With the Technology

The challenge in online learning is to become comfortable enough with the technical components, the medium of instruction, so that it fades into the background. Once the technical part of participating in an online class is no longer a concern it is possible to really get involved with the content. The technical side of online learning should not interfere with the content.

*"Using computers for online learning was not a problem for me, as I am not scared by technology. I enjoy "hands on" learning. Also, I use computers daily in my job, and so I just jumped in and tried things - learning by doing. I did have the luxury of "growing with" the system, having started using computers in my work a number of years ago. Therefore, I've learned about using a Windows platform, how to e-mail, how to use "chat," etc. over time, rather than having to learn it all at once."*

*"One of the frustrations with online learning is having technical problems. I have had situations where I have written an extensive reply and then accidentally hit a wrong key and it has disappeared forcing me to have to try and rewrite it."*

*"In my case it was different. I was already familiar with many of the technical things that might be found in distance education (teleconferencing, online discussions, interactive television). That gave me a lot of comfort prior to starting the class. I was sure what I was getting into before the fact."*

*"I have found that I enjoy learning new things, and enjoy using the computer to do it. I'm not a great engineering mind - I don't always understand how something really works - but I do enjoy using the technology."*

*"I was quite apprehensive because I'm not a computer person. I find it a necessary evil. I assumed that you had to be very savvy and loved to use the computer and had to be highly technical. I think when people of my generation return to school they're not comfortable with all of that technical stuff. I did find that the course didn't require an exceptional knowledge of computers - you only had to do certain basic things. Things that were required were very simple. My fear of technology really wasn't actualized. I think it's important to make that clear to a person before taking an online course."*

*"It is important to be aware that technology should not take "center stage," but should take a back-seat to the content of what is being learned. The focus is not the technology, but the learning. The technology enables the learning, and should become "invisible" to the learner once he or she has mastered it."*

# Giving Structure To the Learning Experience

Being at a distance from the instructor presents the potential for learners to become lost or removed from the progress of the course. It is important for the instructor, ahead of time, to carefully think through the structure that is needed to guarantee that all learners will be able to move through the course at a similar pace with no one being left behind. Appropriate structure is essential in distance education to help compensate for the separation between the learner and the instructor.

> *"I like having some degree of time pressure. If I am too relaxed, if the course is too flexible, I won't accomplish as much. There must be a balance between flexibility and structure."*

> *"I do think it is important for a distance education course to have structure. I have a high degree of internal motivation, and can pace myself to finish course work by the end of the time period allotted for the course. There should be a syllabus, due dates, course expectations. However, the course structure should be broad enough not to replace the opportunity for the learner to incorporate his/her own internal structure. I think this is why distance education courses/programs that are asynchronous are the ones that appeal to me."*

> *"It was very positive to have a syllabus that went from week to week with very clear assignments along the way. If I missed the deadlines I would be out of the loop. I felt very responsible to the others in the group to not get out of the loop and to be there to carry my own weight in the course. The instructor's role was a matter of consistency. He made sure that the online course continued on in a very steady and purposive way. It was then up to us, the students, to make sure we stayed up with the course and to add our substantive input."*

> *"I liked the idea that the course had a combination of specific structure (deadlines) and also lots of flexibility. I knew that I had to complete my assignment prior to Monday - when the new topic would be introduced. I could be flexible all week long but I had to be finished with the topic and ready for the new topic on Monday. Otherwise I would be terribly behind in the conversation that was going on in the class. And, in an online class I couldn't hide - everyone would know I was behind and hadn't done the assignment. If that happened my learning would drop and I would feel very uncomfortable. This kept me very motivated. It was up to me. The instructor didn't have to penalize me - I would end up penalizing myself."*

# Valuing the Role of the Teacher

Online learning does not replace the instructor. Though the technology is powerful, the role of the instructor is still essential – maybe even more than in a face-to-face class. A good instructor can make the online course a success.

> "The instructor tried to make the dialogue more viable. He responded immediately. He was very affirming of whatever the students would say. He was quick to tell students their ideas were good. He worked to try and make it like a conversation. Nevertheless, maybe because of the fact that it was asynchronous and had a time delay, it simply never happened - it never became very spontaneous with the students really contributing their full thoughts."

> "When the instructor clearly loves teaching and loves the material that he is teaching - that comes through very clearly. It is very obvious when the instructor knows the material really well."

> "As an adult you are always looking for insights into how to use ideas - how to apply the learning. Online learning should help to open doors for us. We are not just learning as an intellectual exercise. We are trying to better our life and that should be recognized by the online instructor. The instructor should be ready for those questions that always come toward the end of the course - what am I going to do with this information."

> "The instructor was always very quick to respond to comments that I made - he was very positive. He gave very specific instructions. It was clear what we were supposed to do."

> "I like the way instructors provide a variety of online links that allow you to pursue topics outside of class. The instructor in an online class is able to provide links to learning resources that allow you to explore and to go to places where you have never been. This is very exciting.

> "I have found a lot of concern and genuineness on the part of the instructor in my online classes - wanting us to learn. I didn't feel like he was just doing a job. That type of feeling is really important for the learner to have in an online situation."

## Conclusion

From the words and comments made in this chapter, turning to the learner for insight into how to create a powerful online course seems to be a most logical thing to do. Then, why do we so seldom turn to the learner for such insight? The student is often overlooked, or at best, the last component in the teaching-learning environment that is called on to make input. The eight categories that emerged from these interviews all share a common element – they emerged from a desire on the part of these learners to share what it *feels like* to participate in a powerful and well organized online learning experience. Interestingly, these categories are not defined in terms of specific strategies and techniques that should be done to make an online course effective. Instead they are written in terms of the learner's feelings associated with his/her meaningful and valued participation in an online environment. There is no prescription included that specifies how the educator should proceed. The challenge to the distance educator is to understand the *feelings* expressed by these learners – having a sense of autonomy, being accountable to each other, allowing me to set a flexible schedule, expressing myself in writing, etc – and then creating a distance education learning environment that allows such feelings to flourish.

# Chapter 10

# Promoting Learner-to-Learner Interaction in Online Distance Education

## Lyn Smith

## Introduction

In face-to-face classes we take interaction for granted. We chat with learners, we ask questions, we respond to discussions, we provide feedback and we move naturally and fluidly between a variety of styles and functions. And the result is learning which is greatly enhanced because of the interaction. Learning becomes a consequence of the natural exchange among teacher and learners.

The potential for interaction between learners is what makes an online distance course different from traditional correspondence study or self-paced, independent learning. However, in online distance education the natural exchange among teacher and learners is not automatically present. Interaction can't be taken for granted because it just doesn't happen unless we really work at making it happen.

A significant challenge of the online environment is the asynchronous nature of most of the interactions. We post a message and then wait, sometimes for quite a while, for a reply. We don't have fluid, responsive discussions in the same way. Nevertheless, as the teacher and designer of a course we have instructional goals and objectives that can only be achieved by providing opportunities for, and supporting, learner interaction.

## Learner-to-Learner Interaction

The distance education literature talks about two main types of learner interaction – that between the learner and the content, and between the learner and others. Where learners never or infrequently attend campus classes, it is particularly important to provide an environment where both types of interaction occur. This chapter focuses on the interaction between the learner and others – especially learner-to-learner interaction.

There are many purposes teachers might choose for developing and promoting learner-to-learner interaction. One significant reason is to develop, to some or other degree, an "online community." A second reason, based on the belief that all learners have something valuable to contribute to the learning of others, is that they should be provided the opportunity to take responsibility in doing so.

In order to successfully build the development of a relevant and worthwhile "online community", learner-to-learner interaction must fulfill some or all of these functions:

- enhance social interaction

- aid understanding

- increase motivation by embedding interaction in meaningful activities

- promote the process of feedback through validation and challenge

- encourage reflection

- support learner independence

## Levels Of Learner-To-Learner Interaction

Learner-to-learner interaction can best be viewed in a hierarchical structure with a set of five levels that describes the particular focus for the learner at each level. Each successive level builds on the previous one and adds additional substance to the interaction that is occurring between learners. [1] The five levels, similar to the progression presented in Bloom's Taxonomy of the Cognitive Domain[2], begin with Building a Learning Community (Level 1), advance to Sharing Information and Ideas (Level 2), then to Creating Understanding (Level 3), next to Drawing Personal Meaning (Level 4), and finally to Reflecting on the Experience (Level 4). It is difficult for the learner to successfully move to a higher level until the preceding level has been achieved.

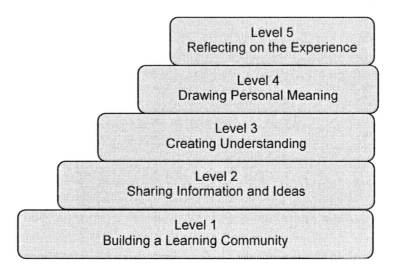

### Level 1 – Building a Learning Community

> *"Online educators who understand that safe, nurturing learning environments are foremost in contributing to learners' happiness, sense of comfort, and ultimately rates of completion, place the creation of community high on their list of priorities."* (Conrad, 2002 in McInnerney)

---

[1] Gilly Salmon (2004) also presents a five level learner interaction model in her book *E-moderating: The key to teaching and learning online*. The Salmon model, though appearing very similar, places primary emphasis on the role of the teacher – e-moderator – whereas the focus of this chapter is on the learner, what he/she is needing, experiencing, and learning via the interaction.

[2] See Chapter Five for a discussion of the Taxonomy of the Cognitive Domain (Bloom, 1956) and how it can be used in the design of distance education programs.

Social interaction is an essential aspect of learning. As teachers we strive to provide support and orientation to learners and, particularly in web-based classrooms, to provide opportunity for informal conversations and ongoing relationship building.

Paloff & Pratt (2002) explain that learners need teachers who get to know learners and how they learn, understand the learner's learning environment and influences on the learners, and understand learners specific needs for support.

Consider someone who has been an independent learner for much of his or her education. How might that person find an environment where participation involves sharing freely and depending on others to complete activities? He/she might struggle to shift thinking from being the sole owner and recipient of knowledge to a co-contributor and creator of shared knowledge.

*What do learners need in order to feel comfortable interacting with each other online?*

Learners need to understand the dynamics of communication in an online space, and to feel comfortable in presenting themselves. They need to be supported to make the transition from 'outsiders' to 'insiders'. (McInnerney, 2003). We can support this process by the choice of social, relaxed and low risk activities we create at the beginning of a course.

The process of warming up and forming the learning community can include a mix of synchronous and asynchronous communication. The goals should be that learners:

1) get to know one another and build relationships,

2) develop comfort with the technology, practicing the skills of online communication and conversation,

3) safely practice revealing themselves, and

4) reflect on their learning possibilities in this environment.

*Here are some starter activities which work well.*

- **Share a bio**, but give it a twist (a formative experience that is central to who you are today; the latest movie you saw and what was interesting about it; an interesting place you recently visited.)

- **Play an online peer game** (a guessing game – who am I for your favourite movie star, thinker, famous person, learners post a description and respond by guessing who others are.)

- **Ranking** (pick your top six strategies for…getting through a course; how to secure the home computer for MY use; getting kids out the door on time; surviving holiday chaos. Learners post and respond to each other's ideas.)

Setting up a forum specifically for "chit-chat" or coffee is always useful. There is a lovely story of the learner who saw the message about meeting in the "Bar" with the class on Friday. He was most concerned about how he could travel that far in time until he realized it was the virtual "bar"!

In some courses teachers have commented that the forum is the place they have seen the most animated discussion and the most revealing comments. Why is this? First, there is little risk – the academic part of the course is somewhere else and there is no assessment associated with the coffee shop. Second, there is the element of choice – learners participate when they like, about what they like and to whom they like, and are therefore drawn to like-minded thinkers who affirm them. There is a lot to be learned from this! Some teachers I know have provided "rules" for this environment (no talking about the course content or assignments, etc.) while others have successfully left it open for the learning community to decide.


## Level 2 - Sharing Information and Ideas

Information sharing activities are those which prompt learners to say, "Hey everyone, look at what I found!" "I've got this great idea!"

Information sharing can be a relatively light, non-threatening process or a getting deeper type activity depending on your purpose. It can relate to a specific formal activity, or be an ongoing ethos of the course. The key is in learners affirming and encouraging one another by contributing to the development of the learning environment. When successful, early information sharing activities can help establish a strong sense of participation and ownership in the online class. There are numerous ways to approach activities of this type.

*Here are some starter ideas.*

- Learners provide a hints list for those who are finding the online environment new or challenging.

- Ask learners to find a topic-related web-resource they really like (website, organization, article, etc) and describe why they like it, how it could be useful or what its quality features are.

- Learners submit their most useful/favorite URL which helps when studying online. The class votes on the best.

- Identify a particular website and have learners suggest 3 things found on the website that demonstrate a particular artistic/technical feature

To help establish the culture of your learning community, it works well to develop activities where learners give feedback directly to those who provide the information. Learners should be encouraged throughout the course to use ideas presented by other learners – and to credit the learner who originally suggested the idea.

*Another activity to share information.*

> Learners select one of the resources provided and write a 50 word summary or abstract that tells a user the main ideas or features of this resource. Identify 3 key words that are appropriate to the resource and select a section heading that would help file this resource. The summary will go on a webpage that lists all resources in one place.

A culture of open acceptance of everyone's valuable contribution will begin to develop as learners see the value of not having to do all of the research alone. Contributing to the shape and design of a course allows learners to feel part of the learning process. If the content is not fully prescribed, then learners might enjoy the challenge of adding a new section; or filling out the resources section as they go on a "treasure hunt" for the best available free things on the web.

Simple pair feedback activities can be effective for promoting learner-learner interaction for sharing information, and for building learner's confidence online. You can choose to use email, or discussion forums.

*Try this pair email activity.*

- Learners are organized in two member teams (an information provider and a questioner). One learner provides the information – a story about something that went well; a solution to a problem; a hint for good essay writing etc. The other learner asks questions – *Why did that activity work in your classroom? How did you get the ____ to work that way? Were there other things happening that might have changed the way that happened?* After discussing this, they post a statement summarizing their findings to the class forum.

At a more sophisticated level, learners can be asked to share and offer feedback to each other on any activities they have completed (drafts, assessed activities, project planning etc). Valuable learning can be had by learners offering up a project, essay, review, or website for fellow classmates to learn from. The learning conversations could center around content of an item, or the process used to develop the item. This discussion benefits both the creator and the fellow learner. An online environment allows teachers to provide exemplars of previous work for learners to view and critique as part of the process of refining and practicing their own skills in the field.

## Level 3 - Creating Understanding

Have you ever noticed it is possible to have a face-to-face discussion without the participants really listening to each other? If we are not careful, online discussion can turn into just such a faceless exchange of information. It can be very discouraging to provide what was assumed to be an exciting activity in an online class and then watch as faceless postings start appearing, one after another, that never move beyond basic information sharing. In such cases the class members look to the teacher's comments as the key ideas to respond to rather than the ideas of each other. In fact, many academic courses struggle to get past this level of interaction.

To avoid this, we need to create an environment where learners are consciously thinking carefully about what others have said, relating this to their own understanding, and responding in ways which promote discussion.

A good place to start is to provide specific structure for a discussion about something of interest about which your learners are likely to have an opinion. Giving learners a simple two stage instruction can help them understand that the purpose of the activity is to grow a conversation – not merely put up a posting. Adding a list of criteria that they can use to check their posting can further helps.

*Here is an example of a simple structured discussion activity to facilitate understanding.*

Reacting to a Newspaper Article

Read the news article on raising the legal driving age and consider – what are some of the interesting social issues surrounding this debate? What are the positives, the negatives? How would you be affected? How would your friends or family be affected? You will need to present a viewpoint on this topic.

Step 1: Create a posting that provides a summary of your thoughts and ideas. Then, state an opinion, ask a controversial question, suggest a resource for us to read to increase our understanding of the topic. End your posting with a lead statement/question for others to respond to – "What do you think?", "Would this work in your situation?" "How would the government respond to this idea?"

Step 2: Read the postings of others in your group. Select a posting which interests you and respond in the following way:

- Comment directly on the message(s) you are replying to – this helps keep the line of argument clear for other readers. Use names.

- Where possible, make your posting respond to several previous postings. This will draw ideas together for you and your readers.

- Be respectful and give positive feedback where you can.

- End your posting with a lead statement for others to respond to – "What do you think?" "Would this work?" "How does my idea sound?" "Can someone suggest a way to improve my idea?"

- Resist being long-winded – no more than 100 words

This example has a clear structure and sequence, gives learners an opportunity to relate the situation to their own circumstances and experience, assumes some independence on the part of the learner, is built on reflection, and offers some choice and a degree of trust – all elements of good adult learning. A discussion will grow more easily out of a worthwhile activity when the learner is clear about what they are to do, and can see value in making the effort.

*Here are some activities that can provide the foundations for good online conversations that promote understanding.*

- Select a concept or model from your course and ask learners to find, share and critique real life examples.

- Provide a single resource – a reading, picture, web page – and ask learners to express an opinion.

- Ask learners to deconstruct a reading – particularly suitable for difficult readings. Do this in sections.

- Find out what the professionals think – working from the theories, concepts or ideas in your topics, ask learners to talk to professionals & share their findings and new perspectives.

- Ask learners to design a solution to a common problem.

- Develop a plan for action & provide feedback/critique.

- Investigate a topic and share the main ideas that arise. This could be a small group activity.

- Host an expert guest – learners can "ask the expert" questions relevant to their studies.

- Write a five minute speech to convince a significant player of your opinion. Other learner's roleplay the response.

- Research and share opinions on the perspectives of various stakeholders.

Early interactions can falter as learners feel tentative and self-conscious about revealing themselves or their ideas. This often comes from a learner's belief that learning is an independent activity, and someone might either "catch me looking at another's work" or "steal my good ideas". Learners may need to be led gently into sharing their thoughts, and scaffold their trust and development. We may need to be very supportive early in a course, and more directive than we would prefer. Meaningful structure can be essential in order to help the learners move toward the level of understanding.

*Here are some suggestions you can give learners to use as conversation starters.*

- My first reaction to this topic was….

- What I don't understand about this topic is….but I do wonder…

- I really was surprised by….

- I am really confused by….

- The main point that I got from this was….

- Quote the part of the reading/resource you think is most important and explain why.

- Select an idea, concept or model and explain why it works in your context.

- Ask a question of the group.

- Explain your understanding of the concept, and ask the group some questions to clarify.

In teaching learners how to respond we need to highlight the importance of helping to move the conversation progressively further. Successive postings should capture the important ideas from previous postings and conclude in ways which further open up the discussion to more ideas and enhanced understanding.

- I like your ideas because… Other things I thought of were…

- I agree with the point that you made… I think we could think about…:

- I (respectfully) disagree with the point you made because… My opinion is…

- I have never thought about this from your perspective before. Did you consider…?

- I did not focus on the point that you discussed; instead, I thought that this … other was more important for me…

Do remember to count the number of potential postings in a discussion and realistically assess what is reasonable. Sometimes it is good to appoint some of your learners as starter posts – if a class of 20 all post a starter-statement to a discussion, it leaves 20 open ends for others to consider – too much processing! In other circumstances small group discussions will be better. This way, learners can have a choice and responsibility as responders.

Our challenge is to support learners to integrate new ideas into their own, without expecting them unrealistically to comment on too many postings. We need to model and encourage the practice of drawing together the ideas from a number of postings into one response. It is important not to let conversations run too long without seeking a summary or conclusion. Summarizing points along the way can be made by the teacher or one of the learners in turns.

## Level 4 - Drawing Personal Meaning

The next higher level of discussion is when you begin to ask learners to engage in a deeper form of learning where "meaning making" is the goal.. Some writers refer to this as academic or professional "dialogue."

*Here is an example.*

> For Assignment #1 you are required to write an essay articulating your views on the differences between management and leadership.
>
> To support you to do this, the next 3 weeks of our online discussions will examine the different views conveyed in the course readings, your responses to these and your personal views and experiences.
>
> The main purpose of these discussions will be debate – for you to clarify what you think, to argue for and test your ideas on others, to relate your personal situation and experiences to the readings and to challenge and be challenged in your thinking. There are no right answers. There are some rules posted on the site for the process of respectful argument.
>
> Your final essay must clearly argue a viewpoint, and show what has influenced your thinking as it has developed over the period of the discussions. You must quote readings, online discussions and other sources in your essay.

This activity focuses on the process of developing a personal and reasoned perspective or argument around an issue. Learners will have considered a wide range of ideas and perspectives and the discussion would involve listening to, critiquing and responding to each other. The motivation for the learners is intrinsic to the activity, they are involved in order to provide evidence of the development of their thinking. In the process of that involvement, they are influencing and challenging other learners.

*Some strategies for enhancing and deepening learning activities.*

- Ensure there is a specific goal or activity to complete within a given timeframe.

- Organize learners to work in small groups.

- Require one member to take leadership responsibility for facilitating the academic conversation around one of your course key topics, issues or tensions.

- Bring in an online expert or practitioner to add their viewpoint and challenge the learners perspectives.

- Establish some guidelines for responses – depth, quality and length.

- Promote inquiry and reflective thinking, and require learners to explain, justify, and reference statements being made.

- Ensure all participants promote open examination of the topic – why are claims, beliefs, assertions held?

- Guide learners to take turns at summarizing the discussion at key points. This helps them practice summarizing skills, and hones the discussion to improve clarity and focus.

- Encourage several threads to run, to allow for learner choice and to enable a deepening of the learning.

- Encourage learners to initiate new threads on aspects arising from the arguments put forward.

- Evaluate the progress of the discussion - Are learner's ideas changing and growing? Is the discussion deepening the group's understanding?

*Some learning activities which promote deeper understanding include.*

- Role plays

- Arguing from a given perspective

- Discussion as a response to:

  - controversial statements/quotes posted for critique

  - a recent speech by a politician/leader in the field

- A discussion developed around "So what…?"

- Information gathered and presented on a specific controversial viewpoint

- Structured debates

- Conversations with experts

- Critical thinking activities

*Using an online debate to help learners draw personal meaning.*

An online debate can be used as a powerful way for learners to draw personal meaning.

Ask learners to argue a position on a controversial issue that is open-ended (does not have an obvious right or wrong answer). Consider a controversial issue such as spanking children. Learners can be assigned to teams and argue for the affirmative or negative on a question such as "is spanking effective when guiding children's behavior?" Learners prepare for the debate by reading, talking to parents and teachers, and by researching the politics and social issues related to the topic. This type of discussion addresses engagement and relevance issues, and is an authentic situation for learners who might be entering the early childhood profession.

For this debate, the format can be synchronous (chat) or asynchronous. Teams can be used to develop and then present an argument. Timelines can support rapid-fire or more slow-thoughtful processes as desired.

*Using a scenario to help learners draw personal meaning:*

The following scenario allows learners to identify alternative actions that could be taken to meet guidelines for good practice. Used in an asynchronous mode, such an online role play would be conducted using parallel teams – each creating their own response to the situation. What actions would seem most appropriate? What should be done? Why? How could such a situation be prevented in the future?

> Fred has called a meeting of all employees to discuss the purchase of a new binding machine. At the meeting, Joanne has voiced a concern that the new machine be equipped with the latest safety features. Fred argues, however, that there has never been an injury at the company on the old style equipment. In addition, the old style equipment is considerably less expensive. Following the meeting Joanne meets with other employees and organizes them to prepare a letter to be sent to Fred that outlines their concerns and urges him to purchase the safer binding machine.
>
> Assume that your group is the group of employees who will be sending the letter to Fred. Prepare your letter. Identify the key concerns that your group has. Why is your option better for the company? Why should Fred listen to your group? Etc. etc.
>
> Make sure each person in your small group has an opportunity to make input into the final letter. When everyone is finished making their input, post the final letter for the other groups to see. You will have one week for this task.

When generating online scenarios make sure the situations are familiar, interesting and accessible. Deeper learning and engagement will develop if learners are encouraged to do some research before becoming involved so that discussion is informed and interesting.

The strength of doing these types of activities online is often in the time delay, giving learners time to think through who they are representing, and what this perspective might be. Each activity needs a clear structure – guidelines for online behavior to prevent learners inflaming a discussion, timelines and word limits, a debriefing period, and a "what did we learn" reflective phase.

*Using small discussion groups to assist in drawing personal meaning.*

The purpose of small discussion group activities should always be to enhance the individual's learning, while contributing to a group process which supports other learners. If designed well, small discussion groups can:

- Reduce the number of postings learners have to work through.

- Add variety to the program.

- Increase the value of participation (provide more input and feedback per learner).

- Help lessen the isolation an online learner feels by creating a small network.

- Promote learner-to-learner interaction with less reliance on the teacher

Of course, if the activity is not worthwhile or well conceived, group work is likely to be frustrating for the learner. There are many practical and simple activities which work well in small groups of 2-5.

- Paired email activities.

- Creation of a plan or a course of action which is presented to the entire class.

- Development of group presentations.

- Pairs of learners working together to better understanding a set of readings.

- Peer review of each other's work.

- Team analysis of a case study.


**Level 5 - Reflecting on the Experience**

The purpose of any reflective activity is to support learners to review and evaluate their approaches, strategies, knowledge or learning. Typical activities which promote reflection include personal journal or diary writing and reflective statements on learning as part of an activity. To engage learners in reflective conversations is more challenging.

*Activity for encouraging reflection.*

> Working with a partner, share a posting you made early in the course and another you made later. Share and discuss how your ideas have developed, what influenced your thinking, and where you might go to from here. The role of each of you is to challenge, probe, question and support the other partner in coming to their own conclusions about their learning.
>
> You will submit your own 200 word statement at the end of this process.

*Suggestions for creating small group reflective activities.*

- Share and give peer feedback on a reflective summary of a significant learning experience.

- Following a practical experience, learners share their learning development – focus on what happened, why, how they responded, what they learned, what they will do next time.

- A critical incident discussion where learners describe a key incident and as a group attempt to provide some strategies for addressing this (eg. the child threw a chair across the room).

- Share a quote from your journal that is meaningful. Discuss how this quote is significant to you, and what it means for your learning – present and future.

- Select one posting from a course discussion that was especially meaningful for you. Share this in your group. Why was it significant? How did it influence you?

- Discuss what process you have been through as a learner and where you feel you now are in the process.

- In your group, reflect on how you might organize this course if you were the teacher.

- Learners examine an assessment activity and some exemplars and suggest what the grading criteria might be. The process of critique and debate could create the framework for the actual grading criteria that learners agree to work to.

## Conclusion

Any good course has a deliberate 'shape' to it. There will be a gradual building of the community of learners into a confident, cohesive and supportive group. There will be ebb and flow of workload, of intensity of involvement, and of level of difficulty and challenge. Activities and learner-to-learner interactions provide the scaffolds to facilitate learning while the teacher provides whatever assistance learners need to enable them to engage in learning activities productively.

In this chapter we have deliberately focused on practical activities and examples from real courses to encourage and support learner-learner interaction. We have identified activities which could be used to create different depths and complexities in your course. In addition, the five levels of learner-to-learner interactions can be very useful as a developmental model for creating the structure for a course. A course might start with basic discussion activities focusing on social aspects, a course could move into information sharing activities as learners come to grips with the content. Higher levels of discussion that call for viewpoint-type activities are effective when the level of comfort with the content and the learning environment is established. More complex collaborative activities rely on learners confidently working together – something that will take time to develop; reflective activities require greater trust, more in- depth knowledge of the content and a willingness to stretch outside the comfort zone – all skills more likely to be evident in later parts of your course. As a course grows, our goal will be to foster positive interdependence among participants - while each unique learner retains a confident independence in themselves as a learner.

## References

Bloom, B. S. (ed). (1956). *Taxonomy of educational objectives, Handbook 1: Cognitive domain*. New York: Longman.

McInnerney, J. M., & Roberts, T. S. (2004). Online learning: Social interaction and the creation of a sense of community. *Educational Technology & Society*, 7(3), 73-81.

Palloff, R. M., & Pratt, K. (2003). *The virtual student: A profile and guide to working with online learners*, San Francisco: Jossey-Bass.

Salmon, G. (2004). *E-Moderating: The key to teaching and learning online (2<sup>nd</sup> Edition)*, New York: Routledge Falmer.

# Chapter 11

## When Learners Lead:
## Building An Online Community

### An Interview with
### Ryan Shaltry

*During the Spring semester of 1997, Ryan Shaltry was a freshman at Michigan State University enrolled in Physics 183 - Physics for Scientists and Engineers I. Though the course was offered in a face-to-face instructional mode, students were also required to spend time each week solving online problem sets. The online problem sets were delivered via asynchronous software called CAPA[1] (Computer-Assisted Personalized Approach) that had been developed by faculty of the College of Natural Science at Michigan State.*

*It didn't take Ryan long before he realized that CAPA was missing some important learner-focused elements. He set about developing his own online system, www.allMSU.com, to supplement the CAPA experience.*

**Interviewer:** Tell me about the beginnings of **allMSU**.

**Ryan Shaltry:** The idea started out as a simple discussion board during the Spring semester of 1997. I was enrolled in Physics 183 at Michigan State University. A big part of the grade was the CAPA homework assignments where you would have to go online and complete problem sets. The problem sets were all standardized — the same for everyone. However, when you would sign in the computer would change the values of the problem sets that you were given. In other words, everyone had the same formula to deal with but different values were plugged into the formula. One night, as I was plugging through these homework assignments, I thought it would make a lot more sense if I could set up a simple message/forum system so that my friends and I could share the formulas of the problem sets we were working on. It seemed that the instructors did not want to share the formulas, they wanted the students to "discover" them on their own. I felt this was a waste of time and my own learning style would benefit from knowing the formulas ahead of time. I wanted to be able to understand the formulas and put them to use. I wasn't interested in going on an expedition to search out the formulas.

By setting up a message forum/discussion board it would allow me and my friends to work independently and then, as we would come up with an understanding of the formula(s) that was needed, we could post it on the message forum and share it with each other. It had a very positive

---

[1] With CAPA, an instructor can create and/or assemble personalized assignments, quizzes, and examinations with a large variety of conceptual questions and quantitative problems. These can include pictures, animations, graphics, tables, links, etc.. The writing and development is facilitated by numerous templates designed to encourage students to collaborate and discuss concepts while insuring that problems differ for each student to inhibit rote copying.

Students are given instant feedback and relevant hints via the internet and may correct errors without penalty prior to an assignment's due date. The system keeps track of students' participation and performance, and records are available in real time both to the instructor and to the individual student. Statistical tools and graphical displays facilitate assessment and course administration. (http://capa4.lite.msu.edu/homepage/)

effect on our learning. And, most importantly, it allowed us to do it asynchronously. We were all busy with jobs, classes and other things so we didn't have times when we could meet together. Sharing our ideas on the message forum fit our lifestyles well.

I set up the entire system on the small computer I had in my dorm room. It was connected to the university's network and allowed me and my friends to sign into it from wherever we happened to be on campus.

**Interviewer:** What happened next?

**Ryan:** It caught on rather quickly. Physics 183, the only class my system was set up to deal with, was one of those very large lecture classes that had multiple sections. There were probably 700-800 students taking Physics 183 that semester. It didn't take long before knowledge of our small message forum got spread throughout the class. We never really promoted the website. It just caught on via word-of-mouth between students. It was exciting to see the number of messages and conversations that were being initiated. And most importantly, people were getting the kind of help they needed.

By the end of the semester I received a request from some of the students to put up a new message forum for the next semester's class – Physics 184. So I added another layer to it. When you signed on to the website you would be given a choice to enter either the discussion board for Physics 183 or the one for Physics 184. Once on the discussion board you would be presented with a simple list of messages for the class that you selected. And, of course, you could post a response to a message if you wanted. It was very straight forward. The system that was used was still the one that was set up for my friends and myself. The other users were a bonus that we hadn't really planned on. It was working fine for just us and apparently other people were also benefiting from it.

Things started to get rather big by the end of the second semester. We were getting well over 400 students logging in on a consistent basis. Actual feedback on how the users were using the system was pretty minimal. Very little came directly to me. However, I would overhear in-class conversations between students discussing how they were using the website to solve their problems. Everyone seemed to like it.

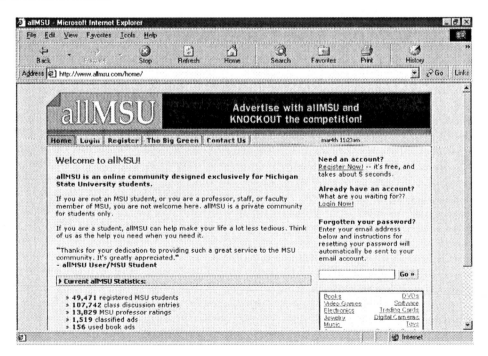

**Interviewer:** When did you start to realize the potential of how big your system might become?

**Ryan:** The reality of what the system could turn into began to occur to me at the end of the second semester. It was at about this time, after two semesters of offering the discussion board, that I started to realize the potential of the system. If it was helping us in Physics 183 and Physics 184 it could probably help lots of others as well in their classes. There had to be other classes that needed a similar service. After all, MSU had over 40,000 students on campus.

At the time MSU was not offering any form of online collaboration system so I felt it was up to me to make something happen if anything was actually going to happen. During the next year we expanded to include 10-12 classes on campus, all of which used the CAPA system, as a way to help students practice the class material.

When someone would request a new class be added to the system I would do a bit of research on the University's website to learn more about the class. Was it an actual class? Did the class use CAPA? If they did offer CAPA I would be more likely to add it to my system. I knew that students would definitely use my forum if CAPA was being used in their class. I didn't like setting up message forums that would not yield any traffic. Such a forum would take up space on my server and wouldn't be helping the students.

**Interviewer:** Were you still using the same basic discussion board?

**Ryan:** One of the first major changes I made in the system was to add a registration procedure. As students registered to use the system they were asked to sign an agreement licensing their use of **allMSU**. Within this licensing agreement are two major concerns.

First, the license had them state that they were not an MSU faculty or staff member. The system was designed exclusively for students and I felt it would only work well if there was a level of trust that existed. And, one way to promote trust is to ensure that only students are participating. Another important reason for keeping faculty out of the system was that I was still a student and I had some level of fear that I might be thrown out of the university for encouraging students to share their ideas about their homework with each other. I remember at one point, after an exam I had in a class, the professor singled me out and wanted to know who I was and who the guy was behind this website. Of course, I had always kept my own identity out of the website, I really wasn't looking to become famous or popular, I just wanted to set up a meaningful website where MSU students could feel comfortable in sharing their thinking with each other. I felt there was a real need for such a thing. Evidently this professor didn't think so.

A second concern that the user license dealt with was the issue of copyrighted material. The potential users had to agree they wouldn't post any copyrighted material from their homework assignments into the discussion board. We wanted to make sure we would not be involved in any intellectual property issues. In the license agreement we clearly stated that all content posted by the system users was their responsibility and those responsible for operating the system assumed no responsibility for the posted content.

**Interviewer:** How could you possibly police your system to see if students were complying with the rules? After all, **allMSU** currently has almost 50,000 registered users.

**Ryan:** Certainly there are violations of the rules. For instance, I really don't know the exact number of non-students who use the system. However, I suspect that there are quite a few. When it comes to actually policing the system, though, I find that I don't have to spend a lot of time doing it. It really takes care of itself. Occasionally we get some offensive content that we have to delete. And when that happens we usually get emails from students who are concerned or offended that alert us to what's going on. We deal with these things on a case-by-case basis. In addition, I have a few friends who regularly monitor the website for problems. We have worked hard to develop a sense of community within **allMSU**. It's that community spirit that helps make it work so well.

**Interviewer:** Certainly the development of **allMSU** hasn't been without its problems along the way. For instance, an article written by the developers of CAPA refer to you when they stated, "An enterprising student developed an elaborate web discussion forum where students could get answers and formulas, often with little understanding…" (Kashy, et. al. 2001) They went on to say that students who use **allMSU** "tended to score lower on midterm exams, quizzes, and the final." How do you respond to that?[1]

---

[1] Mixed reaction continues on the MSU campus. The CAPA developers have started calling allMSU a "cheat site" and have included the following on one of their websites. "In addition to the official collaborative venues, such as the helproom and the online moderated discussion groups, a culture of "cheat sites" has been developing, most notably http://www.allmsu.com/, which currently advertises "73,408 class discussion entries" (Kortemeyer, 2003). The MSU Office of the Ombudsman advises faculty that, though no university policy requires a statement about academic honesty and integrity in their course syllabi, they may consider including the

**Ryan:** Once **allMSU** became popular we started to see a certain level of friction between what was happening on the website and the university faculty. I've heard reports of teachers threatening to give students a zero grade for their homework if he/she found out that the students were using the **allMSU** discussion board to help with their homework. In fact, this semester a professor threatened to give the entire class a zero on their homework assignments if he saw any messages from his students discussing their homework assignments on **allMSU**. I was able to effectively deal with this threat to the students by changing that particular class section so that when a student would log in and share their questions about their homework it would show that it was from "Anonymous." So, all postings were done anonymously. That took care of the problem quite nicely. It protected the students and allowed them to continue to get the help they needed.

One aspect of **allMSU**, that has not yet been substantiated but I think exists, is the idea that students who most need help turn to **allMSU** more often than they turn to their instructor. This may be because of the hour of the day (or night) when they need the help or the type of relationship they have with their instructor. On the other hand, those students who are doing well and don't need any extra help are able to move through their class without the assistance that **allMSU** can provide. This would explain why **allMSU** students "tended to score lower." It could be that we're filling an academic void and working with a "lost" segment of the student population – those who are most in need of help.

I think that the professors/faculty seem to think that they need to take control of the entire learning process. They don't realize how much learning is going on outside of the classroom and outside of their control. The professors often say that there is lots of misinformation being shared on systems like **allMSU**. Of course, that's very similar to life and we have to develop skills in recognizing good and bad information. The **allMSU** system facilitates real dialogue between students which is so very important for effective learning throughout life.

**Interviewer:** I understand that CAPA eventually added a message forum/discussion board to their software, much like what you created with **allMSU**.

**Ryan:** Yes, that's true, the CAPA system now has their own message forum to support their drill and practice homework sets. It's interesting that the same professor that had singled me out in his class and wanted me to tell him who was behind this online system came back to me a year later and asked if I would be interested in creating a similar message forum for including in the CAPA system. He offered to pay me to create just such a system. I accepted the offer and worked for CAPA for almost two semesters – creating a message forum system similar to what I was doing from my dorm room. However, after working there for a couple of months I realized that if I did a good job for them I would probably end up destroying my own system. So, after I created the basic message forum for them I quit the job. Today that message forum is still operating but it does not have nearly the popularity of my own system. The reason, of course, is that the forum that is tied to CAPA is focused exclusively on the homework problem sets and is carefully monitored by faculty and teaching assistants to ensure that it stays focused and accurate. There is nothing on that system that attempts to

---

following. "Therefore, unless authorized by your instructor, you are expected to complete all course assignments, including homework, lab work, quizzes, tests and exams, without assistance from any source. You are not authorized to use the www.allmsu.com Web site to complete any course work in this course." (Office of the Ombudsman, Michigan State University, 2004).) And, to the contrary, the doctoral program in Educational Policy in MSU's College of Education values allMSU.com and includes a hotlink on their online Resources page (Educational Policy, College of Education, Michigan State University, n.d.). Meanwhile, the campus newspaper reports that, "Created more than five years ago by former MSU student Ryan Shaltry, allmsu.edu has established a strong following with more than 50,000 registered users" (The State News, 2004).

appeal to other aspects of the lives of the students as we do on **allMSU**. As such, it seems to have only limited appeal for students. Their website is heavily teacher/content focused whereas my website is heavily learner focused. That makes a significant difference if you're trying to appeal to people who would like to control their own learning as a part of a community.

**Interviewer:** You have said that **allMSU** is a community. How were you able to make this happen?

**Ryan:** Certainly this sense of community didn't happen over night. It took a lot of work and continual adjustments of the **allMSU** operating system to begin to see the community side of it. For instance, we slowly added a variety of features to **allMSU** in addition to the message forum for sharing homework. This added tremendous diversity to **allMSU** – much like the diversity you find in the student body.

I don't think MSU likes us infringing on their learning process. However, they haven't been able to come up with anything that caters to the student's needs as well as we have. We have gone way beyond just establishing a bulletin board. We have worked to establish an online community that allows students to deal with class learning concerns along with a host of other things in their lives.

Students aren't so narrowly defined as the University thinks they are. They have complete and busy lives and have crazy hours when they are able to join in a community for the sharing of ideas. The asynchronous web-based community of **allMSU** makes a lot of sense for this type of person. **allMSU** tries to accommodate and respond to that.

The University's attempt to provide a forum for the students is limited to just the academic part and isn't seen nearly as valuable by the students. This may be because the university isn't interested in getting that involved with that much of a student's life. I think they see their role as dealing with only the educational part of the person – not the whole student.

**Interviewer:** I've had a chance to compare today's **allMSU** with what it looked like at the beginning. It has really changed a lot.

**Ryan:** We began to add features to the website as students would suggest them. We added a section of classified ads where students could buy, sell and trade things. As with the other aspects of **allMSU** there was no charge for the classified ads. We also added a link for users to suggest new message forums so that we could expand to other courses where students felt the opportunity to dialogue would be helpful. We also added some general message forums on topics such as sports and music that we felt could further build the community. There's now a Dating section, a Used Books section which is very popular at the beginning and end of each semester, and a section where you can Rate Professors you have had in class and share your reactions with others. There's also an Events Calendar where students can post information about upcoming events, and a College Life section which includes apartment reviews, information about computers/technology and dormitory forums. Each of these sections has come about through the suggestions and recommendations of students in the online community.

Recently we added a section to the website called "The Big Green" which is a student run *ezine*, an electronic magazine. There are 15-20 writers and a number of photographers who now regularly put together this electronic magazine and use our website as the way to disseminate it. We gave them space on our website and created a system whereby they can autonomously administer that section of the website. They can post their stories and pictures, correspond with their readers, and generally maintain their own magazine – at no cost to them. We felt it was another opportunity to support the student electronic community that had been established and, based on the response to the magazine, it was a good decision.

**Interviewer:** It sounds like **allMSU** is now dealing with the more popular topics of student life rather than staying with its original focus on helping with homework.

**Ryan:** No, I'd have to disagree with that. Certainly we've expanded as any community would. However, the academic part of the website is the backbone of the community. There are some other online communities available to MSU students, but nothing that has been successful and lasted as long as ours. I think the reason we have been successful is due to our ability to mix academic content and recreational content on the same website. Students can choose which part of the website they want to visit. Depending on their own mood they may choose to work on their homework or, instead, check out the classified ads. The academic section of the website provides a certain degree of substance to this project that isn't readily seen in other websites that attempt to get students participating.

I have always been concerned about maintaining the focus for **allMSU**. I think that there is a lot of value in this website for the students and I am concerned that I not lose the focus by getting too absorbed in trying to make money or exploiting the student community in some way. I think that would easily be picked up by the student users and the website would fail immediately. There is a lot of loyalty that the students have to the website and I have to respect that. I try to be honest and straight forward and offer them something that has value for them and their lives. Something that they can really use.

The area that I think that we most contribute to is that of learning how to effectively communicate. After all that is what the website is all about – whether it is sharing thinking about homework problems, posting a classified ad, or sharing information about a professor. The ability to communicate is the key to all of it. Technology is becoming such a large part of our lives and we have to learn how to effectively use the technology to communicate with others.

**Interviewer:** You've been gone from MSU for a few years. Yet, you still are able to maintain **allMSU**.

**Ryan:** There was a time after I had moved to Arizona, a period of nine months in 2000, when the site did not exist. I decided that I had other priorities in life and the website really wasn't my focus at that time. Plus, I was a considerable distance away from MSU and had little contact with the on-campus community of students. However, I started getting personal emails from students wanting to know what had happened to the message forum and why couldn't they find it anymore. Where is it? What happened to it? We miss it! So I finally invested a few hours of learning time, made some needed modifications in the software and put it back online.

After I finished the redesign of the website I again used word-of-mouth and a few flyers posted on campus (by some of my friends) to advertise the availability of the message forum. Word just kind of spread by itself.

**Interviewer:** Are you surprised by what you have done?

**Ryan:** Yes, I am surprised by what I've done. Not because of the success but because of how easy it was. By merely listening to the students and following their leads and suggestions it has been possible to create a meaningful system that has turned into a vibrant electronic community.

## References

Educational Policy, College of Education, Michigan State University. (n.d.). *Resources* Retrieved June 14, 2005 from http://ed-web3.educ.msu.edu/edpolicy/msuresources.htm

Kashy, D.A., Albertelli, G., Kashy, E., & Thoennessen, M. (2001). Teaching with aln technology: benefits and costs. *Journal of Engineering Education*, 89, pp 499-505.

Kortemeyer, G. (2003, November) R*esearch themes and methodology*. Retrieved June 14, 2005, from http://lectureonline.cl.msu.edu/researchthemes.html

Office of the Ombudsman, Michigan State University. (2004, April 20). *Cheating from where the instructor sits*. Retrieved June 14, 2005, from http://www.msu.edu/unit/ombud/dishonestyFAQ.html

The State News. (2004, April 14). *Web sites created by 'U' connect many to services, make some a quick buck*. Retrieved June 14, 2005 from http://www.statenews.com/article.phtml?pk=23603

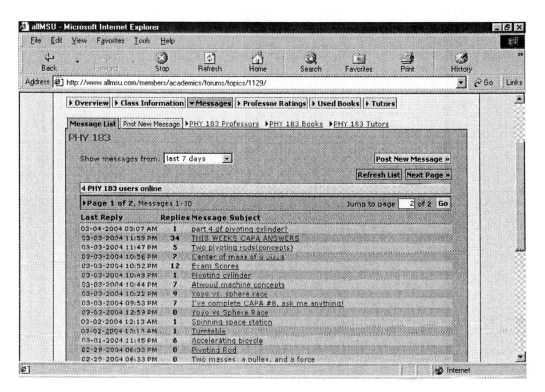

**allMSU Class Message Forum**

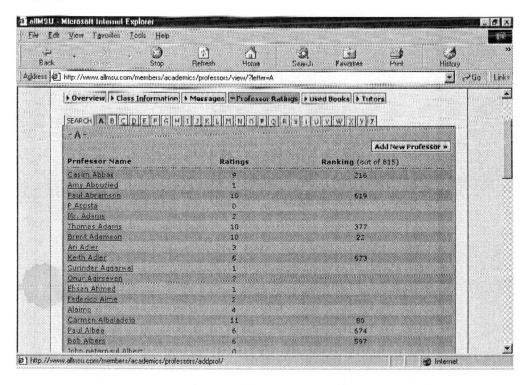

**allMSU Professor Rating Section**

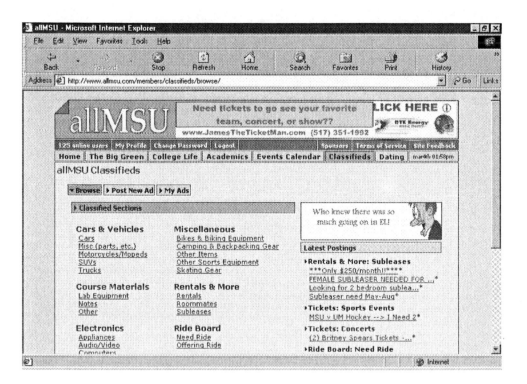

**allMSU Classified Ads Section**

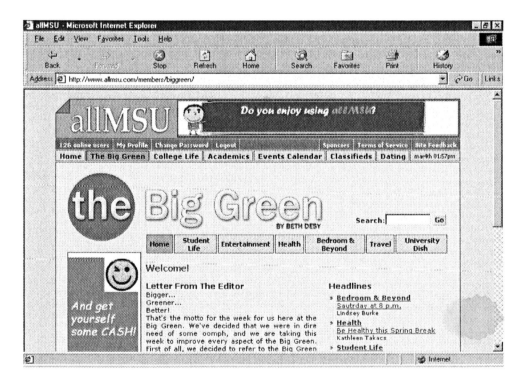

**the Big Green on allMSU**

# Chapter 12

# A Guide for the
# Distance Education Learner

## Simone Jonaitis

*This chapter is a bit different – it is written to the distance education learner and not the educator. It focuses on four areas that are essential to the learner for a successful distance education experience: personal commitment and motivation, familiarity and attitude toward technology, communication skills and preferences, and personal support systems. Also included are ideas about the role of student services and the importance of assessing the institution's commitment to the distance learner. It has been included in this book to provide the educator with a clear view of those skills and competencies that the learner must possess in order to be successful.*

## Overview

So you've decided to take a distance education course. It's just another course, right? Well, not exactly. Distance education can be an exciting and wonderful way to learn, especially if time and location constraints dictate your life. There are, however, a number of things you should consider before taking a distance education course or enrolling in a program. The following discussion is intended to provide you with a set of questions and tools you can use to assess your understanding of distance education, the meaning of learning at a distance and some other key considerations.

We as learners sometimes fail to recognize our own immense responsibility and commitment required for the learning process to take place. It is easy to place the responsibility for learning on the instructor, the environment, or the institution. What this accomplishes, however, is giving up control over our own learning. In order to have a successful learning experience, it is critical you retain control and take ownership over your learning experience. It is important that you truly understand your own learning objectives, style, and expectations, as well as take steps to address any potential concerns. No one can be better equipped to evaluate your own learning process than you.

With this understanding as background, there are four questions that will form the basis for this Guide. These questions are:

> *What do I need to know before deciding on a distance education course or program?*

> *What set of personal skills do I need to be successful as a distance learner?*

> *What support services should I expect from my institution?*

> *How can I further develop my skills as a distance learner?*

# What is Distance Education?

Distance education or distance learning can be any type of instruction that is centered on bridging time and/or location limitations via the use of technology. It is important to define what type of distance education course or program you are taking, as this defining will greatly determine how you approach your learning experience. There are a variety of delivery methods used. The most common are interactive television courses, satellite, audio conferencing, Internet and telecourses. Your instructor may also opt to use a combination of these technologies and will structure the course or program in a synchronous or asynchronous format or may select a combination of delivery formats.

It is important to understand the differences between asynchronous and synchronous formats from the standpoint of your expectations and responsibilities as a learner. If your course or program is being offered synchronously, the instructor is assuming that he or she and all learners will be available to interact together at the same time. With this format you will be expected to be somewhere, whether it be in an actual classroom or on-line, at the appointed time for your class-at-a-distance. On the other hand, asynchronous learning assumes learners are available for instruction only at times that are convenient to each individual. Learners are able to study, send, and receive information on their own time schedule. Whenever you have available time for participating in the course, you are able to participate.

Make sure you know how the course will be delivered to ensure you know ahead of time what will be expected of you. You may assume that because it is a distance education course there, will be no specific time or location requirements placed on you – an asynchronous course. Look again. In some cases, courses offered as distance education use technology for certain portions of the course and then also require students to meet on-site on specific days and times for seminar discussions. Take the time to find out in advance how the course will be offered and what will be expected of you. Most importantly, evaluate whether the course format will realistically fit into your own schedule.

# Personal Commitment and Motivation

>   Why am I taking this class?
>   What really motivates me?
>   Are my time management skills strong?
>   What is my level of commitment to learning?

To ensure a successful distance education experience, one of the very first things you need to explore is your motivation and commitment to learning. Similar to any other formal learning experience, self-discipline and self-direction are essential, but learning at a distance will emphasize these skills even further. For the most part, you are in a situation where you and you alone manage and budget your time. It is essential you understand the relevance of these skills and are able to recognize your level of commitment to the process. Without self-discipline and self-direction skills you may find that a distance education course is an inappropriate learning activity for you.

There are a whole host of reasons why individuals participate in programs that allow them to learn at a distance. Most of them center on specific time and location constraints. Many individuals believe that distance education will save time. To an extent it does. You may not be required to spend several hours driving to arrive at a specific location or perhaps you won't have to leave work early to ensure you will arrive at class on time.  These are all very valid reasons.  However, check your thinking, especially if you believe distance education in and of itself will save you time.  In many cases, distance education courses tend to take up more time than a traditional on-site or in-person class.

Some individuals take a course or program by distance education with the belief that it will require less time and commitment or that it will somehow be easier than a traditional face-to-face course or program.  Quite the contrary!  Not that the material will be any less or more difficult, but it will require you to stay committed and schedule your time accordingly.  You will be amazed at the amount of reading you are expected to do and the amount of interaction you will have with both your instructor and classmates.  Please don't make the mistake of thinking you won't have to work hard.  Your instructor and classmates will have certain expectations of you, and you will be expected to fulfill them.

Given this criteria, ask yourself how disciplined you feel you are.  Do you generally tackle projects and immediately get things done before the deadline or do you have a tendency to wait around until the last minute and then scurry to get it done?  Be careful.  Make sure you are allotting appropriate amounts of time for your coursework, and you are doing it all along the way.  Remember in a traditional classroom you may spend 3 to 4 hours in class per week and then an additional 6 to 8 hours outside of class reviewing the material presented and working on assigned projects and readings.  This general time allotment doesn't change just because you are not physically sitting in a classroom at a prescribed time and place.  You will spend 3-4 hours reading and familiarizing yourself with the initial content and then another 6-8 hours working toward a true understanding of the presented material.

Study habits and time management skills are not something you learn in a few hours.  These skills take time and personal commitment to develop.  Chances are you have spent many years  developing these skills and continue to enhance and master them. Remember in a distance education environment, because in many cases you are not being asked to be anywhere at any specific time, it is easy to procrastinate.  Don't let the lack of boundaries fool you. You will be expected to read what others have to say, comment on what they have said, and most importantly, to be prepared.  If you are not prepared and do not keep up with the material, not only your instructor, but also others in the group will know it.  Not only are you placing yourself at a disadvantage, you are doing a disservice to the others in the group.  By not contributing and being prepared, you are reducing the exchange of ideas and diminishing the experience for everyone else in the course.

Although there are plenty of good reasons to take a class, probably the best reason is because you have a genuine interest in the material.  By being genuinely interested, you will be more likely to concentrate on content rather than the mechanism by which it is being delivered.  Chances are you will also be enthusiastic about exploring the many resources that will be available to you.  For those less interested in the content, they may become distracted by the format and less enthusiastic about the actual content and the opportunity to learn.  In fact, a real warning sign that a distance learner is losing interest in a course is when he or she becomes most concerned about the media or technology being used for delivering the course and much less concerned about the content.  There are many, many benefits to learning at a distance, but learning at a distance requires discipline.  You are way ahead of the game if you genuinely want to understand the material and see the format as simply a vehicle to transmit that information.

## Technology

Do I own or have access to the technology necessary for the course?

Am I comfortable with my skill level?
Do I have appropriate technical support?
Do I have a positive attitude toward technology?

If you are enrolled in or planning to enroll in a course or program via distance education, your interaction with technology is about to increase. It is essential you have access to all the necessary equipment that will be required. Without it, you simply won't be participating in the course. Sounds rather logical, but sometimes we don't always think things through thoroughly before engaging in a new activity. For example, do you own a computer? If so, does it have all the necessary software needed for the class? If not, do you know where to purchase it and how to install it? What about access to the worldwide web? Do you have an Internet service provider? Will it be OK if you're tying up the phone line while on the Internet? Should you consider a second line? If you don't own your own computer, do you have convenient access to one that will serve your purpose? Most of the specific equipment is relatively easy to acquire or access, but the key is making sure these things are in place before you actually begin the course. It will be extremely frustrating if you are still working on your plan for accessing equipment while the other learners are moving forward with the course material and assignments.

Once you have enrolled in the course or program, make sure you understand the instructor's expectations. It is important you understand the basic elements of the technology that you will be using and possess basic computer skills. You won't be required to know all about the wires and cables and specifics about the hardware, so don't get unnecessarily concerned if you're not a technical genius, but do be sure you know how to use the technology. More than likely you will be expected to know how to send and open attachments, sign on to listservs, use basic word processing applications and be able to navigate the worldwide web with relative ease. If these are new skills for you, then plan on some practice beforehand.

Many learners in distance education environments comment on the importance of keeping up with the material. We have discussed this concept and will continue to discuss it in terms of your academic performance, but it is also important from a technical standpoint. Learners comment that they find that if they don't keep up with the required technical skills on a regular basis, they find that they may have forgotten how to use some of these skills when it is essential to their progress in the course. Remembering passwords, particular sets of directions for locating a special website, a sequence of actions needed to find a pre-set location on a DVD, or a program for a modem to dial a particular computer can all be skills that can be forgotten when not used. Learners find if they have waited too long in-between sessions, they may have to relearn certain skills. Practice with and using the technology often may not make you perfect, but it will certainly keep you proficient and will save time that can be used for learning content.

So what happens when you have technical problems? We all know that technology is a tool and can break down. Consider your reaction to basic technical problems you may encounter on a daily basis. When the VCR at home doesn't work correctly or the copier at the office jams, do you generally fix the problem or do you walk away in frustration and wait for someone else to fix it? Your reaction to common everyday technical frustrations can be a cue to how you might react while working with technology as a tool for learning. Frustration levels can increase dramatically if you have an assignment due and you are having difficulty logging onto the worldwide web or you can't remember how to access the discussion page for your class. These things all happen, and although you may not be able to avoid the problem itself, you certainly can develop mechanisms that will help diminish the frustration you may feel.

First and foremost, make sure you've given yourself ample time to complete work assignments.

Second, make sure you are aware of the technical support available to you through your institution. Is there a toll free number (email address, online technical support material) you can use to reach a technical support person? Is the service available 24 hours a day or just during certain hours? Are the technicians specifically assigned to work with distance education learners or do they provide technical support for the entire institution? This last question is important to confirm. Sometimes technical support personnel are well trained in the use of computers and software but may not be trained to address the specific needs of the distance learner. Although useful and necessary, do not rely wholly on the technical support provided by your institution. Enlist a friend, co-worker, or family member to help out when you encounter technical problems. It is better to have a network of individuals who can provide you with information than to go it alone. And finally, don't let your inexperience with technology deter you from enrolling in a distance education course or program. Remember that technology is a tool and it can be mastered.

## Communication Skills and Preferences

Are my reading comprehension skills strong?
Am I comfortable with others reading my work?
Am I able to transfer my ideas into words fairly well?
Do I like to learn by participating with others in a group?

Our ability to receive the ideas of others and to express our own ideas to others is essential if we are to be a good learner. In the distance education situation there are some very key limitations on how we receive and express ideas. It will be important to make sure that we are not constrained by these limitations. Sitting in a face-to-face learning situation – the regular classroom – is usually dependent upon our ability to listen and speak. Learning via distance education – the virtual classroom – i9s very different and we are dependent on our ability to read and write. At first this difference may not sound like a major shift. However, it can be very frustrating if we are not prepared for it.

A considerable amount of the coursework in a distance education program demands that you read it. Though we tend to think of distance education in terms of the technology that is used, the bottom line is that reading is usually the foundation of the course and the information we receive. And when we are not reading we are probably sharing our ideas by writing them to others. Yes, there are exceptions to this characterization such as conference call sessions, satellite video programs, or correspondence via compact disc recordings. However, even these exceptions rely heavily on printed material to support concepts that are presented and to provide needed structure to ensure that each learner stays clearly on track. Without good reading and writing skills you may find that the distance education course that you are taking is very frustrating and hard for you to maintain the pace.

It is always a good idea to do some testing of the water, that is, try some distance communicating before actually signing up for a course. Sure, you send emails back and forth like everyone else. However, this time try to do some "academic" emailing. Find the email address for the instructor of a distance education course you might consider enrolling in. Compose an email that tells the instructor a bit about yourself and ask some key questions. Was it easy to compose the email? Difficult? Did you reread your email? Did it still make sense? How could you have improved your email? After you receive your reply, read the response carefully to see if all of your questions were answered. Does the instructor's response make sense? Are there additional areas that you should respond to? Does the email you received make you want to take a course from this instructor? Why? Why not?

Another "academic" practice exercise can be similarly carried out with some other learners. Think of a person you know who has taken a distance education course. Instead of calling this person on the phone and asking about the experience, email him or her in the same way that is described above. You should again be able to get a good idea of how comfortable you are with using email for sharing information in a more formal or "academic" setting. You will be developing a good sense of what a distance education learning environment can feel like.

When communicating in a face-to-face situation, we have the advantage of being able to sense many different cues that let us know how our message is being received. These cues help us understand when we can trust the other person, when we feel we can share ideas more openly, and when it is important that we respond in certain ways. In the distance education situation these cues may be entirely absent. Without this form of feedback it becomes difficult to understand how to shape our messages. We run the risk of saying things that may get misinterpreted and misunderstood. Distance education demands a considerable amount of trust in the others with whom we are communicating. Trusting others in the class and developing comfort in having others read what you have to say can be a real key to your success as a distance learner.

The learning that goes on in a distance education course is often built on a reciprocal relationship. If we would like to receive feedback from the others in the class, it is important for us to reciprocate by responding with our feedback to their ideas. In a truly reciprocal relationship each person in the course is responsible for sending and receiving ideas, offering his or her thoughts and reflecting on the thoughts of others, providing constructive feedback to others and receiving feedback in a positive manner, and generally viewing the entire experience as a learning partnership that is built on the skills of reading and writing.

## Personal Support Systems

> Have I shared with my friends or family the idea that I may be taking a distance education class?
> Do I understand when I may need the help of others to be successful in a distance education class?

Becoming involved in learning at a distance is going to force you to make some shifts in your life. They may be as simple as merely rearranging your schedule a bit or they may be very complex calling for you to end your involvement with certain activities and greatly reducing your commitment to others. In all of these decisions, it will be very comforting to know that your family and friends are supportive of what you are doing and willing to help, if called upon.

If we are the only ones to be affected by these shifts, it would be fine. However, the reality is that there are many others around us who will also be affected by our decision to take a distance education course. It will be important that these significant people in our lives understand and encourage the decision we are making. And the way to enlist their support is to involve them in your decision to learn at a distance at a very early time. From the very beginning it is wise to share your thinking with others. Do they think it is a good idea for you to try a distance education course? What cautions do they have for you? Have they had similar experiences that they could share with you? Do they know of others who you should speak with? Keeping your family and friends updated with your latest thinking is a good way to ensure their help later on when you may really need it.

Exactly what is a support system? A support system can be many things. For a learner, though, the most important thing that we hope that a support system can provide is the emotional support that will help us be successful in our learning endeavor. A viable support system consisting of family and friends will know when we need quiet time to work on assignments, telephone time to be online, or a friendly ear to hear about the things we are learning. A solid support system will give you a feeling of strength knowing that you are not standing alone at the end of a long distance communication network.

How can they help? A well functioning support system of family and friends will be able to give you the freedom to go about your learning agenda without feeling guilty about reducing your time with them. They will be available to encourage you when needed and to make suggestions for helping you past road blocks. Ideas of where to find local learning resources, advice on topics for a term paper or strategies for analyzing a problem, or reading the first draft of a paper you are working on can all be excellent functions for a support system.

Once we recognize the value of a support system in being successful at learning at a distance, it will also be important to recognize the need for the relationship to be mutual. To sustain our support system it must be a two-way street. Asking for a special favor of our family members is so much easier if we regularly look for ways to openly express our appreciation for their help. If we know that we will have to spend a number of evenings locked away with our CDs, books, and computer, we can balance ahead of time with evenings we spend with them. The distance education adventure can turn into a very consuming activity – consuming of time, friends, and relationships. So, be sure to nurture these relationships, so they will continue to be there for you long after the distance education experience.

## Causes for Attrition and their Solutions

This topic is not enjoyable, but it has to be said! *The attrition rate – dropout rate – in distance education courses is considerably higher than in regular face-to-face courses.* Why? There are two key reasons why people drop out of distance education courses. One, they do not know what to expect when they enrolled in the course. Second, the anonymity that comes along with a distance education course lets them "sit in the back of the virtual classroom" and not participate.

Hopefully this guide will help you develop a stronger sense of exactly what will be expected of you in a distance education course. Carefully think through your decision. Sure, the distance education approach may be considerably more convenient for you. However, will your learning style work well with what is demanded by distance education? Do you sense that you have the personal commitment and motivation that is needed? Are you familiar with technology to the point that you can use it with ease? Are you comfortable communicating by reading and writing? And do you have the support of friends and family to help you when needed? If you feel that you are able to effectively deal with these concerns, then you will have successfully avoided the first reason why people dropout – you really do know what to expect.

About anonymity, yes, sitting quietly in the back of the room can be very acceptable at certain times. However, in distance education courses it is important to carefully select those times. And during the other times, it is essential that you be active and fully participate in the class. No one will call out your name loudly to force you out of your anonymity. No, it will be up to you to step forward and to assume an active role. Try keeping a small diary, so you can jot down a few reflections after each segment of the distance education program. How did you do? Did you try to find at least one opportunity to send a question, share a thought, or respond to the ideas of some one else? If you didn't, what was holding you back? If a bulletin board is available for the class, have you been able to regularly read the postings of others and add your own thoughts? Becoming less anonymous takes a bit of work but is certainly achievable!

## Assessing the Institution's Learning Environment

Now that we have discussed how critical it is to assess your personal style and have examined the personal responsibilities and level of commitment you need for a successful distance education experience, it is equally important to assess what your institution will do to help you be a successful distance learner. Institutions offer degrees and programs by distance education because they recognize that you, the learner, are insisting on more convenient formats that accommodate your schedule and lifestyle. They recognize that you are also insisting on quality. Your institution's level of commitment to quality will be reflected not only in the type of faculty or instructors teaching in the distance education environment, but also the type of services that are provided to you. It is amazing how many resources are available to learners particularly if they have taken classes in a more traditional format on a traditional campus. You have access to academic advisors, library services, career information, and financial aid. Many times it is easy to take these things for granted, until you are separated from these services by distance. The last thing you want to do is spend countless hours trying to take care of the operational details such as enrolling or getting your books. You want to have easily accessible services.

Not sure exactly what questions you should ask of your institution? The following is a suggested list of questions that you should consider asking. The key is to anticipate areas of concern, ask questions, and make sure you understand what is available to you.

> *How do I register? Is there a toll free number?*
> *How do I pay my tuition bill?*
> *What type of technical support exists?*
> *What are the hours of all of the students services available to distance learners?*
> *Is there an orientation I must attend?*
> *How do I access library services?*
> *How do I get my books?*
> *What type of advising and/or counseling services are available?*
> *What if I need a tutor?*
> *Are there different costs for distance education courses?*
> *What computer and/or software will I need?*
> *Is there financial aid available specifically for distance learners?*
> *Is there an institutional/departmental/program website available?*

# Chapter 13

## Distance Education Inventory

or

### *So You Are Considering Taking a Distance Education Course!*

**Simone Jonaitis**

This Distance Education Inventory provides an opportunity for the distance education learner to be challenged to really consider the idea of participating in a distance education course. The Inventory consists of groups of statements designed as a tool to help the learner think about what it means to learn at a distance. There is a different set of statements for each of the four key areas touched on in the Guide (Chapter 12) – **Personal Commitment and Motivation**, **Technology**, **Communication Skills and Preferences**, and **Personal Support Systems**. A short discussion section follows each group of statements to help the learner further reflect. Time should be spent carefully considering each statement before responding to it. The response to each statement should best represent the real behavior of the learner. By carefully considering each statement and the response that is made, the learner will have an opportunity to reflect on how his/her personal goals, expectations, style and situation will impact on learning at a distance

| Distance Education Inventory<br>A. Personal Commitment and Motivation | Very much like me and my situation | Sort of like me | Not at all like me or my situation |
|---|---|---|---|
| *For each of the following statements circle the letter (X, Y or Z) in the column that corresponds with how similar the statement is to you and your situation.* | | | |
| 1. I am considering taking this distance education class in this format because it looks interesting. | X | Y | Z |
| 2. When taking a class I make sure I stay on schedule with the class (I budget my time, prepare my assignments, don't have to play "catch-up", etc.) | X | Y | Z |
| 3. Taking a distance education course sounds exciting. | X | Y | Z |
| 4. I am familiar with others who have taken distance education courses. | X | Y | Z |
| 5. The subject matter for this distance education class is important to me. | X | Y | Z |
| 6. I usually don't get bored easily in classes that I take. | X | Y | Z |
| 7. Having a "live" instructor to keep me focused is not important to me. | X | Y | Z |
| 8. My attendance habits are good. I rarely miss a class. | X | Y | Z |
| 9. I am prepared to spend more time taking this course since it is offered at a distance. | X | Y | Z |
| 10. I enjoy learning by myself. Having others around me in a class setting is not so important. | X | Y | Z |
| 11. The subject matter for this distance education class is of interest to me. | X | Y | Z |
| 12. I enjoy learning. | X | Y | Z |

# A. Personal Commitment and Motivation

*If the table shows many Xs, consider the following:*

Chances are your motivation and commitment to learning are high and you understand learning is more than completing coursework – it's understanding the content. More than likely you enjoy learning and have developed strong study habits that guide you through most tasks you undertake. Keeping up with readings and assignments is critical in a distance education environment. As with any course or program, if you want to get the most out of the experience, then you must stay on top of the coursework and be ready to discuss and ask questions. You should do well.

*If the table shows many Ys, consider the following:*

Taking a class because it is a requirement is certainly motivation. Perhaps it leads to an increase in pay or an increase in professional responsibility. However, it is important to continue to explore why the course or program is required and examine your level of commitment as well as study habits. For example, if you are not strongly committed to completing a degree or if you feel forced into taking the course without any real interest in the content, you may find yourself focused on finishing the course rather than focusing on learning and understanding the material. If you are not particularly interested in the material or content, then you may find it more difficult to focus on the course. Try to be well organized as a learner and keep up with the pace of the course. Continue to focus on goals, keep up with the material, and don't forget to enjoy the experience.

*If the table shows many Zs, consider the following:*

If you feel you are motivated because a distance education course will save you time, please reconsider. There are certainly many benefits to taking a course at a distance. However, be advised that many students who have taken a class via distance education have found that even though they were not required to be at a particular place at any specific time, they found they spent more time taking a distance course rather than less time. Also, if you have found you tend to procrastinate and put things off, you may find yourself falling terribly behind in a distance course. You are going to find in a distance education environment you have to push yourself to get things done. It's easy to be fooled into believing that because you are not forced to any specific place or time, you have all the time in the world. You might neglect logging on to your computer as often as you should, and when you finally do, you might find that the rest of your group has been engaged in an extensive conversation and you're going to have to do a lot of catching up to bring yourself up to their level of the others in the group. Chances are that you will find that there is a lot of reading – more than you had anticipated – and a level of participation that won't allow you to "sit in the back of the room." Remember the only way your instructor knows you are in the group is when you post your thoughts to discussions and listservs. If you are falling behind in your reading, your assignments, and your participation, it is going to be obvious not only to the instructor, but also to your fellow classmates as well.

| Distance Education Inventory<br>B. Technology | Very much like me and my situation | Sort of like me | Not at all like me or my situation |
|---|---|---|---|
| *For each of the following statements circle the letter (X, Y or Z) in the column that corresponds with how similar the statement is to you and your situation.* | | | |
| 1. When I have a technical problem with a machine or equipment, I am generally successful if I work through the problem alone. | X | Y | Z |
| 2. I like to understand how equipment or technology works. | X | Y | Z |
| 3. I am able to easily use the Internet to do personal research, browsing, and communicating with friends and family. | X | Y | Z |
| 4. Watching a teacher on a video allows me to stop the presentation when needed, so I can replay a section that I don't understand. | X | Y | Z |
| 5. I think technology can improve most courses. | X | Y | Z |
| 6. A FAX machine is a very helpful device. | X | Y | Z |
| 7. I feel as if I am in control when I am able to learn on my own with a computer or recorded materials. | X | Y | Z |
| 8. I often volunteer to help others who may be having difficulty with technical equipment. | X | Y | Z |
| 9. My friends turn to me if they have questions about how to use their computer. | X | Y | Z |
| 10. Cellular telephones are easy to use. | X | Y | Z |

# B. Technology

*If the table shows many Xs, consider the following:*

It certainly appears you have a good familiarity with computers and are comfortable with technology in general. It's true, knowing everything there is to know about technology is impossible, but having a positive attitude toward technology is important, if you are to succeed in a distance education environment. Learning at a distance isn't learning *about* technology. It is learning via the technology and to be successful the technology must stay in the background and not be a major concern. Your profile suggests that you are comfortable enough with technology not to be concerned about it. You are off to a good start! Technology is only the vehicle used to deliver the information for the course, and it can be a wonderful tool to help in learning. What is important, however, is to remember technology is only a tool and by being familiar with it, you can enhance the power of the learning experience.

*If the table shows many Ys, consider the following:*

Chances are that you are somewhat familiar with the basics of technology and will not have too much difficulty navigating your way around a distance education environment once you become familiar with the environment. Take time at the beginning of your distance education experience to become very familiar with the technology that will be used. Try it out. Rehearse the different situations in which technology will be used. Find a few friends who have considerable experience with technology and would be willing to help you, if needed. Make sure you know how to access technical support from your institution and don't be afraid to call on them when needed. With a bit of practice you should be able to master the technology and get on with the learning.

*If the table shows many Zs, consider the following:*

You may not be an expert with technology and may not want to rely very much on technology. Learning at a distance can be a problem for you with the technology getting in the way of learning, if you don't take enough time at the beginning of the course to learn the basics of all of the technology you will need. Invite a friend who is good with technology to join you during the first session or two to lend a hand, if needed. Following the session have the friend stay a few minutes longer to allow you to review the key technical skills that were needed. Rehearsing the use of the technology is an important way to master the technology, so it will not be in your way. Having little or no experience with technology may indicate an underlying negative attitude toward technology and may lead you to frustration. Be sure to ask the instructor and the institution about the technology requirements for the course. Be honest with yourself when considering the type of technology use that will be required for you to be successful in a distance education program. If this level of use will be uncomfortable and frustrating for you, you may be wise to think twice about participating in a distance education program, especially one that makes extensive use of technology.

| Distance Education Inventory<br>C. Communication Skills and Preferences | Very much like me and my situation | Sort of like me | Not at all like me or my situation |
|---|---|---|---|
| *For each of the following statements circle the letter (X, Y or Z) in the column that corresponds with how similar the statement is to you and your situation.* | | | |
| 1. I usually grasp written information quickly. | X | Y | Z |
| 2. I tend to be spontaneous and enjoy exchanging ideas with others. | X | Y | Z |
| 3. I try to read at least one book every month or so. | X | Y | Z |
| 4. By writing essays and reports I am able to re-read my work and make improvements. | X | Y | Z |
| 5. I enjoy being the discussion leader in a group discussion. | X | Y | Z |
| 6. Browsing at a bookstore is a fun activity for me. | X | Y | Z |
| 7. I enjoy using email to share my ideas with others. | X | Y | Z |
| 8. I prefer a take-home exam, so I can spend a good amount of time preparing my response, rather than an in-class exam with a limited amount of time. | X | Y | Z |
| 9. I am good at providing feedback on the papers that are prepared by my friends and classmates. | X | Y | Z |
| 10. I am very familiar with the word processor on my computer. | X | Y | Z |
| 11. The thought of sharing my written work with others appeals to me. I look forward to the feedback. | X | Y | Z |
| 12. Being able to answer questions by writing allows me to think and rethink how I will respond. | X | Y | Z |
| 13. I enjoy the interaction that comes from a good group discussion. | X | Y | Z |
| 14. Email is a good way for people to share their ideas with me. | X | Y | Z |
| 15. An important reason for preparing papers and written reports is so I can get feedback from others. | X | Y | Z |
| 16. I am a fast reader. | X | Y | Z |
| 17. I enjoy putting my ideas into written form. | X | Y | Z |
| 18. I can quickly pull out the key ideas when I read a paper. | X | Y | Z |

## C. Communication Skills and Preferences

*If the table shows many Xs, consider the following:*
Reading and writing are critical skills in any learning environment, but especially so in a distance education environment. You will be amazed by how much reading and writing you will do in your course. It is really the only way the instructor and the others in your class can discuss topics. Chances are your reading and writing skills are strong and you enjoy both. Your skill in these areas will be a real asset to you and will enhance your distance education experience.

*If the table shows many Ys, consider the following:*

You may find you are putting in more time reading and writing that you thought you would. You will be expected to share your thoughts with the others in the class and expected to react to the ideas that others have presented. It is unlikely you will have trouble. However, you may find you are spending more time reading things over carefully in order to make sure you understand the material clearly and you also may find you are spending more time composing your ideas and reworking them before submitting them to be read by others. At first it may not be comfortable having others provide feedback to you on your ideas, but it is something that you will probably get used to. You will also be expected to carefully read what others in the group are writing and provide thoughtful feedback to them.

It is unlikely you will have any trouble with this, but do be alerted to the fact that you will probably spend more time doing the readings, composing your thoughts, and reacting to the thoughts of others than you think. Remember, it generally takes more time than you thought it would!

*If the table shows many Zs, consider the following:*

Strong reading and writing skills are absolutely critical in a distance education environment. Without constant use of these basic skills how would the others and the instructor know whether you understood the material and how would you ever be able to share your ideas with the class? How would the instructor or the others even know you were present if you didn't write your thoughts for them to see? And certainly, if you are going to write your comments and ideas to the group, you certainly will want to be sure you understand the material. One thing you may find is that you will be spending quite a bit of time reading the material, so you truly understand what is being said. You will need to develop your confidence in this area. It is not always easy to put your ideas out for everyone to see and critique, but it is the most effective way to do so when your classmates are scattered all over the city, state, or nation. If you truly feel your skills need to be sharpened, contact your institution's student services office or tutoring area. Perhaps you should speak with someone trained to work with students in the areas of reading and writing to help you better evaluate your skills and provide you with a personal developmental plan.

| Distance Education Inventory<br>**D. Personal Support Systems** | Very much like me and my situation | Sort of like me | Not at all like me or my situation |
|---|---|---|---|
| *For each of the following statements circle the letter (X, Y or Z) in the column that corresponds with how similar the statement is to you and your situation.* | | | |
| 1. My friends and family are very supportive. They understand the importance of my education. | X | Y | Z |
| 2. I have a number of friends who are also involved in educational programs. | X | Y | Z |
| 3. It is easy for my family and friends to see when I am having difficulty in a class. | X | Y | Z |
| 4. The place I plan to do my studying is quiet. I can study without being interrupted. | X | Y | Z |
| 5. My employer is very supportive and encourages me to take classes. | X | Y | Z |
| 6. I can depend on my family and friends to encourage me when my classes are difficult. | X | Y | Z |
| 7. I have a favorite place where I like to study. | X | Y | Z |
| 8. My family and friends are very aware that I would like to take a course using distance education. | X | Y | Z |
| 9. I try to help others who are taking classes. | X | Y | Z |
| 10. Sometimes it is important for me to have someone who can listen to my concerns. | X | Y | Z |
| 11.My friends think my decision to take a distance education course is a good decision. | X | Y | Z |
| 12. I try to remember to make time for my family and friends, so my studying does not always get in the way. | X | Y | Z |
| 13. I enjoy telling others about the classes I am taking. | X | Y | Z |
| 14. I usually can handle stress quite well. | X | Y | Z |

# D. Personal Support Systems

*If the table shows many Xs, consider the following:*

It looks like you have strong support mechanisms in place. Going back to school or taking a class is time consuming and requires a lot of commitment and energy. If you are like millions of people taking classes, you probably have many other responsibilities competing for your time and energy. It is incredibly helpful and absolutely necessary to have supportive people and environments to keep you motivated throughout the process. It is also important that you allow others to help you when needed. As you probably already know, managing multiple responsibilities can be very stressful. Don't hesitate to use your support systems. It certainly appears that everyone is behind you!

*If the table shows many Ys, consider the following:*

Learning takes time and energy and without the proper support systems you may find yourself adding unnecessary stress to your life. Take a look at the types of things that produce stress in your life and enlist your friends, family, and employer to help you manage some of these things in your life. For example, is it possible for another family member to pick up the children after school or from the baby sitter? This can help you gain another hour or two to do some of your coursework rather than rushing home where you may get involved in the daily routines of the household. Perhaps you can share cooking responsibilities with your partner or maybe a teenage son or daughter. When family and friends offer their support to you, it will be important to allow their assistance. Sometimes this aid may be difficult to accept, but you will learn that it can be very helpful and allow you to focus more attention on your studies. Does your job allow you some flexibility to do personal errands? Managing your time and enlisting others in helping with daily responsibilities will help you ease into learning at a distance and will provide you with more time to concentrate on your studies. Having a well functioning support system can be essential to your success in a distance education program.

*If the table shows many Zs, consider the following:*

If you are like so many of us you have a variety of responsibilities and probably already struggle to keep up with everything. Taking a course is just another thing to add to your list of things to do. Remember, taking a class at a distance, despite the benefits of participating when your schedule best permits, requires enormous amounts of energy and time, if you are to do it well. Take a look at your schedule. Are there certain things that can be altered in order for you to make more time for studying? Are you taking on too much? Are there people in your life, friends and family, who can help you make the changes in your life that will free up valuable time for you to be a better learner? When you need someone to share an idea with, who will you turn to? Are you ready to ask others to help in this way? Sometimes we expect to give 100 percent in everything we do without examining how much it will cost us and how important others can be to helping us. Seriously evaluate the support systems you have. If you are not finding the level of support you feel you need from family, friends, employers, or co-workers, does your institution have any resources you might be able to tap into? Talk with your instructor and share your concerns with the others in your class. Building a system of support that you can lean on when necessary can spell success for you in a distance education course.

# Part Three:
# Implementing Distance Education

**Examples of programs and initiatives which are based on learner-focused distance education.**

# Chapter 14

## The Internet for the Aged Professor-
## Some Surprising Pluses

### George H. Axinn

Life can be an exciting, rewarding, and surprising challenge, even in its latter years. These are some personal reflections on the teaching of a web-based graduate seminar by an aging Professor Emeritus. This adventure has been full of surprises.

In the eyes of many of my colleagues, the attempt to try teaching on the Internet was a surprise, and viewed as a mixture of foolish technological whimsy and serious threat. To me, what started out as a challenge to creativity has developed into a promising improvement on the traditional graduate seminar, taught in a small room, around a table, at a fixed time each week. Could it really be done on the Internet, with students scattered around the countryside (if not the globe)? Could it be done by a professor shifting from wintry Michigan State University to sunny Tucson - and even continuing while the teacher attends a summer school at Cornell?

My colleagues were not convinced. Many said, "You can't do that!" Some told me I was too old - only kids have the necessary computer skills to surf the web! Others said graduate students need to see each others' faces for a seminar to really work. And colleagues of my age said, "You won't be able to teach if you can't see their faces."

In truth, I wasn't at all sure myself. The Vice-President in charge of our Virtual University told me that a "producer" would be assigned to me. Some academics might have asked, "What is a producer?" or, "Why do I need a producer? I've been teaching for decades without one." But for me, who had pioneered the use of television for university instruction in the 1950s, I understood. As a TV producer who had enabled other professors to use that strange new media - back then - I was delighted to have a producer. Only later did I discover that the producer had a programmer and an artist, and that the team was going to produce this "on-line" class.

Preparation time was an unknown. Without offering the details here, I estimate that it took me about eight to ten times as long to prepare each lesson as I had been spending for preparation for classroom seminars. But I had been teaching a similar class for decades - updating readings, case studies, assignments, and supplementary materials each semester - but I had always worked from an outline before, never a written script. For this three credit graduate class, fifteen 3-hour lessons had to be prepared on the Internet. Each would have an introduction page, a table of contents, and a series of other pages with what might have been called a lecture, assigned readings from a text book and from other web sites, assignments, and instructions to students about posting their term papers, etc.

So where are the surprises? What are the pluses? After fifteen consecutive semesters of teaching this course online the evidence is beginning to become apparent. Here are some of the surprising pluses:

1.  The quality of participation in this simulation of a live graduate-level seminar has been better in many ways than earlier experiences with a live group sitting around a table once a week with the professor. This has been particularly evident with international students and minority students.

2.  The flexibility of timing of participation is appreciated by both students and teacher. The asynchronous conversations have been ideal for this type of seminar. Student participation begins slowly in the first few weeks, but then becomes lively through the most of the class, tapering off somewhat in the last few weeks when students are occupied by production of their term papers.

3.  From the professor's perspective, there are some other positive surprises. International students, whose English language skills are more limited, seem more willing to express themselves than I have experienced in the seminar room. Women students, and particularly international women students, have been very active participants. Perhaps there is more balance in the interactions than in "live" classrooms, as no individual student can monopolize the conversation, and anyone who wants to pitch in to any conversation can easily do so!

4.  The end-of-semester student evaluations show student enthusiasm for the virtual course, which has increased over the years.

## Costs for the Aging Professor

Like almost everything else that has value, there are some costs. One is the preparation time, mentioned above, and the actual "teaching" time. This was a semester class for three graduate credits. Typically I would be in the seminar room with my students for three hours each week, in addition to some office visits, and increasing email exchanges with students, plus reading, commenting on and grading assignments and term papers.

A log I kept for the first offering of my 15 week Internet course showed online activity averaging 6 hours and 16 minutes per week for a class of five grad students. That does not include any of the preparation during the previous semester. It does include all time actually on the web with students, in e-mail communication with students, and in communication with the technical support team, and my own department technical support.

As the years have gone by, student numbers have grown, and (not as a surprise) I learned that my time invested in this class grows in proportion to the number of students. Since I try to give each classmate feedback with positive reinforcement in response to each of their inputs, and the student number has ranged from 6 to 24, I now think the ideal number of students for this particular on-line seminar is 12 students.

## Benefits for the Aging Professor

Here are some of my positive reflections on teaching via the Internet:

> **No repeating of old stories.** In my normal, informal seminars, there is some probability that I might (on rare occasions) tell something to my students that I had told them the week before - or possibly even an hour before. With several people involved in proofreading each

web-course lesson in advance, that does not happen.

**No confusing statements with items stated backwards.** Although I hate to admit it, sometimes in class I may say "North" when I mean "South," or "down" when I mean "up." Again, I don't make those errors in the Internet course.

**No regular schedule of class hours at a fixed time each week.** That gives me more flexibility in time-use. The students appreciate it even more. When one student suggested that we try a "chat room" at a fixed time each week, other students rejected the idea. They preferred the asynchronous conversations - as some "went to class" in the evenings, others on the week-ends, and one "attended" very early in the mornings, before going to work. And some live in different time zones around the globe

**More accurate record keeping for grading.** Because student inputs are all available for review at grading time, both students and the professor have more reliable evidence for assigning grades.

**No additional office hours for students.** By being available daily for personal e-mail conversations, as well as the conversations on the appropriate web pages for each aspect of the class, there are very few occasions when a student wants to see me in my office. Such requests have been rare.

**No travel from home to classroom in bad weather.** Thirty or forty years ago, I never thought of that as a burden. But, as I am past seventy, and especially when there is snow or rain, it has become an issue.

**No interruption of class for urgent bathroom calls.** Again, my pattern has long been to break up a three-hour seminar with coffee for all students and myself along the way, and a break in the middle. But nature's calls are not as predictable for some of us "seniors," and the whole question does not arise while teaching via computer on the Internet.


## Benefits for the students

Here are some of the things students have reported to me:

**Increased dialogue between individual students and the professor.** Students tell me they have more opportunities for personal conversations with me than they normally do in conventional seminars.

**Increased tracking of individual students' inputs.** Students can go back to earlier lessons and see what they had said. They can also surf to earlier conversations, and see what their classmates had said. That is also useful to me.

**Increased flexibility of timing for class attendance and submission of assignments.** This has made it possible for students to leave the country for several weeks in mid-semester, and keep up with the class. Several students have had unexpected time pressures from the workplace, for which we were all able to make adjustments.

**Increased willingness to participate in class discussion for students with weak English**

**language skills, particularly international students.** I mentioned this above, but students also mention it to me. They notice the difference.

## Here are some examples:

Poonsin, a woman student from Thailand was a vigorous participant in the asynchronous conversations in the seminar. She was fearless in challenging responses to class questions; even some from men students. And she made excellent inputs of her own. One of those men students sent me an e-mail after a few weeks of class, to comment that he had been in another graduate seminar with Poonsin in the prior semester. There, she attended each week and took notes, but never opened her mouth. What a difference!

Barry, a domestic male student needed only a few more credits to complete the requirements for his Master's degree. But he had a full-time job that required travel. What to do? He enrolled in the Internet class, took his laptop with him, and completed all requirements on time!

Maria sent me an e-mail one day. The snow was over a foot deep, and she was able to stay in her warm room, and do this week's lessons without getting either cold or wet!

Tom was the type who "knows" the answer to everything, is always the first to have his hand up, and who requires special pressure from the teacher to stop talking. In this class he was "under control." He could respond to every question if he wished; but so could every other student. And he could give a "long-winded" response if he wished - but others could skim it, or skip it, if they wished. He did not hold up the class discussion, or prevent others from having their opportunity.

## And here are some quotations from the students' end-of-semester evaluation forms:

*What surprised you about taking this virtual university course?*

"It is easier and more convenience than I ever thought."

"Ability to communicate effectively with classmates that you have not met before. In fact this was even easier than a face to face discussion where sometimes this becomes tainted with attitudes observable in body language. The fact that technology makes it possible to learn for someone who cannot always be able to go to class at certain specific scheduled times. The fact that it is possible to learn even for people outside US in this system."

*What did you like about it?*

"It is more understandable than a classroom teaching. I did not miss any point the instructor needed me to know. All my questions were answered by the instructor right after he got my messages."

"The pace of the course."

"It made learning available and accessible."

***What did you dislike about it?***

"The VU (Internet course) depends on the server which somehow sometimes did not work appropriately. I sometimes have to reconnect for several times within an hour!"
"The difficulty in engaging other classmates with discussion."

"Once a relationship has developed between people, the tendency is to want to actually meet the people and share experiences face to face. This course did not provide that."

## So what do I know now that I didn't know before?

The combination of the computer and the Internet is not going to replace the classroom, the seminar room, or the laboratory. But like the printing press, the radio, television, the overhead projector, and "PowerPoint," it is one more excellent tool which can improve the quality of higher education, as well as increase access to it. And for us older professors, it can be a real blessing!

# Chapter 15

# Bringing Eleven Universities to Town!

## Marguerite Cotto

## Background

The Northwestern Region of Michigan is well known for sparkling lakes, wonderful scenery and resourceful communities built around agriculture, light manufacturing, and tourism. Since the 1970's the region has experienced population growth at a far higher rate than the rest of the state, including some counties that have led the state in population gains since 1990. Interestingly, with over 100,000 residents in the region, no locally chartered four-year higher education institution has been established to serve them.

How could such a situation exist? The answer - by design! Northwestern Michigan College (NMC), a comprehensive community college founded in 1951, avoided the urge to reinvent itself as a four-year college and instead went about luring universities from across the state of Michigan to offer their programs to the people of the Northwestern Region. And, thanks to distance education, it's working. There are currently 11 participating four-year universities offering 58 programs leading to Certificates, Bachelor degrees, Master's degrees and beyond.

## How It All Started

In 1988, an economic development study conducted for the Grand Traverse Area Chamber of Commerce by the Battelle Institute in Grand Rapids noted the lack of baccalaureate and advanced degree opportunities in the five counties of the Northern Region and identified this as one of the significant problems in attracting prospective business and industry (Battelle Institute, 1988). The report struck a sensitive chord within the community and at Northwestern Michigan College. Degree opportunities beyond the first two years were only available through limited off-campus programming (such as a bachelor's degree completion program in nursing offered on the community college campus), or by commuting directly to a main campus. For most employed adults, the time required to even travel to a campus close to Traverse City seemed to be an almost insurmountable hurdle, and they were applying pressure on Northwestern Michigan College to begin the process of converting from a 2-year open-access college to a 4-year regional university.

A study conducted by the State of Michigan Board of Education in 1991 entitled "Project Outreach" determined that 81 percent of surveyed citizens in the College's service area felt that the College needed to "either become a university or expand baccalaureate and advanced degree offerings" (Michigan Board of Education, 1991). Furthermore, the strategic planning process developed by the Grand Traverse 20/20 Steering Committee for the Citizens of Grand Traverse County in 1991, referred to as *Grand Traverse 20/20*, determined that within the area of education, the highest regional priority was for NMC to meet this educational challenge (Smith, 1991).

The community identified advanced educational opportunities as a key factor in the region's capacity to encourage economic development. Concerns over relative geographic isolation, gaps in rural infrastructure, particularly as this would apply to communication systems and access to technology, as well as a sense that the area was paying a disproportionately high percentage of state taxes without the benefit of closer access to a public university all contributed to a grass roots effort to work with the College to create alternatives. This group of civic leaders and interested citizens called themselves the "Founders 21."

In 1993, *Founders 21* presented a set of recommendations to the Board of Trustees of Northwestern Michigan College (Founders 21, 1993). The vision behind the *Founders 21* report was best articulated by Les Biederman, the primary driving force behind the creation of the College in 1951, who had anticipated that NMC could become:

> "...an association of colleges, a university of satellite institutions of learning. In Traverse City, grouped around the central campus...it seems, of course, overwhelming to think about starting other four-year colleges, but if NMC's resources, already available and functioning, were to be utilized, would-be schools could be helped on their way to opening" (Biederman, 1982, p.148)

So with the idea of helping already available and functioning colleges and universities "on their way to opening" in Northwestern Michigan, NMC began the process of creating mechanisms to make it happen. The Board of Trustees, upon the recommendation of the founders group, took action and identified the fall of 1995 as the date when this new enterprise would begin. The initiative would be formally known as the "Northwestern Michigan College University Center" (UC).

## The First Steps

With an eye toward this prize, the College partnered with the regional intermediate school districts to develop "Project Interconnect." With a major grant from the Kellogg Foundation and in collaboration with area cable companies, "Project Interconnect" was designed to provide two-way interactive television capabilities to the 15 high schools in the College's service area, and to build the base of interactive classrooms that would become the backbone for delivery of university classes to the region.

In 1993, the distance education movement in the state was beginning to invest heavily in these facilities as a primary strategy for delivery of courses and degree programs at a distance. Northwestern Michigan College was planning to become a state-of-the-art regional facility as part of its strategy to encourage the participation of universities. At the time, the cost of developing one classroom exceeded $80,000. NMC managed to develop seven such rooms within two years.

A significant portion of the Kellogg Foundation grant was dedicated to the training of faculty who would be teaching in this new venue, and NMC became a central training facility for faculty from around the Midwest interested in the potential of the technology.

## Developing the University Center Concept

The movement toward higher education partnerships in which one institution becomes the host through which other universities deliver programs is certainly not new to Traverse City. In the early 1990's, Mott Community College (Midland, Michigan) and Macomb Community College (Macomb County, Michigan) were both developing relationships with 4-year partners to facilitate bringing bachelor degree completion programs to their communities. Northwestern Michigan College's

150

approach was to facilitate the development of a dedicated campus in which multiple universities would co-locate and share resources that would reduce the overall cost of bringing programs to the area.

From the academic side, NMC worked closely with its faculty and with the faculty of prospective university partners to improve communication between schools and to assure support for the students who would be learning in a very different and somewhat experimental environment. Multiple agreements were developed to make administrative partnerships work smoothly as well; everything from how students would apply for admission and financial aid, register, purchase books and supplies - even sweatshirts - was considered before the project was announced to the public.

To support this significant enterprise, the College developed a $5 million dollar community capital campaign to fund the development of a new campus, purchase needed technology, develop an electronic library for students, and to establish an operating endowment. A measure of the community support for this project was the remarkable success of the campaign that raised over $8 million dollars in support.

## Opening the Doors to the First Learners

Through an extraordinary effort by hundreds of citizens and educators, the Northwestern Michigan College University Center officially opened its doors to eager learners in August 1995. Six hundred twenty-three students enrolled in over 25 degree program options, both undergraduate and graduate, offered by an inaugural group of 12 public and private state universities.

The typical UC student at that time was 34 years old. Sixty percent of the students were women, 70 percent worked full-time, 60 percent had families. Eighty percent said their principal reason for returning to school was career related. Forty percent were preparing for their first professional career. Sixty percent came directly from NMC (Northwestern Michigan College University Center, 1996).

## Life at the University Center

Programs at the University Center are offered almost entirely in evening and weekend formats. In 1995, 30 percent of all courses were offered through the two-way interactive system, with Traverse City and two or three other communities linking to the university's main campus classroom. By 2002 this percentage had dropped to between 20-24 percent which reflected two trends - growth in online course options and a higher percentage of faculty choosing to commute to the Traverse City campus.

The largest degree programs are in education, followed by nursing and business. Students graduating from professional programs are finding employment in their home communities, fulfilling a portion of our mission to improve employability through education and to support the stability of communities by building learning resources that keep people in the area. Some specialized programs, particularly in education for teachers, are offered daytime in the summer.

Although the University Center was chartered to support adult learners in the five county service area of the community college, students regularly travel from a ten county service region, some as far away as 100 miles one-way. Traverse City is still the closest hub for advanced education in the northwest region.

# The Organization of the University Center

The University Center itself is organized so that Northwestern Michigan College is closely working with each partner university at two levels. As the facility owners, NMC manages the schedule production for the several hundred courses offered each year. Facility support is crucial in maintaining a comfortable environment for students and visiting faculty alike. The UC provides direct support to students through the Zonta Library, a "virtual" library environment where students can connect to the main campus libraries, or receive technical assistance from staff as they do homework and research.

At the program development level, the University Center works closely with each school in identifying new areas of interest and determining areas where programs should be phased out. Each partner school is responsible for staffing an office, a concept that has been described as a "one-stop shop" where all services for the student are available, from admissions and advising through graduation.

An interesting outcome of this approach is that a prospective student can easily make comparisons between programs and schools - just by walking down the hall. Customer service is the beneficiary of this competitive force, and happily, improved collaboration between schools in order to assist in student needs is also evident.

# Distance Education and the University Center

In 2003, approximately 1200 students were enrolled in programs through the University Center. Teacher education programs were the most popular and this trend is expected to continue for the next decade. Over the seven years of operation, two universities have phased themselves out, and two additional universities have joined the partnership.

Several degree programs have online offerings, but this delivery mode is not expected to grow to more than 10 percent of all course offerings. Students appear to enroll in online courses when this reduces the time needed to complete their degree. With University Center students averaging 8 credit hours per semester, an online course becomes the more feasible approach for those who want to add a class. However, through the annual Student Interest Survey, students indicate that online is not their *preferred* learning mode, although access to the Internet has become widespread. In 1995, for example, approximately 85 percent of students reported they did not have computers or ready access to the Internet. Interestingly, by 2003, student responses indicate that this percentage has changed drastically with 83 percent of students now reporting computer ownership and Internet access, but not necessarily reflecting a preference for online learning (Northwestern Michigan College University Center, 2003).).

Two-way interactive television, which was considered the "leading edge" for the distance-based delivery of educational programs in 1995, is finding new life serving as the "linking" technology for teacher professional development activities between the schools of the original Project Interconnect. The University Center will push two-way interactive applications to a new horizon with its *demonstration laboratory*, a science lab facility designed to connect to other labs via web-based video streaming at Northwestern Michigan College's Great Lakes Campus, however, it is unlikely that additional interactive television classrooms will be added to the network.

# Being a Voice for Learners at a Distance

The University Center is a learning enterprise built to the needs and expectations of the citizens of the Greater Grand Traverse Region. In ways we could not have imagined in the dreamscape of 1993, the University Center has become the *communiversity* of its vision statement, a learning environment in which distance has been transformed from barrier to opportunity. As such, the College holds dear its role as an advocate of adult learners. From the very beginning, NMC has worked to give voice to the lifelong learning interests of the community it serves. In the University Center story, technology has been a resource for the facilitation of learning. Learner commitment, however, has been the true heart of its success.

As the University Center looks toward its 10th anniversary, few remember the skepticism over interactive technology (it will be too distracting for teachers and students), or over the comparability between learning experiences on a main campus and off campus (teachers seem to believe that what adults bring to the classroom in their off-campus setting creates a rich and unique learning environment), or whether universities would even remain in the partnership for more than a few years.

The questions for the future will be of a different nature than those that led to its development. The University Center will have to understand and anticipate the changing economic landscape and its relationship to the employability of our graduates. And, it will have to develop creative options that encourage universities to deliver new programs in even more flexible configurations. The role of being a host to universities will expand to include a more systematic and comprehensive approach to market assessment, as well a more visible role working with increasingly diverse learners who now expect to be able to continue their learning without leaving home.

Our learners have taught us incredible lessons in tenacity and persistence. The University Center is undertaking a comprehensive study of the impact of the UC project on the lives of graduates since 1997, the first UC graduating class, hoping to learn more about the economic impact of degree completion as well as to capture their ideas about our next steps. The doors continue to open at the UC!

## References

Batelle Institute. (1988). *A report to the Grand Traverse Regional Economic Development Corporation on barriers and opportunities to economic development in Northwestern Michigan with recommendations.* Unpublished report.

Biederman, L. (1982). *Happy days: An autobiography by Lester Biederman.* Traverse City, Michigan: Pioneer Study Center Press.

Founders 21. (1993). *A report to the Northwestern Michigan College Board of Trustees.* Unpublished report, Northwestern Michigan College.

Michigan Board of Education (1991). Project Outreach. In M. Smith (Ed.), *Grand Traverse 20/20 futuring sessions and summary conference: Summary report / prepared by the Grand Traverse Steering Committee for the Citizens of Grand Traverse County.* Lansing, Michigan.

Northwestern Michigan College University Center (1996). *Student survey results: Enrollment profile, including student's responses for enrolling in classes at the Center.* Unpublished report.

Northwestern Michigan College University Center (2003). *Student interest survey, including student profile.* Unpublished report.

Smith, M. (Ed.). (1991). *Grand Traverse 20/20 futuring sessions and summary conference: Summary report / prepared by the Grand Traverse Steering Committee for the Citizens of Grand Traverse County.* Traverse City, MI: Grand Traverse 20/20 Steering Committee.

# Chapter 16

# Equine Instructor Reaches Irish Students Via DVC

**Steve Evans**

As we continue to become more and more technologically literate it appears there are certain assumptions that guide our use of technology. One of the key assumptions is that "more is better". Our computers operate at faster and faster speeds with bigger hard drives. Hardly a day goes by without being enticed by advertisers who suggest that our old 35mm camera should be replaced with a digital camera. A printer is nothing without an integrated FAX, copier and scanner. And, a web-based search that yields less than a million hits probably is flawed in some way.

Our ability to effectively communicate with sound and pictures has not been left behind either. New generations of interactive communication systems continue to be developed - components have been reduced to being microscopic in size, transmission of information over large distances is easily accommodated, and black and white images seem to be something only our ancestors can remember.

> *"Every generation that has grown up since the 1950s is part of the video age. This age has given rise to visual immediacy. In this age, television has shaped the world's social, political and economic climate. The video age has evolved from a store-and-forward environment to a real-time bombardment of information and images." (Rosen, 1996)*

As can be expected, the evolution of interactive communication systems has had a tremendous effect on distance education. And, it is this effect on distance education, especially a concern for limiting the cost of the technology that can be used for 2-way interactive television, that is the focus of this article. The frame of reference for the article is the use of distance education within higher education and the challenge of building distance education programs around technology that is affordable. Certainly, it would be wonderful if we had all the resources in the world to provide distance education programming - but we don't. As institutional resources become more scarce it is incumbent upon us to explore the effective use of less expensive technology that may have been prematurely discarded and to identify ways in which such technology can serve a viable purpose.

## Personal Videoconferencing

Personal videoconferencing is just a case in point.

> *"Personal videoconferencing includes desktop, laptop, palmtop, TV set-based videoconferencing, and real-time video kiosks. These are primarily personal communication devices." (Rosen, 1996)*

A few years back the focus of personal videoconferencing was Desktop Video Conferencing (DVC) for the home P.C. - it was the rage. It seemed that everyone had to own one of those miniature cameras, carefully taped to the top of the monitor, so that you could communicate with voice and picture over the Internet. For most DVC owners, the equipment, which transmitted signal over dial up telephone lines, was inexpensive enough to allow you to purchase it and gamble that it would work. And, for many, it was fun the first few times. Then interest waned when the pictures, transmitted over a 56k modem, weren't very clear, the motion was rather jerky and annoying, and sometimes you had to wait forever to get your screen to "refresh" and show a new image. It seems that DVC had been destined to gather dust sitting atop the monitor like a hood ornament on an old Hudson. Ahh - the wonderful world of disposable technology!

In spite of these inherent problems, Michigan State University Extension felt that the investment that had been made in DVC was worth further exploration. DVC units had been purchased for 70 of the 83 Michigan county extension offices when the technology was first introduced. Were there appropriate instructional applications that could successfully use desktop video conferencing, even with its inherent limitations?

## Understanding DVC

Desktop Video Conferencing (DVC) is computer facilitated two-way interactive voice and sight communication between two or more individuals at distant locations. DVC allows users to communicate face-to-face over distances from a few feet to thousands of miles. In a state as large as Michigan, where a trip from one end to the other is nearly 12 hours in good weather, the DVC systems are a convenient way of getting a group of people together to discuss an issue without scheduling a meeting that would require extensive travel. In such cases, users forgive the lack of high-resolution images and the slow scan rate. The idea of having visual images to supplement voice communication without having to travel great distances seems to be a large enough reward to encourage people to use this rather basic form of personal television.

Desktop video conferencing units transmit signals over a variety of communication lines. Low-end systems use dial-up telephone lines at a rate just less than 56 kilobytes (KB) per second. Higher end systems, such as the early systems used by MSU Extension, communicate via dedicated ISDN[1] telephone lines at a rate of 112 to 128 KB per second. These systems come with the rather significant cost of a fulltime ISDN line. It is quite common for ISDN users to pay as much as $150 per month for an ISDN line. Add to that the cost of using the line on a per minute basis and it is easy to see that using ISDN as part of the communications infrastructure for a DVC system can be cost prohibitive for many small and medium sized businesses and educational institutions.

For Desktop Video Conferencing to be cost effective, the operating costs need to be lower. One key to the success of today's desktop video conferencing system is its ability to operate over the Internet and therefore not needing costly dedicated telephone lines for transmission. An added bonus is that these newer systems can run over most networks comfortably at around 256KB per second. And, the picture quality is improved substantially over earlier systems. For educational institutions and many

---

[1] ISDN is an acronym meaning "integrated services digital network." It is an international communications standard for sending voice, video, and data over digital telephone lines or normal telephone wires. ISDN supports data transfer rates of 64 Kbps (64,000 bits per second).

small and medium sized businesses that already have internet access via cable modem, DSL[2] or T1[3] phone lines, this is another way of maximizing the potential of those lines without having to pay for a dedicated line. The software in your computer translates the audio and video DVC signals into small packets of digital information and sends them zooming back and forth via the Internet to their destination.

Many secondary and higher education institutions use two additional forms of 2-way interactive audio/video. At Michigan State University we commonly refer to these as conference room-based and classroom-based CODEC[4] systems. The conference room based systems are typically comprised of a camera, microphone and two video monitors communicating to a similar system over a pair of ISDN telephone lines. A classroom-based system typically consists of multiple cameras and microphones with multiple viewing monitors communicating to a similar system over T-1 telephone lines. These systems, though superior to DVC in picture quality, audio quality and speed of transmission are considerably more expensive. And, of course, one of our main goals was to see if we could achieve the instructional objectives with an inexpensive system like DVC.

**Comparing Audio/Visual 2-Way Communication Systems**

| System | Advantages | Disadvantages |
|---|---|---|
| DVC via internet | System can be used with an existing high speed internet line | Heavy internet traffic can negatively impact signal quality |
| Conference Room-Based Systems | Dedicated lines guarantee basic signal quality | Dedicated lines can cost $150 per month |
| Classroom-Based Systems | Dedicated lines guarantee highest level of signal quality | High grade dedicated lines can cost hundreds of dollars per month |

## Using DVC for Classroom Instruction

MSU Animal Science Assistant Professor Brian Nielsen's specialty is Equine Exercise Physiology and he provided an ideal opportunity to try out the DVC system in a purely instructional context. Yes, DVC could facilitate meetings at a distance but could it also facilitate classroom learning at a distance? Could the disadvantages of DVC be overcome to the extent that such disadvantages would not stand in the way of learning?

---

[2] DSL stands for "digital subscriber lines." DSL technologies use sophisticated modulation schemes to pack data onto copper wires. They are sometimes referred to as last-mile technologies because they are used only for connections from a telephone switching station to a home or office, not between switching stations.

[3] A T-1 line is a dedicated phone connection supporting data rates of 1.544 Mbits per second. T-1 lines are a popular leased line option for businesses connecting to the Internet and for Internet Service Providers connecting to the Internet backbone.

[4] CODEC is an acronym standing for compressor/decompressor. A CODEC is any technology for compressing and decompressing data. In telecommunications it is a device that encodes or decodes a signal, often a television signal, so that the signal can be efficiently transmitted to another location.

In the spring of 1998, Nielsen accepted the invitation of an Irish colleague, Professor Gary Connally, to travel to Ireland's Enniskillen Agricultural College to guest lecture in a number of classes. One of Nielsen's lectures to Agricultural Engineering students on how various horse track surfaces impact the mobility of horses went over very well. So well, in fact, that Connally asked Nielsen to deliver the same lecture to a new group of students the next year. The cost and time of flying to Ireland just to deliver one lecture was prohibitive. Fortunately, both Enniskillen College and Michigan State University Extension had made investments in desktop video conferencing. Neilsen, in reflecting on the experience, said:

> "We got started with Desktop Video Conferencing after having spent two weeks in Northern Ireland at Enniskillen Agricultural College. One of the lectures I had given to the Irish students dealt with training surfaces and how they affect the way a horse moves and potential injuries. It turned out that the instructor for the class had no expertise in that area and really enjoyed the lecture. As a result, he asked me to give this lecture to his class the following year. Since making a trip to Northern Ireland to give a single lecture was not economically feasible, we did the next best thing and gave a lecture using Desktop Video Conferencing."

Nielsen is now in his second year of teaching the class from a conference room in Agriculture Hall at MSU. A dozen undergraduate students, many of whom will someday manage a horse training or breeding facility in Ireland, have learned what physical impacts a poorly designed track surface can have on a horse's ability to run. And they learned it "live" via the Internet from an expert who was thousands of miles away.

At MSU, Nielsen sat at a computer where he could see the students on the monitor. His image and voice were carried back to Ireland through the small video camera mounted on top of the monitor and an audio headset with a built in microphone. Nielsen's slides of actual track surfaces and the injuries caused by them were incorporated into a PowerPoint presentation. Recognizing the bandwidth problems associated with trying to use a PowerPoint presentation in real time over the Internet while the DVC class was in session, the presentation was emailed to Gary Connally at Enniskillen the evening before the class. For the class, Connally loaded the PowerPoint presentation into his computer and projected it on a large screen for the students to view as Nielsen made live remarks via DVC keyed to each slide. The DVC image of Nielsen lecturing was also displayed on additional monitors throughout the classroom. Students were able to ask questions through microphones that were fed back into the DVC system.

The system worked well. Nielsen could call on a student as he saw him/her raise a hand. And the students were able to learn from a PowerPoint presentation that was facilitated live by a guest instructor in Michigan. According to Neilsen:

> *"At first it seemed a little strange, basically teaching to a video screen while a camera recorded you. However, it turned out to be a great way to interact with the students. To begin with, I made them go around the room and introduce themselves and tell me a little bit their horse experience. As they were doing so, I tried to personalize my comments to each one of them. That helped them fully realize that this was a two-way interaction that was occurring. Then, as I began to lecture, in order to get the students to better comprehend the material I presented, I made students stand up and demonstrate how they would walk "if you were walking on slippery ice" or "if you were in deep mud." Obviously such actions made for humorous moments. To be able to watch the students demonstrate such conditions, and to be able to laugh with them while they were doing so, really helped me connect with them. Such connections couldn't exist if they were watching a video-tape of a lecture or if only audio was*

*available. It definitely requires some effort to put on a good lecture. There is a slight delay in signal so there is a little pause before you receive feedback from your group. That takes a little getting used to. However, that is a minor inconvenience considering the advantages this system offered. To be able to provide a lecture at such a low cost to a classroom on the other side of the world, and to be able to interact with the students on a very personal level, certainly make this technology a wonderful tool to have at one's disposal."*

The project has worked so well that Nielsen and Connally have begun talking about the feasibility of teaching a 15-week course for students in Ireland using desktop video conferencing.

**Design Considerations for Making Effective Use of Desktop Videoconferencing**

| Design Consideration | Rationale |
|---|---|
| Use the DVC in a Supportive/Secondary Role (not a primary role) | Don't try to use the DVC segment as a "stand alone" teaching activity. Instead use it in combination with other instructional media – PowerPoint presentation, live instructor, on-site discussions, models, note taking guide, etc. |
| Try out the technology ahead of time | Use the system a day or two ahead of time to identify unique characteristics that must be accommodated, technical problems that may occur, and how to operate special features. |
| Establish meaningful objectives | Define both instructional and learner objectives that can be fulfilled through the instruction that takes full advantage of the unique capabilities of DVC. |
| Rehearse the Presentation | Carefully review the content to be presented, the order in which it will be presented, and how it will be integrated with DVC. |
| Minimize unnecessary instructor movement | Be seated while teaching in order to minimize distraction that may be caused due to the slow scan rate (non-continuous motion). |
| Reduce the use of print material | Minimize the difficulty of trying to read on-screen print material by sending handouts to students ahead of time. |
| Maintain audio quality | Use a small headset-mounted boom microphone to maintain uniform instructor speaking level. |
| Use a remote location facilitator | Have a person on-site with the distance learners to help facilitate as needed. |
| Keep the presentation interactive | Provide opportunities for the distance learners to participate by sharing ideas, respond to questions, and ask for clarification. It can be very helpful in identifying communication problems that may not be obvious to the DVC instructor. |
| Prearrange "signals" between the two sites | Establish simple signals that can allow the remote facilitator to let the DVC instructor know when audio quality is low, presentation is too fast, picture is distorted, etc. |
| Send supplementary materials ahead of time | Reduce bandwidth requirements during the class and allow more local control of supplementary materials by having them distributed at the remote site – not attempted to be seen on the screen. |

# References

Rosen, E. (1996). *Personal Video Conferencing: Chapter 1.* Retrieved June 14, 2005, from http://www.manning-source.com/books/rosen/rosen_ch01.zip.

# Chapter 17

# Distance Education In The Workplace: Practical Problems And Sensible Solutions

## Neil VanderVeen

## Introduction

It was a hot August day in Meridian, Mississippi. The supervisors from the night shift were assembled in the dining room of the local Elks club for an all-day training session. The topic of the training was "building empowered work teams."

John had worked at the plant for nearly forty of his fifty-eight years and had managed to survive an endless string of "workplace transformation initiatives." It seemed to John that the older he got, the less patience he had with "head office garbage."

John tolerated the training for the first couple of hours. When ten o'clock rolled around, with no break and no opportunity to go out and have a cigarette, John stood up and proclaimed, "This is a bunch of crap. We don't need empowerment. We just need to be left alone to do our jobs."

Meanwhile, while John and the other supervisors were being exposed to the virtues of "empowered work teams," the training director and director of human resources were back at the plant talking about a new direction in training being introduced by the corporate offices. The corporate folks were planning to reduce the cost of training at all of the plants through what they were calling "enterprise-wide distance education solutions."

Of course, none of the corporate folks had ever met John. They had no idea that many of the end users would be people who were very much like John. Would distance education be the answer that would be able to bring new skills and competence to all of the employees?

Training directors used to think their biggest struggle was managing the tension between content-centered and learner-centered approaches to instruction. However, the emergence of technology-centered approaches has created a variety of new tensions not previously envisioned. Nonetheless, integrating technology-centered approaches into employee and organization development strategies is currently the challenge we are facing. Whether curriculum designers approve or not, line managers in business, industry, government, and the military are demanding rapid reductions in classroom training with corresponding increases in distance education. And, the assumption that often is the basis for such decisions is distance education is quicker, better, and cheaper! This is the world in which we now live.

| Comparing Training Approaches in Business and Industry | | |
|---|---|---|
| Content-Centered Approaches | Learner-Centered Approaches | Technology-Centered Approaches |
| <ul><li>Instruction is defined by the organization</li><li>Use existing media to deliver instruction</li><li>Learner involvement and motivation are desired</li></ul> | <ul><li>Instruction is defined cooperatively by employees and organization</li><li>Use highly interactive media to deliver instruction</li><li>Learner involvement and motivation are essential</li></ul> | <ul><li>Instruction is defined by the organization</li><li>Use highly technical media to deliver instruction</li><li>Learner involvement is essential and motivation is desired</li></ul> |

In this chapter some of the major challenges will be explored as we move toward distance education in the workplace. For distance education to become a successful and powerful learning system demands that we face these challenges and creatively design strategies to accommodate the challenges.

## The Challenges Facing Distance Education in the Workplace

In general terms, the challenges facing distance education applications in the workplace involve the design of the distance education product itself and the circumstances surrounding the implementation of the distance education initiative. Many resources exist that do an excellent job of presenting design ideas and the issues surrounding the development of designs that can be effectively used in distance education. Beyer and Holtzblatt (1998) present a detailed approach to understanding customer needs and designing, through a systems approach, to meet those needs. Iuppa (1998) provides a more technical look at design issues, particularly as they apply to interactive digital media.

Similar books that describe the challenge of implementing distance education in business and industry are not nearly as prevalent. This chapter is concerned with presenting the issues surrounding implementation and ideas and suggestions for effective implementation. So what are the challenges facing the person about to implement distance education in business and industry? Let's look at some of the major issues of implementation.

*Homogeneous solutions often fail to meet the needs of heterogeneous organizations* – Specific distance education programs are often adopted as single solutions to perceived learning needs within organizations. The result is often a one-size-fits-all situation that is inappropriate to many of the sub-cultures within the organization. For example, the U.S. Navy is considering replacing a residential course that includes problem solving with a web-based offering through "Navy Knowledge On-line." Although the existing face-to-face course is nominally a single offering, in practice, participants are assigned to table groups within each class based on their job specialization - surface warfare, aviation, sub-surface warfare, medical, or some other Navy community. This practice results in fitting the face-to-face problem-solving solutions taught in the class to the needs of the different sub-cultures who are in attendance. Members of each sub-culture, or group of learners, in the face-to-face class work together to customize the content to their unique needs. Such customization is much more difficult with enterprise-wide distance education solutions that are not mediated by instructors and learning groups. However, it is not impossible.

Distance education that is designed to be effective with a heterogeneous workforce demands a strong sensitivity to the variety of learners who will be involved. Distance education is sometimes viewed in the context of a single mode of delivery when in fact a wide range of learning activities can be implemented quite effectively. Such diversity of learning activities can be effective in helping meet the needs of heterogeneous learner groups. Some of these learning activities can involve web-based programs with high levels of interactivity while others may be little more than books transferred to computer files, or homework assignments periodically sent from a central location. In some distance education activities the performance of the learners is monitored, while in others the learners are on their own. Some distance education can involve cooperative learning through chat rooms while some may attempt to engage the learners in a completely solitary and isolated mode. In computer-based distance education, learners can download worksheets, complete online forms, or be referred to print resources that may be available. And, in some distance education applications learner performance is assessed while in others there may be no evaluation at all.

*Reduced opportunities for cooperative learning* – Cooperative learning often occurs within the context of classroom instruction whether the instructor supports it or not. Students get together in *ad hoc* study groups. They share information. They talk about class material they may be struggling with. They find reinforcement for learning from each other. The processes and implications of cooperative or "peer" learning are discussed at some length in O'Donnell and King (1999). The authors discuss the ideas of Piaget and Vygotsky and their implications for peer learning. They also consider the implications of peer learning for teaching and teacher education. Techniques for implementing cooperative learning can be found in Johnson, Johnson, and Holubek (1993). These authors discuss the research on cooperative learning, the role of the teacher in cooperative learning, issues associated with group processing and evaluation issues. There is little doubt that cooperative learning can be a powerful force in employee development. There is also little doubt that the effective use of cooperative learning becomes much more difficult in the context of distance education.

Though there are numerous examples of ways to provide for cooperative learning in a distance education environment, most distance education products developed for commercial consumption are not set up to make use of cooperative learning. The challenge must be to build in appropriate cooperative learning opportunities so that learning becomes powerful. Chat rooms can be added to encourage communication between participants. Group projects that are assessed or evaluated by an on-line mentor can add substantially to a sense of community among learners and the creation of opportunity for learning in a cooperative manner. Team efforts in an online setting can bring together employees from distant locations who can gain by learning from each other. The concept of cooperation is essential in all well-functioning organizations. It makes a lot of sense to model cooperation by using cooperative learning strategies in distance education.

*Course materials are often designed and developed by people who are unfamiliar with the environments in which the materials are to be used* – People who design and develop classroom learning materials often have a clear image of a rather specific audience of learners and the classroom experience is designed with that specific audience in mind. On the other hand, people who design and develop distance education materials may not have nearly as clear a view of the learners for whom they are designing the instruction. If their product is to be widely marketed, the actual audience for their products can be much more varied than they would imagine. The opportunity to interact with the learners who will be receiving the instruction is often very limited and it makes the tailoring of learning materials very difficult. The usual approach to "packaging" instructional materials for face-to-face instruction never works quite so well in a distance education situation. The designer of distance education materials must consider a variety of alternative strategies to provide for the variety of learners that may use the materials. Building in the use of local facilitators, providing of alternative case studies, learning in small teams, and providing resource materials to be used following the distance education session are some of the ways that can compensate for an instructor's lack of understanding the environment in which the materials will be used.

*Lack of meaningful contact between learners and subject matter experts regarding how the learning can be applied* – Teaching at the application level in a face-to-face situation is a challenging task. It is much easier to simply dispense information without a concern for actually putting the information to use. However, in business and industry the application of learning is the bottom line. Without application there is usually little support for on-the-job learning.

For distance education to be successful there must be a focus on application. But how can that be accomplished when the person offering the instruction often doesn't "see" the learner? Try including provisions for on-line mentoring or for cooperative learning. Create simple ways for the learners to ask questions – individually and in groups. Have learners participate in distance education programs in the same groups in which they work within the plant. Build into the distance education application problems that are similar to what the learners will be expected to face. Reduce the use of simple-to-correct multiple-choice tests and replace them with more open-ended tests that demand the learner use analytical skills.

In very heterogeneous organizations, the on-line mentor may be completely unfamiliar with the environment in which the application is to take place. General Motors Corporation has a foundry in Northwest Ohio and a large financial services operation in New York. Both groups may be participating in the same distance education session at their respective locations. It would make a lot of sense to involve distance education mentors who are familiar with both locations so that unique questions from the different work sites can be dealt with as they occur.

*Lack of on-going support to keep distance education materials up-to-date* – Face-to-face instructors in non-academic settings are continually challenged to maintain the currency of the learning materials. After all, classroom participants can make it very uncomfortable for instructors who fail to keep their materials up to date. Face-to-face instructors in business, industry, government, and the military must be responsive to the demands of their classroom participants. The fact that feedback on outdated learning materials, in a classroom setting, is both immediate and forceful creates a very powerful incentive for the face-to-face instructor to continually update and improve the learning materials.

There really isn't a similar demand placed on the distance education instructor. Computers don't feel embarrassment when caught dispensing the wrong information. Unlike printed materials that are always present and available for leafing through and spotting things that need changing, distance education materials are usually hidden away and the instructor in search of things that need changing must purposely pursue each page wherever it is located. When a learner does dash off some feedback about a problem with the instruction he/she often has the feeling hat the feedback has been dropped down bottomless pit with little chance for a meaningful response. After all, when you can't see the learner there is an entirely different sense of accountability when it comes to updating the material.

Even when the instructional developers involved in a distance education initiative are of the right mindset and want to continually update the learning materials to supply consistently high-quality product, the funding for unlimited life-cycle support is usually not available. This is often a function of the distance education course being seen as a solution, not as a tool. Viewing something as a tool implies that it will have to be worked with, changed and improved as time goes by. Viewing it as a solution implies that we can simply buy it, apply it, and forget about it. The investment has been made once and the instruction is expected to last a long time.

*Failure to tie the distance education initiative to broader organization development goals* – Many organizations have a cherished history of throwing training at problems and imagining that the

164

problems will disappear. "We've trained everyone in diversity so racism is no longer present in our organization." Or, "Everyone has viewed the training video on 'Safety in the Workplace' so our accident prevention program is complete." This has been a problem with classroom-based training and it continues to be a problem with distance education initiatives. In many ways, distance education has less of a potential to effectively respond to broader organization development goals. Without actually seeing the learners and interacting with them during a face-to-face learning session, the challenge of identifying those broader goals that may need attention is very difficult. It is important for distance education initiatives to link more closely to the organization, make the instruction as real and personal as possible, and provide meaningful opportunities for the employee to provide substantive feedback to the organization through the distance education technology. Though more difficult, it is not impossible for distance education to contribute in a meaningful way to broader organization development goals.

*Underestimating bandwidth needs and overestimating bandwidth resources* – The term "bandwidth" has become an everyday term since the Internet has become a part of life and it helps clarify yet another major challenge facing distance education. Bandwidth refers to the capability of a site to receive and transmit information. Instructional planners usually begin by taking into account the bandwidth required for delivering information from their site. However, they often underestimate the amount of bandwidth needed because they don't consider the amount of traffic that will be created to manage on-line help, to support chat room activities related to the design of the curriculum, or to encourage direct communication among the learners.

Similarly, planners often overestimate the bandwidth available to individual users. They may assume that most people have the same sort of high-speed Internet connections as the planners have. Or, the learners are able to easily upload complex diagrams or drawings in response to problem sets. They may assume that the various remote workplace sites have the same available bandwidth as the organization headquarters where employing a streaming video presentation would be a simple task. It is essential for the distance education designer/instructor to spend the time necessary to develop a clear picture of how bandwidth affects both the organization's ability to deliver and the learner's ability to receive.

*Keeping the kids off the lap while Mom or Dad are "going to school"* One advantage of classroom learning is that the learner goes to a place that is designated for learning activities. This may sound rather foolish, but it can be really helpful to learn in a place specially reserved for learning. You don't have to explain what you're doing – you're going to do some learning. You can leave the distractions of home behind.

A popular aspect of distance education is that it often encourages the learner to work from home. However, there is often little if any assistance provided to help the learner understand the necessity for a special place for learning and then to assist in establishing such a location. Learning is attempted in the midst of all of the distractions that normal, active families can provide.

Managing to complete the learning tasks without alienating family relationships can sometimes be difficult to accomplish. Spouses have needs. The ball game is on the TV. The neighbors just dropped by. Young children just don't understand why Mom is not available since they she is just on the other side of the closed door. After all, Mom has been at work all day and now she is home and should be available.

*Instructors can often be motivational forces and establish the relevance of the learning* – The need to establish motivational links between the audience and the material to be learned is well established. Morgan, Ponticell, and Gordon (1998) discuss a broad range of approaches to adult education and training. Many of these approaches involve engaging learners with that which is to be learned. There are many instances where the relevance of a learning activity is not immediately apparent to the learner. This is often the case with learning activities that are required by the employer. In such cases the instructor can provide an essential service to the face-to-face learner by helping to clarify relevance, link to application and generally provide a motivational setting in which learning can occur.

To create a similar sense of response in a distance education environment is often very difficult. It demands that learners be listened to as individuals and not so much as a large faceless grouping of people – usually from varied locations. Personalizing distance education to allow the establishment of a relevance framework is extremely important. More than just asking the learners for feedback, the designer of distance education activities must find ways to challenge the learners to initiate comments, respond to situations and interact around substantive ideas. Using cooperative learning strategies, on-line mentors and enhanced opportunities for interaction among learners can work to motivate learners and help underscore the relevance of the learning.

*Distance education is often presented as a one-size-fits-all solution to a host of undifferentiated organizational problems and target audiences* – A major company in the distance education arena reports that they have over 20,000 learning objects that can provide 5,000 hours of training to their 3,000 customer organizations. Plus, they suggest that their learning programs can help their customer organizations gain a competitive advantage, improve customer loyalty, increase productivity, reduce costs, increase job satisfaction, and train globally.

That's a rather impressive listing, and it's only a part of the total list! And, of course, there are numerous other providers with similar sorts of promises made regarding the power of their distance education instructional materials.

The reality, though, may be far from that which is promised. And the reason is that the assumption is made that the distance education product is fully responsible for guaranteeing the learning. The reality, of course, is that only the learner can guarantee learning! And without significantly involving the learner in the creation of the distance education situation there may be very haphazard results. If only life could be so simple to guarantee human outcomes in response to nonhuman interventions!

*Distance education solutions lack a translator to overcome language problems* – The issue of language problems occurs in a number of different ways in training. There are problems of colloquial language or jargon when the training is developed for financial institutions but used in the factory setting. There are problems of value-laden terminology when the training is developed for social workers but used to train law enforcement officers. There are problems of vocabulary when the training is developed for an audience with college level education but is used for an audience made up of people who have not completed high school. Such language problems can have very detrimental affects on learning at a distance.

Taking time to tryout distance education materials on each unique audience is an absolutely essential activity. To distribute distance education materials widely without a tryout can create some enormous problems – especially with language. Using an advisory committee made up of learners representative of your end users can help avoid problems that are sure to crop up later.

## Strategies for Responding to the Challenges

Before describing some strategies for dealing with the challenges, a general word of warning is in order. *Although distance education is a powerful tool, there are a number of learning tasks for which distance education is simply the wrong approach.* It would be appropriate to use distance education to teach **rules of conflict** management but developing the ability to actually **manage conflict** needs to be accomplished in a live classroom where learners can go "nose to nose" and feel the heat of the conflict with real people. Similarly, distance education can be used to teach the provisions of the National Labor Relations Act but developing the skills to negotiate a labor agreement is definitely best done in the classroom where mock negotiating sessions can be held. Generally learning that is at the higher cognitive levels and includes a strong affective component is best accomplished in a setting that is very similar to where the learning will be applied. Such learning does not work well in the more academic setting of distance education.

With the above warning clearly in mind, the power of distance education is so enormous that the desire to deal with the challenges is very strong. To successfully deal with the challenges means implementing strategies that are not only creative but also draw on the involvement of the learner as a meaningful "partner" in the learning environment. The following are some specific strategies for placing the learner more centrally in the instructional process so that the many challenges to distance education in business and industry might be more effectively dealt with.

*Incorporate cooperative learning wherever possible* so that learners can support one another in understanding the learning content and in figuring out how to apply the content to their lives. There are essentially two categories of cooperative learning opportunity associated with distance education.

> Off-line learning groups – If learners are in the same geographic area they can get together for cooperative support. Those responsible for the learning endeavor can encourage cooperative learning by arranging for meeting space and other resources. Another method of encouraging cooperative learning is to build cooperative exercises into the learning materials.

> On-line learning groups – When learners are in different geographical areas, cooperative learning opportunities are more limited but can still be accomplished through chat room technology. These chat room activities can be managed on an *ad hoc* basis where the learners structure the interaction or specific cooperative learning activities can be incorporated into the learning materials.

*Make mentors, or at least monitors, available on-line to help learners* use the software and to act as advocates for the learners when system weaknesses are revealed. There are a number of different kinds of support personnel that can be made available to learners in distance education applications.

> Process mentors – These are support personnel who are informed about the learning processes. They may not be experts in the subject matter but they can provide guidance regarding what is expected from the standpoint of instructional design.

> Content mentors – These are the subject matter experts who can answer questions about the content of the instruction. They can also direct learners to resources so that self-managed learning can occur.

> Applications mentors – These support personnel can provide learners with help in managing the software applications that are required to make the distance education possible.

*Analyze the intended group of learners carefully* and consider making several versions of training materials available to sub-cultures within the learner population based on experience, values systems, educational level, and so on. Of course this approach is expensive because it involves a number of activities.

Identify relevant sub-cultures – The first step is to examine the intended audience to identify all of the relevant sub-cultures. For large, heterogeneous organizations that are geographically dispersed this can be a difficult undertaking but the consequences of not doing it are harmful to the organization.

Conduct differential formative evaluation – Formative evaluation involves testing learning materials on samples from the intended audience before the content is in its final form. This process can assist in demonstrating the validity of the content. A target audience that is very heterogeneous suggests the need for multiple formative evaluation activities in order to ensure that the content is valid for the various sub-cultures within the audience.

Develop parallel forms of the instructional materials – Of course, differential formative evaluation is without value unless the findings are translated into differential content. All parallel forms of instructional materials should accomplish the learning objectives but don't necessarily have to use the same instructional strategies to do so.

*Provide users with tips on how to manage the problems associated with working at home.* There are materials on the web and in books that discuss this issue. For example, Sandy Anderson's book *"The Work at Home Balancing Act: The Professional Resource Guide for Managing Yourself, Your Work, and Your Family at Home"* provides many useful ideas. Examples of these tips include:

The need for interaction with other learners – Find out who else is participating in the learning activity and set up *ad hoc* learning groups.

Managing boundary issues with family members – Negotiate with family members to clarify your needs and their needs and how both sets of needs can be met during "learning time."

Personal time management issues – Schedule the learning session in your calendar the same way you would any other activity and then stick to the schedule

Absence of learning through class discussion – Some of us learn very effectively through listening to and participating in class discussion. This absence can be partially compensated through the use of chat rooms, emails discussions or phone conversations with other learners. If that is not possible, talking about the issues with co-workers or spouse might help. (Anderson, 1998)

*Incorporate motivational content into the distance education material.* This should help the learner understand how she or he can benefit from the content. Taking this step will not replace the motivational instructor but it can help. The following are some examples of motivational content:

Stories about how the ideas presented in the learning materials are being used in other organizations.

Ideas about how the material can improve the success of the learners' organization.

Suggestions about how the information can make the learner's job safer, easier, or more satisfying.

*Be careful about purchasing a bushel basket of courseware to replace residential training offerings.* Each distance education product should be individually examined for appropriateness in terms of the following:

The learners – The material must be appropriate for the learners including sub-cultures within the intended audience.

The content – The content must be complete and accurate and must support application to the actual jobs being performed.

Life cycle support costs – The cost of life cycle support for one course may be entirely appropriate whereas the cost for the next course on the list might be unreasonable.

The longevity of the material – If the content of the training is perishable, distance education is probably not a viable solution.

Is the subject matter something that requires a classroom approach rather than distance education – We've returned to the idea that started this section. If the learning objective requires real-time, face-to-face interaction between learners and classroom facilitators, distance education approaches should be rejected.

*Be realistic in estimating bandwidth requirements and availability.* These estimates should take the future into account as well as the present. Although we exist in a graphics-rich environment, resist the temptation to load up on graphics that create large files that are slow to load.

*Be careful about assuming that "blended training solutions" are really blending.* Like oil and water, dissimilar approaches may simply not mix without a lot of attention to emulsifying strategies. Monitor outcomes carefully and continually. Some of the monitoring issues include:

Specify what outcomes are expected from each of the blended solutions. It is difficult to determine whether all learning objectives have been covered unless one specifies all of the objectives and maps learning content and strategies to each of the objectives.

Determine exactly what outcomes are to be monitored. This involves translating learning objectives into observable phenomena capable of being monitored.

Determine how selected outcomes are to be monitored. Establishing an appropriate metric to represent the desired outcome to be monitored is often a challenge in itself.

Learner-monitored outcomes. Consider the learners as a valuable source of data. They will be able to describe the extent to which the various blended solutions fit together to create the desired cognitive and affective gestalt.

*When considering purchasing distance education content, envision the life-cycle support requirements,* plan for the support, budget for the support, and, most importantly, provide the support. This will increase the apparent cost of distance education and make that cost closer to the actual cost. There are a number of cost factors that should be considered.

Content revisions– It is frequently necessary to revise training materials because of changes in technology, materials, processes, regulations, and so on.

Upgrading because of IT systems capability – It is often the case that training materials developed just five years ago do not run very well on today's equipment and operating systems. Despite this obvious limitation, development of distance education materials is frequently amortized over a much longer period.
Live support – The need for support from mentors, subject matter experts, computer applications personnel, and so on was discussed earlier. These support requirements will continue throughout the life of the distance education project and should be included in life cycle support budgeting.

*Consider all learning initiatives, not just distance education, within the context of broader employee and organizational development interventions.* This provides for broader, more systemic solutions with increased probability of success. The kinds of organizational development interventions that can and should be linked to learning initiatives include:

> Needs analysis – This should not be limited to training needs analysis but should include all of the organizational needs that might impact the desired end state for which the training is being considered.

> Training situation analysis – Training occurs within an organizational context. One can't predict the outcome of training without understanding that context. An environmental scan can be used to identify all of the forces that may support or impede the training so that supporting forces can be maximized and impeding forces can be minimized.

> Strategic planning – Wherever possible, training should be linked to the strategic plan of the organization. The link may not be immediately apparent because strategic planning is macro while much training is micro but, the link should still be present.

> Tactical planning – Relating training to organizational tactical plans makes it much easier to get funding for the training. It also reduces the perception that training interferes with mission-critical activities.

Root cause analysis – It is too often the case that training results from a "knee-jerk" response to a problem. Root cause analysis techniques that are used for quality management initiatives can be applied to training analysis with highly beneficial results.

## References

Anderson, S. (1998). *The work at home balancing act : The professional resource guide for managing yourself, your work, and your family at home.* New York: Avon Books.

Beyer, H. and Holtzblatt, K. (1998). *Contextual design: Defining customer centered systems.* San Francisco: Morgan Kaufmann Publishers.

Iuppa, N. (1998). *Designing interactive digital media.* Boston: Focal Press.

O'Donnell, A. M., King, A. (Eds.). (1999). *Cognitive perspectives on peer learning.* Mahweh, New Jersey & London: Lawrence Erlbaqum Associates, Publishers.

Johnson D., Johnson T., and Holubek, E. (1993). *Cooperation in the classroom.* Edina, Minnesota: Interaction Book Co.

Morgan, R., Ponticell, J., and Gordon, E. (1998). *Enhancing learning in training and adult education.* Westport Connecticut: Praeger.

# Chapter 18

# Establishing a Distance Education Program in Higher Education

## Tim Brannan

## Introduction

As we envision the potential of distance education in higher education a number of learner-based scenarios draw our attention.

> A student stops by the COW on his way to class, not for milking lessons, but to take a laptop from the Computer on Wheels. He is instantly connected to the wireless network. He has just left a face-to-face class and has signed on to the college's course management system so he can complete his next assignment virtually. Connected learning in the form of hybrid classes is beginning to take hold. Instructors hold classes once each week and post case studies, discussion topics or even host chats in lieu of an additional face-to-face session. Working parents are not required to commute to campus as frequently thereby freeing up classroom space for the college.

> A soldier enrolls in a computer networking class from her barracks in Korea. She completes Week One and Week Two, submits her assignments online and heads off for a two-week training maneuver. When she returns she will sign-on again and complete Week Three and Week Four. She feels good about having the opportunity to complete her Associate's Degree while in the military and is even beginning to consider the idea of completing a Bachelor's Degree once the current program is finished. She's never visited the campus of the college where she is enrolled.

> Due to economic conditions and the changing workplace, a factory worker decides to take classes in hydraulics to "cross-train" for a better position on the shop floor. He visits the college's computer laboratory and takes Hydraulics Theory I & II on CD-ROM and then goes to the laboratory "hands-on" portion of the course where he puts theory into practice. When he feels that he has both the theory and practical requirements of the course mastered, he performs the required assessment for the laboratory technician and receives a certificate of completion. Open entry/open exit forms of modularized instruction are available for the changing needs of the workforce in the area the college serves.

Fiction? It would have been just a few years ago. But thanks to current distance education technology it has become today's reality. It's all part of what a Midwestern community college is doing to create an "electronic campus" to meet the needs of students, faculty and employers.

Lansing Community College (LCC), serving over 19,000 students in a tri-county area of Central Michigan, is now moving miles beyond its campus with flexible programming to better meet the needs of a variety of different learners. Starting out in very traditional ways, the college spent its first 40+ years building a campus and offering a variety of programs from technical training, to two-year degree programs, to short term training sessions for local businesses and government agencies. Recognizing from the very beginning the need to extend programs beyond its campus, the college also worked to establish satellite centers in secondary schools in the region. These centers, operating during the evening hours, provided a vital link to learners in locations close to where they lived. As the "distance education revolution" has gained momentum Lansing Community College has worked diligently to develop an even broader base of operations.

Lansing Community College was the first community college in the state of Michigan to introduce an online certificate and degree program in 1997. In 2000, the college decided to expand current course offerings and to provide access to online learning tools for faculty. Between 2000 and 2003, Lansing Community College increased courses offered online from 40 to 130 and increased the number of degrees and certificates offered from two to sixteen. Annual enrollment in online and hybrid courses increased from 1,200 to almost 10,000 in less than three years. In Figure 1, you can see how the enrollment trend has increased over 100% each semester compared to the previous year's respective semester. This article describes the way in which the college has attempted to bring distance-bridging technology online to keep up with the demands of today's learner.

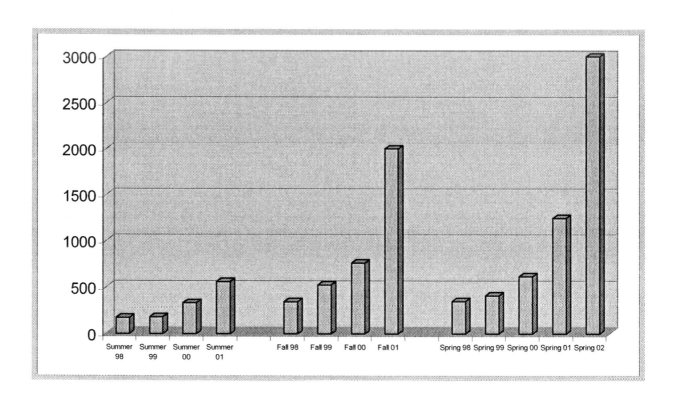

Figure 1: Semester Enrollment

## Electronic Campus Initiative

Lansing Community College adopted the Electronic Campus Initiative as the program under which the college would move significantly in the arena of distance education. The idea was that LCC needed to be poised to offer quality educational opportunities regardless of time and place constraints faced by students. LCC has been able to maximize the Electronic Campus concept by providing a learner-centered/community-focused type of education that uses the latest technology to provide on-demand educational opportunities. Wireless connections, modularized learning for credit and streaming media are becoming the norm for learning experiences offered at LCC. Faculty members digitize lectures for students who miss class and their virtual sections. They create "virtual field trips" to take the place of excursions that in the past would need extensive planning and were subject to Michigan weather.

The lines between face-to-face and virtual classes are beginning to blur with asynchronous discussion boards becoming a very common and accepted practice. Electronic student services, once available only to students who traveled to campus are now available at-a-distance from early in the morning to late in the evening. In addition to online textbook sales, Lansing Community College now offers tutoring, student training programs and advising – all online.

For Lansing Community College to successfully implement and support the Electronic Campus, three support elements needed to be planned for, implemented and well functioning:

1. Technical Support – integration of student management and course management systems; student and faculty technical support via online and telephone-based help desk.
2. Instructional Support – faculty support for online course conversion and development; instructor training program for online teaching.
3. Student Support – rapid response to student advising inquiries; consolidated location for students who need answers to administrative questions.

In the summer of 2001 Lansing Community College formed a group that was charged with the task of designing and implementing these three essential support elements in order to infuse instructional technology across the institution.

## Technical Support

By fall semester, every course section had a *coursesite* created automatically in the course management system and each student, faculty and staff member was issued a *userid* and password to access the system. A seamless link was created between the student information system and the course management system. Each faculty member would be able to post discussion questions and supplementary materials online for students to access, regardless of the course delivery type.

In addition, the college piloted eight hybrid courses during the first fall semester of the Electronic Campus. The hybrid courses consisted of a combination of face-to-face instruction and online instruction. It was hoped that the hybrid courses would provide an "easier" transition for those faculty and students not yet involved with online learning.

Five very different groups had to be considered during this planning and development stage:

- Students – Once online and authenticated, students would have to be able to view their schedules, grades, bills and transcripts as well as other appropriate student information. They needed to register electronically for courses and have their course schedules available for viewing. Membership in student organizations had to be recognized so students could have access to their organization's materials.

- Prospective Students – Those interested in attending the college would need access to information to assist in making their application/admission decisions. In the existing system prospective students would gather information passively via the college's websites. By providing direct access to the electronic campus, students could preview actual courses and "chat" with an advisor online.

- Alumni – Alumni of the college would have access to reunion information, including the ability to register on-line for events. Online registration for lifelong education programs would be available as would opportunities to financially support the college through an e-Giving program of the Alumni Development Office

- Faculty and Staff – The faculty component of the electronic campus would be a major implementation point of the educational technology initiative. Connected learning or "web-enhanced" environments would include class syllabi, course materials, homework assignments and student projects to support face-to-face classes. Logging on to the electronic campus would allow faculty and staff full access to all resources needed to successfully fulfill their job assignments. Job postings, administrative services, and web forms would be included in a college-wide intranet.

- Associations – College-based associations are a strong and important part of the total college-learning environment. The electronic campus would be a major entry point for students to access associations and the varied activities of these groups.

By taking into account the individual needs of the above-mentioned users, the electronic campus infrastructure had to be supported. The support system that was chosen by LCC was a web-based portal environment. The portal would have the following features to support the Electronic Campus:

- Communications Mechanism – The Electronic Campus would be the primary source of information for all LCC constituents. Users would become accustomed to going to one source for College information.

- Calendars – A master calendar of LCC events should exist and offer 'drill down' capabilities to calendars containing group specific information. A user may wish to see what is happening on campus next Friday evening and then be able to view Athletics or Theater calendars separately.

- Chat & Bulletin boards – Each constituent group would have access to their own organization site where they can hold chat and bulletin board forums. Employee groups could collaborate on projects via this method. Students, prospects and parents could use this function to communicate amongst themselves.

- FAQ – Would be designed as an on-line help mechanism for current and prospective students, faculty and staff.

- Electronic Campus Search engine – The search engine would be used to find information in our electronic community. Some site visitors rely solely on search engine capabilities to locate information of interest.

- Access to Lansing Community College Resources – All faculty, staff and students should be able to access the applications software they are using in their job easily. Accessible systems would include: the student information system, Library resources as well as any other appropriate system.

- Access Web Resources – There should be a Web search engine as well and allow users to access information on the Internet. User defined URL links are common to most portals as are links to media resources. This would allow individuals users or groups to "bookmark" links for others to access.

- Customization – One common component of most portals is the ability for individuals to customize the look and feel of their own portal while still maintaining a consistent format defined by Lansing Community College. Individuals would be able to use templates to define preferred screen layouts and what information is important to them. This functionality should also extend to the group and campus level. Our security model would determine which applications and access levels an individual would be authorized to use and allow faculty to share content that is customized to the discipline being taught.

- Content Management – Lansing Community College departments publish information to the Web site continually. The timeliness, accuracy and relevance of this information need to be constantly monitored and updated.

## Instructional Support

In order to support the faculty and new instructional delivery, Lansing Community College partnered with facultytraining.net to offer Online Instructor Training. This program was designed to provide faculty with an overview of the Blackboard Course Management System, online teaching strategies and LCC policy and procedures for virtual instruction. In addition, it was the college's goal to set up what was termed "base courses" for each course converted online. This would provide an instructor with basic course documents - syllabus, assignments, and assessments - that they could modify for their own use. This would ensure an element of consistency between courses to maintain quality and allow for academic freedom for the faculty member to individualize the course by adding or deleting certain elements.

In order to target which courses would be initially converted to the online/hybrid environment, college staff reviewed credits generated on an annual basis for each course and found that 10% of the courses offered on an annual basis generated 50% of the tuition income. It was decided that the focus of the first two years of course conversion would be on the 80 courses that generated the most tuition income and had not yet been developed for the online environment. These courses represented eight subject areas: Math (transfer and developmental), Writing (transfer and developmental), Biology, Humanities, History, Arts, Management, and Computer Information Systems for Business. To ensure a smooth transition online and to maintain quality, 8 full-time faculty were released half time to work with the Distance Learning Office as Virtual College Liaisons for two years. The faculty chosen for these jobs either had experience teaching online or had a strong interest in doing so. Their job would be to work with colleagues in their departments and mentor them during the first time they taught online or the first time they converted a course for online delivery.

In addition to the Virtual College Liaisons, the Distance Learning Office employed four instructional designers, each assigned to a specific division of the college, and an instructional programmer. Their roles were to work with the liaisons and individual faculty members in converting/creating online content.

As a part of the master contract for faculty, all hybrid and online instructors were required to be certified in online instruction by attending a 40-hour program in teaching online and on Electronic Campus Policies and Procedures. Lansing Community College contracted with facultytraining.net to provide this faculty training. Table 1 shows the specific seminars offered in online teaching strategies, background information on the college, policies and procedures.

**Table 1 – Faculty Training Seminars**

| **Seminar One—Building an Online Learning Community** | **Seminar Two—Models, Theories and Strategies** |
|---|---|
| A. Online learning environment<br>   1. Getting connected<br>   2. Communicating<br>B. Blackboard communication tools<br>   1. Email<br>   2. Student home page<br>   3. Discussion forum<br>C. Learning communities<br>   1. learning partner<br>   2. current educational experiences<br>   3. online assignments | A. Characteristics of distance learners<br>   1. current research<br>   2. motivation<br>   3. gender and cultural issues<br>   4. accessibility<br>B. Elements and models of distance education<br>   1. flexibility and design<br>   2. technologies and methods<br>   3. learner support<br>   4. evolution of distance education<br>   5. education business strategies<br>C. Web resources for research<br>   1. web research assignment and rubric for evaluation |
| **Seminar Three—Instructional Design and Course Customization** | **Seminar Four—Making Connections** |
| A. Instructional design fundamentals<br>   1. Course syllabus<br>   2. Learning outcomes—Bloom's taxonomy<br>   3. Learning activities<br>   4. Assessment and evaluation schemes<br>B. Course customization<br>   1. Incorporating media<br>   2. Online tools<br>   3. HTML<br>   4. Bandwidth Considerations | A. Assignment types<br>B. Managing interactivity<br>C. Evaluation Schemes<br><br>**Seminar Five—Course Administration**<br>A. Time on task analysis<br>B. Online education and copyright law<br>C. Student and faculty support policies |

```
Electronic Campus Policies and Services
        A.  Electronic Campus Course Standards
        B.  Intellectual Property Rights
        C.  Virtual College Operations
            1.  Paychecks
            2.  Mail (interoffice and outgoing)
            3.  Telephone
            4.  Miscellaneous Services
        D.  Student Services
            1.  Registration and Academic Advising
            2.  Student Blackboard Basics
            3.  Test Proctoring
            4.  Library Services
        E.  Glossary of Common Terms
        F.  Help and Support

    Student
            1.  LCC on-site student orientation
            2.  LCC Student Orientation Guide
            3.  Blackboard Student Manual
            4.  Remote Service Technicians (RST's)

    Faculty
            1.  Distance Learning Office
            2.  Center for Teaching Excellence (CTE)
            3.  Technology Helpdesk
```

# Student Support

Although technical and instructional supports are important components of an Electronic Campus, student support is key to ensuring the end users of the system have available resources to thrive in a new environment. At Lansing Community College, the critical component to ensure success was to create a single access point, which could be accessed via telephone or email, for students to ask questions. The virtual college advisors, or "cyberadvisors" as they became known, handled all student questions from hardware necessary to take an online course to questions regarding course transfer.

A "rapid response" system was created whereby a student would receive a response from a "live person" via email or telephone. Telephone responses would occur within 4 hours from 8 am to 6 pm and email responses within 6 hours from 6 pm to 8 am the next day. In addition, instead of restricting students from taking online classes, as was the previous practice, by requiring them to take a pre-assessment, the new focus was on providing tools that would ensure students would be successful in taking a class online. Each student was enrolled in an online virtual college orientation that provided instruction on the use of the course management system. Students could also elect to attend face-to-face orientation sessions on campus at the beginning of each semester.

As the enrollments grew so did the services available online. By the fall of 2003 not only was access to advising and help provided online, but so was tutoring services, book ordering and other ancillary student support services designed to provide access to all of the necessary campus services needed for distant students. In fact, if a student wanted a t-shirt from Lansing Community College all he/she had to do was contact the online bookstore and it would be sent. They didn't have to even fight for a parking spot!

A student in Speech 120 – Dynamics of Communication, provides interesting feedback on four student support factors that hc feels are essential for a student to be successful in an online course. Speech 120 is a "high enrollment" required course for all online degree programs. It examines communication theory and has students put theory into practice by requiring two speeches, participation in a group project and the preparation of two papers. The group project is completed using the online tools in the coursesite and the speeches are either submitted via videotape or on CD-ROM. Here are the student's words:

"My personal experience with distance education has, for the most part, been a pleasant experience…in order for students to be successful, several key factors need to be addressed:

1. **The course needs to be well organized.** Assignments were sent out to us in a weekly email. This made keeping track of assignments extremely easy. A syllabus was also mailed out to us the first week of school. This was also a helpful guideline to follow in addition to the posted syllabus located on the website. The course website itself was laid out in an easy to navigate manner, making it easy to use for even those relatively new to the internet. The course material was relevant to and directly aided students in broadening our understanding of the course subject.

2. **The instructor needs to take an interest in his students and encouraged them to enjoy the course instead of viewing the work as a burden.** The instructor repeatedly expressed to us, his students, that we should look at the assignments as an enjoyable part of the course. It was stressed to us not to treat the coursework as a burden. I personally think instilling this positive mindset in students is a very helpful approach to reduce the levels of stress students normally have when dealing with college-level coursework.

3. **The instructor needs to make every effort to make the course as accessible as possible for his students, taking into consideration the nature of the course (that it was completely online) and that many of his students lived out of the school district – some even out of the country!** There were numerous efforts made by the instructor to make this course successful while delivering the material online. The instructor was easily reachable via email, which for an online course should be an essential aspect of the course. I, for one, lived overseas, so this was the most convenient means of communication. Submitting assignments was made as easy as possible.

4. **The textbook used for the course was an interesting read and relevant to the subject matter of the course.** The textbook used for the course (Essentials of Human Communication by DeVito) was a very informative book that did a very good job of covering the topic of communication. The textbook was very relevant to the course, and it helped to build a firm foundation for the understanding of the course topic.

# Lessons Learned

In retrospect, it would be easy to second-guess the best way to set up an Electronic Campus. However, the implementation of Lansing Community College's Electronic Campus went fairly smoothly with the allocated resources. There are several lessons learned that would be beneficial to the reader if he/she is contemplating the implementation of a virtual learning program of this magnitude.

First, hire the virtual college liaisons early on in the process so they can be "peer faculty champions" of the cause. Many times during the first year of planning/implementation, faculty on campus viewed the conversion of courses and decisions as "top-down" and that they had very little input. It was easier to gain buy-in from several departments once they saw the good work that was being done and the virtual courses were held to the same quality level as the face-to-face courses. These were not just "an easy A" correspondence course.

Second, an institution needs to ensure that the integration of the information systems is seamless to the staff and students and that the internal information systems area of the organization has the capacity to make these systems work together. Lansing Community College outsourced the applications/hosting (ASP) of the online content, as internal capacity was limited and other organizations were better equipped to handle the scalability issue.

In regard to lessons learned on course conversion, at Lansing Community College the goal was to create online "base courses" that would have "standard" course features – syllabus, assessments, course content, etc. This allowed the college to offer multiple sections of the same course by copying basic course content without requiring each faculty member to convert or create their own content for each course section. This allowed for a starting point so the instructor could customize the course to his/her liking and provided for academic freedom without compromising quality. Required assignments and assessments were provided ensuring outcomes and course objectives were included for each course.

Creating hybrid courses would be an excellent starting point for an institution that has yet to put content online. These courses save students time on campus and free up classroom space as the same course can be offered twice a week. In fact, one of the psychology faculty members taught the same hybrid class scheduled on Tuesday and Thursday at 10:00 am in the same room. He let the students know they could attend either class as his lectures and the online assignments would be the same for each class.

Work still has to be done in the area of modularized, open-entry/open-exit coursework. Traditional colleges and universities are still reluctant to allow students to take "mini" courses and then apply them for credit versus a traditional semester length course. Time will tell if tradition gives way to necessity.

The final lesson learned is that implementing an Electronic Campus is costly up-front with large investments in information systems, faculty training, and course conversion. However at Lansing Community College the pay-back was seen after just the second year of implementation. In fact, the virtual and hybrid offerings were true enrollment growth to the college because as online sections filled, so did face-to-face sections. There was no "internal seat siphoning" of the face-to-face sections due to an overall increase in enrollments at the college.

## Conclusion

Distance education has taken a firm hold at Lansing Community College and shown significant growth over a very short period of time. Focusing on the three major areas of support – technical, instructional and student – has been an essential aspect in the transition from a traditional community college to one that has begun to significantly embrace the concept of an Electronic Campus. The challenge for the future will be to continue the same spirit of encouragement and change that has focused on supporting the people of the college – the students, the faculty, and the alumni.

Chapter 19

# Dealing with Instructional Technology and Surviving: The Creation of a Student-Focused Online Education Program

Diane Golzynski

As a new doctoral student I was really excited about the opportunity to do some "real" teaching. While working on my Master's degree I had enjoyed teaching classes with as many as 30 students. However, I was now beginning a doctoral program and I was going to be able to spread my insight and knowledge to well over 100 students in a basic Foods/Nutrition class. I couldn't wait.

I was teaching very traditional basic mathematics to a Food Service Management class. It was an undergraduate junior/senior level class and the entrance level mathematics ability of many of the students was extremely low. We were using paper and pencil exercises and trying to get the students moving from simple addition and subtraction into fractions. I had assumed that everyone knew this sort of stuff. I was wrong.

It soon became clear that a third of the class really needed a lot of extra help. It was that group that couldn't remember the math rules for dealing with a complex equation. They couldn't take a fraction and convert it into a decimal. They couldn't express a decimal as a percentage. These were all critical skills for someone working in food service and I needed to find a way to effectively teach these skills.

It would have been nice to break the class into two separate groups, but that would have meant twice as many teaching hours for me and I really didn't have the time. I saw no other option than to drag everyone in the class through basic mathematics and hope that we could move on once the basics were established.

Before long I was spending most of my free time creating remedial take-home assignments for the students to practice these skills. These practice assignments were handed out in each class and returned to me the following class. I was aware of the importance of immediate and personalized feedback so I would try my best to read the homework each night, correct it, add comments and get it back to the students as soon as possible. It tuned into an unending task. I quickly learned that there were far too many students that needed help for me to personalize my instruction for each of them.

The two hour class session soon turned into two one-hour segments with the first hour devoted exclusively to reviewing mathematics concepts and the second hour focused on the content I was supposed to be teaching. I encouraged those students who didn't need the remedial mathematics to skip the first part of the class and only come to the second hour so they wouldn't be bored with the class. As the instructor I started to feel rather helpless. I was not moving ahead with the curriculum in the manner that I had planned. Was this what teaching was all about?

At the end of my first semester I had my worst fears confirmed. The final examination showed that, even with all of my extra attention to mathematics, a large number of the students were terribly deficient. Their math competence was far below the level that was required of their profession. I was in trouble and I felt that I had failed.

## A possible answer

As I was commiserating over my situation I spotted an announcement for an upcoming seminar entitled, "Teaching Large Classes: How To Get Students To Understand The Content." It sounded like it might be an answer to my problem. And even if it wasn't a complete answer I could probably learn a few strategies to help me manage the hours that I was spending teaching mathematics. I enrolled in the seminar and was surprised to find that it dealt with some new computer software named CAPA (Computer-Assisted Personalized Approach) that had been created by the physics/astronomy department on campus. It was being used to teach math concepts to chemistry and physics students.

With CAPA, an instructor could create and/or assemble personalized assignments, quizzes, and examinations with a large variety of conceptual questions and quantitative problems. It could include pictures, animations, graphics, tables, and links. The program provided the student with immediate feedback and relevant hints and allowed the student to correct errors, without penalty, prior to an assignment's due date. The system kept track of each student's participation and performance, and records were available to both the instructor and the individual student.

## Rolling up my sleeves and building the problem sets

So here I was, a doctoral student in food science with negligible computer/technical skills, attempting to learn how to write computer code from a group of scientists. It soon became apparent they had never considered that someone outside of the basic sciences might want to learn how to create curriculum that could be used with CAPA. They thought I had lost my mind but agreed to give it a try. I spent the entire Christmas break sitting at a computer terminal in the Cyclotron Laboratory, talking to the software designers, and learning how to code in CAPA - trying to understand how I might be able to use their system for teaching math concepts to my students. I knew that there had to be a better way of teaching math than what I was doing and I was hoping that this software would be the answer.

The following Fall semester, almost a full year since I had first heard about CAPA, I was ready to try it with my students. And what had I accomplished in that time? I had figured out how the CAPA system operated and was able to develop a total of 5 problem sets – each problem set included 25 different mathematical problems that I felt were important for the students to be able to master.

That year had also allowed me to clarify exactly what it was that I wanted to achieve with my students through the use of this technology. First, the use of the technology would have to free up the large amount of time that I was spending to teach remedial math. And second, this technology would have to significantly improve my ability to graduate students who were competent in using math concepts in their professional life.

## It Worked! However...

As we began that Fall semester I was really excited about being able to use this computer-based method for teaching. Then all of the problems started to surface. Some days turned into nightmares! These problems occurred in two areas. First, there were coding errors where the student selected the right answer for a problem and was told it was wrong. And, secondly, there were numerous typos that had managed to escape the many times I had proof read the problem sets.

That first class did get some things out of it. However, they appeared to be very frustrated with all of the errors. And, of course, due to my errors in coding, it turned into a very popular excuse for why a student might have gotten a problem incorrect – "You must have coded this one wrong." Being a bit insecure with the technology I always assumed at the beginning that it was my problem rather than assuming it had been a student error. I think this was very important for the eventual acceptance of the program by the students.

The other major barrier was the material that I was teaching them, the mathematical concepts needed in food service, was not available in a textbook. I had searched everywhere for a textbook from which I could merely "lift" the problem sets and insert them into the CAPA software but I wasn't able to find one. So I was not only trying to create a unique way of presenting the material to the students through the use of the computer software but I was also faced with creating these materials based entirely on my own mathematics knowledge and what I thought needed to be done to help them understand how to get to recipe conversions.

This added another major dimension to the significance of the challenges that the students created for me. If the student had a problem/question, I found that I would begin by questioning myself. And, of course, I would often wonder if I knew what I was doing. If there was an error, was it a function of bad programming or was it a function of bad pedagogy? My role had to be both a programmer and an educator.

By the end of the semester I began to feel, for the first time, that all of this effort might have some payoff. In fact, I had something to show for my efforts. A major group of problem sets had been created that would be very useful for our program of studies, regardless of whether or not the CAPA software was used to present the problems. With this bit of good news I was able to get the Provost to provide funding for the Spring semester that would allow further editing/refining and the creation of additional problem sets to make the material more comprehensive.


## Moving to the Next Level

I felt like I was doing something unique. And, I truly believed that in the end the students would benefit. I never dreamed that my efforts would go beyond this class and that was okay. I had always assumed that the students in my class, and the development of their mathematical competencies, was as far as this project would go. However, that Spring semester, as part of my own graduate studies program, I took a class in the area of instructional design.

The semester assignment for that class was the development of an instructional manual that would be supportive of some aspect of my own teaching. The teacher provided a format and then I was instructed to take my topic and organize it into a manual that would guide my students, in a self-directed manner, to the class materials. What a great assignment. I was now able to create a manual that could accompany the problem sets that I had developed. This new piece of the puzzle fueled my resolve to continue the efforts to develop the instructional materials.

This manual became a very significant add-on to the development of the teaching materials. The manual, 50 pages in length, gave the student something to visually focus on during their computer exercises. It provided instructions on how to use the computer software, a clear outline of what needed to be learned and samples of the different problem sets. It provided the missing link – the student could now be guided through the problem sets by the manual, be fairly assured of success, and there was now no need to spend class time for any of it! Though I had started with the idea that CAPA would be the central curricular element, the manual now took over that role and CAPA became secondary. The manual was the curriculum guide and the CAPA software became the drill-and-practice system for helping the student learn the material. This was such a revelation to me. At the beginning I had no idea this is where I would end up.

The next Fall I was able to implement the homework sets, delivered via CAPA, with the manual that I had developed in my graduate class. The materials were introduced to the students as self-learning activities. They were to cover the materials completely on their own without any class time devoted to the materials. The students, of course, could schedule time to speak with me about any of the problems that they had worked on in the self-directed mode for which they still had a concern.

The exciting thing for me was that I was now able to check into the CAPA system on each homework "due date" and easily see how my students were doing – how many each person had gotten correct, how many they got wrong, how many times they had to answer each question before getting it correct, which problems were causing the most difficulty (and could use some additional computer-based instruction), etc. As an instructor, the computer-based system was now allowing me to feel very empowered in being able to understand my students and how I might be able to better assist them in their learning. The program not only provided feedback to the learner but it also prompted them in better understanding the concept that was involved so they could be successful the next time.

## Turning the Program into a Distance Education Offering

After the third semester of implementation on campus, when the program seemed to be working quite well, the word got out at a national meeting and all of a sudden we started receiving requests from other institutions to make our problem sets and software available for others to use. The concerns that we had been having with our students were the same on other campuses and they were in need of the same kinds of assistance.

Since the system used the Internet as a way to deliver the problem sets to the students, it was now feasible for us to consider offering it at other locations. However, the Family Educational Rights and Privacy Act created a major hurdle for us. Student data and scores/grades were the responsibility of the student's home educational institution and since scores on the problem sets were being stored on MSU's server it created a liability issue. This forced the development of a legal agreement between MSU and each institution that wanted to use our online program. The agreement would allow MSU to maintain the grades without being in violation of the privacy act.

The next few hurdles were related to how we would provide the grades back to the instructor at the student's home institution. How would we do it? What form would it take? How would we charge the student/institution for using the materials? Who would collect the money? How long would the students have access to the homework sets?  Would the faculty at the other institutions have full access to the system?  How would we assign login names and passwords to students form other institutions?  Would our system be able to recognize these "foreigners" as valid users of the system?  And finally, what would we name our system and how much would we charge?

Luckily we found a campus unit that was able to step in on our behalf, establish the necessary legal agreements and market the program for us – including all of the needed interfaces that would allow distant students to interact with our on-campus system (which had not been created to facilitate such a plan).  Whenever I would receive a request from another institution to use our materials I would contact out campus unit and they would set up the system.  I would then receive the student roster from the other institution and I would go about assigning login identities and passwords, log them individually into the server, print their homework sets, go to a local print shop and duplicate their self-instructional manual, and bring the whole thing to the marketing unit that would then assemble the individual packets and send them directly to each registered student.  It was a rather laborious process for me, setting them up to effectively use the system.  However, without this front-end time there would have been no strong guarantee that the students would be successful with the program.

Issues of students attempting to access the system and do the work for others was a responsibility of the instructor at the student's home institution.  We had early realized that any attempt on our part to police the system from a distance would probably create major problems.  We felt it would appropriately be a responsibility of the contracting institution.  In most cases this concern was dealt with by the contracting institution by offering the problem sets at an on-campus computer laboratory at which the student would have to use their local login to gain access.  Also, the use of locally proctored examinations was another way that concerns of cheating could be effectively accommodated.  It was essential, of course, that the local instructor still knew his/her students.  We weren't attempting to completely remove all responsibility from the other instructor.  We were only attempting to provide one specific module of instruction that could be added to their existing curriculum.

Food Service 2000 was born.  Approximately 50 different institutions have been involved with offering Food Service 2000 to their students.  And, approximately 800 students each year have been enrolled in the program at a distance.

The next major hurdle occurred when the product started being noticed by non-educational institutions that wanted to offer the problem sets to their employees.  Hospitals, prisons, hotel catering departments, dietetic internship programs and other similar settings that regularly trained food service workers began to see the value of what we were able to offer through this type of instruction.  Suddenly we were facing an entirely new set of very diverse problems.  What to do if the employees were prison inmates and they were not allowed access to the Internet?  Or, what if the institution wanted to offer the instruction at a time that didn't coincide with the beginning of a semester?  Could the program be used in a continuing education format rather than as a semester-long graded course?

For these non-traditional learners we allowed 6 months of access to our system.  We assumed that the learner, in that amount of time, could meaningfully work their way through the problem sets with enough repetition and feedback to learn the concepts and be able to put them to use.


## What Would I Do Different the Next Time?

The process of discovery was such an important part of the development of Food Service 2000.  I don't think it would have turned out nearly as well if I had known, at the beginning, what I was about to become involved with. As it turned out, though, I was able to treat each step along the way as a significant learning event. And the most important aspect of that learning for me was my concern for the student. I wanted to make sure that the outcome of my learning would not only be a viable approach for teaching but it would also be the best possible outcome for student learning.

I was able to deal with each problem along the way as it occurred. The area that turned out to be the most foreign for me was learning about marketing and pricing. I had never imagined these aspects as very essential to the development of an educational program. I had always assumed that they would be done when the time was right and they would sort of just happen. That was far from the truth.

As the program moved to an Internet-based distance education offering, marketing took an inordinate amount of my time and energy. Unlike the development of the curriculum, which was always guided by my concerns for the student, the marketing/pricing part of this project had me working in an unfamiliar area without any referent to help guide me. This segment of the project had been thrust upon me when it appeared the university began to realize that there was potential money to be made. They wanted to make sure that they were appropriately "positioned" if there would come a time when a profit could be realized.

Would I do it again? Certainly I would. The challenge of creating an instructional program for my students was an unbelievable journey and a wonderful set of learning experiences for me. Plus, moving the program to the Internet so that it could be used by students at a distance taught me so many things about people, how they learn and how the distance education instructor must respect the individualistic qualities of each learner in order to be successful. My success was clearly dependent on the success of my students.

# Chapter 20

# Creating a Viable Educational Web Resource: Lessons Learned from the Worldwide Web

S. Joseph Levine

## Introduction

Posting educational material to the worldwide web has now become an accepted part of life for those in academia. Papers, reports, class outlines, reading lists, and so many other materials have provided new resources for learners to explore just about any topic imaginable. The technical challenge of creating an educational webpage has been gradually reduced so that anyone, with minimal technical ability, can now post whatever they would like and invite the world in to see it. But is it really that easy? And will people really flock to your website? This case study describes a journey along the cyber highway as an educational resource, one that would take full advantage of the power of the worldwide web.

## The Original Idea for the Educational Webpage

Back in the early 1980s, I put together a mildly popular small publication that detailed the ins and outs of getting through the preparation and defense of a dissertation or thesis. It was a printed publication with only two different type sizes and a few words highlighted in bold. The graduate students in my department all knew about it and made sure some of their friends were also able to get a copy. In the first 15 years, almost 200 copies of the *Dissertation Guide* were printed and distributed.

In 1997, as I was about to restock the supply with another 25 copies, it occurred to me that the Guide would be an excellent candidate for placement on the worldwide web. The image that danced through my mind was of a counter at the bottom of a page that was zooming out of control as one graduate student after another swooped down to get his or her own Internet-delivered copy. I could then get out of the printing business, and the *Guide* could become easily accessible to all who wanted a copy.

Now all I had to do was to find out exactly how I would do such a thing. Like so many of my colleagues, I felt the web seemed to have wonderful potential as a source of information, but the technical ability to actually create web pages was something quite beyond my ability or my interest.

Luckily, I was familiar with a graduate student who knew the secrets of preparing web documents. Unfortunately, he was in another department, and I had no power to persuade him to take on this project. When I suggested that it would make a wonderful project for him, he smiled warily, suggested he had way too many "wonderful projects" at the time, but would be happy to teach me how to write in hypertext markup language (HTML).

Hypertext markup language? It sounded like a legal term or a phrase that I had heard in a hospital emergency room. However, without any other viable prospects I went along with the offer, and without a lot of investment of time and energy, I was soon writing phrases on my word processor that consisted of important words and letters sandwiched between the lesser than (<) and greater than (>) symbols. Somehow when I viewed this with my web browser, it turned into rather pretty looking material that could easily be adjusted in a variety of ways to make it more readable.

Being an academic at heart, I also purchased a reference book that I could keep by my side and consult whenever I got in over my head. Lots of books are available, and I found one that was clearly organized and allowed me to quickly turn to a specific page, see how a certain tag was written, and then write it into my webpage. I wasn't interested in a book that I had to read from cover-to-cover on the way to becoming an HTML expert. I just needed the information presented clearly and succinctly. I was on my way.

Now, five years later and approaching half a million visitors, I think it is a good time to reflect on what has transpired. Based on the many email messages I get each week, it seems that my small publication has managed to reach and help many people looking for the answers that I have to offer. And I have been able to do all of it with less of an investment than it cost to produce those first 200+ printed copies.

When I consider all of the things I have had to learn along the way, it would appear that there has been a considerable investment of my time in this project. But I consider it a good investment. Let me describe the main lessons that I learned:

## Getting Some Expert Opinion

From the very beginning I felt good about the content of the *Dissertation Guide*. After all, I had been distributing it with periodic updates for a number of years. Feedback from graduate students had always been good, and whenever I would get some new ideas, I'd make revisions to improve it.

Nevertheless, I thought getting some expert feedback on the web-based version of the *Guide* would be a good idea. Did the content come through easily? Was it easy to use? Were the users able to go directly to the information they needed? Were the sections too short or too long?

At first I tried a few colleagues, but I found they were still intrigued with the worldwide web and not yet prepared to offer substantive comments on how to design educational materials for it. My computer friends, on the other hand, seemed to be most concerned about the colors that could be used and other technological issues of the page and not its contents. I would get comments such as:

> Why don't you break up your single page into multiple short pages that could be linked from a main page? After all, one of the exciting things about the web is that you can click on a link and you will be immediately taken to another page! Zoom, zoom, zoom.

> Hmmm. Sounds a bit of a nuisance to me.

Then I realized that the "experts" I needed to speak to were the students themselves, that is, those who would be visiting the website. So I emailed a few students, asked them to visit the website, and then let me know what they thought about it. In a few days I had the feedback I needed:

> One page works just fine – no need to break the page into small linkable pieces.
> Please don't use frames; it makes the screen size too small.

Provide an outline at the beginning, so you can immediately see the topics covered and in what order.

Keep the content light and enjoyable – minimize the lecturing.

Stay away from bulleted points; this isn't a PowerPoint presentation.

Search out some good links to other websites and include them.

It didn't take long to make the changes that were suggested. Now I was ready to sit back and watch the action start.

**Figure 1**

**A Very Basic Website**

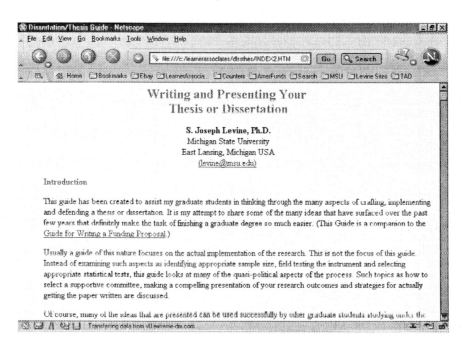

## Waiting for the Hits to Begin

Part of the excitement of posting a page on the worldwide web is the thought of the number of people who will visit the website. Naturally the inclusion of some form of counter to accurately record the number of visitors is essential. I was able to find lots of "free" counters on the web, and I selected one that wasn't very obtrusive when placed on the webpage.

Once the counter was placed on the webpage and running, I started checking the *Dissertation Guide* every few hours to see how I was doing. Although it soon became immediately clear that I wasn't going to establish any new hit record, I was pleased to see that one more visitor was counted each time I checked. Then it occurred to me. I realized that the counter was counting *my* visits and no one else's. Once I got over this initial shock, I sat down and planned a real strategy.

I spent a half day during Thanksgiving 1998 searching the web for websites that might be interested in posting a link to my webpage. I found about 30 such websites. I then composed an email to send to each one, inviting him or her to consider linking to my website. My email was written in a very academic manner, and my full university address was included. I wanted to make sure each one knew that my website wasn't a commercial enterprise. With that communication activity on my site improved noticeably. Hits started to be recorded on the counter.

Then, I stumbled onto a lucky find. One of my emails had gone to the Department of Computer Sciences at the University of Wisconsin-Madison, publisher of the Internet Scout Report. It selected the *Dissertation Guide* as one of the featured Internet resources they would describe in its weekly Scout Report that would go to hundreds of researchers, educators, college librarians, and others. The Scout Report was disseminated electronically on December 11, 1998, and the effect was immediate. People were beginning to visit the website in significant numbers.

**Figure 2**

**Early Hits and the Influence of the Internet Scout Report**

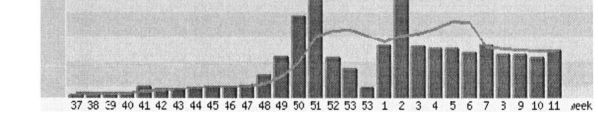

Although the heavy hits from the Scout Report lasted only a week (Week 51), and then returned briefly after the New Year (Week 2), it was clear that the weekly level of hits following the release of the Scout Report was significantly improved (Week 3 and after). The Scout Report had clearly disseminated to the "right" people, that is, those who were spreading the word to others.


## Turning on the Search Engines

One of the fun things about the worldwide web is that you get ideas from every website you visit. Checking the "Page Source" immediately shows you the specific codes that the designer has used to create the effect that is presented. And with a little practice, you can easily borrow from here and there to develop your own unique style.

One of the things that I discovered during a clandestine visit to someone else's website was Meta Tags. These are coded words and sentences, embedded at the very top of a webpage, that help search engines identify the focus of your page. Search engines might read the title of your webpage, but what they're really looking for are these Meta Tags. There are Meta Tags devoted to a "description" of your webpage and those devoted to "keywords" about your page. It didn't take me long to embed Meta Tags on my webpage.

190

**Figure 3**

**Meta Description and Meta Keywords for the Dissertation Guide**

| |
|---|
| <meta name="description" content="A practical Guide to assist in the crafting, implementing and defending of a graduate school thesis or dissertation.  Authored by S. Joseph Levine, Michigan State University (levine@msu.edu)."> |
| <meta name="keywords" content="graduate, graduate education, dissertation, thesis, doctoral, phd, master's, defense, adult education, research, guide, practical, social science, thesis guide, thesis handbook, dissertation guide, dissertation handbook, thesis writing, dissertation writing, thesis defense, dissertation defense, thesis help, dissertation help, graduate school, thesis ideas, dissertation ideas, thesis steps, dissertation steps, successful thesis, successful dissertation"> |

Then I spent another half day visiting the different search engines and looking for the ways in which I could let them know that my page was available to be indexed by their engine.  It didn't take long before I could spot a small link that said, "Add a Site," "Submit a Site," or "Submitting Your Site."  To keep things consistent I used my Meta Description to complete the "Submit" form for the search engine.  Then I waited a few weeks and did it all over again.  I wanted to make sure that I was listed on the different search engines.  Two or three months later I started seeing my website appearing on searches that I would do.

## Finding out who was Really Visiting my Website

I felt good that I now had people visiting my website.  In fact, thanks to the counter, I could tell you the most popular hour for visiting the website, the country from which they were accessing the worldwide web, and what search engine they had used.  I could even tell you what words were used in their query that had landed them on my site.

But who were these people?  Were they spending an appreciable amount of time with the information I had on the website or were they just surfing by?  The material I had posted on the web was designed to be used by graduate students, but were these the actual users?  Were they all from similar academic disciplines?  I had lots of questions but very few answers.

In October 1998 I posted a small plea on the website, asking visitors to complete a short online survey form that could be anonymously emailed to me.  This was another "free" service I had found on the web.  The survey had a total of twelve fixed response items, three short-answer items, and one open-ended "Comments" item.  I left this request up for six months.  During that period a total of 9,500 hits were recorded.  Of that number, 326 (3.4%) took the time to respond to my survey.  At first I thought the percentage response rate was rather low; however, after further contemplation it became apparent that getting 326 visitors to stop surfing for a minute to complete a survey form was pretty good.  I was happy.  And the results were fascinating and gave me my first real sense of who was visiting the website.

Table 1

Selected Survey Responses

| Survey Question | Responses | Meaning |
|---|---|---|
| 1. *How did you happen to find the Dissertation/Thesis Guide web site?* | 43  I found it strictly by accident<br>120 A search engine found it for me<br>86  It was listed on another web site<br>69  A friend told me about it<br>02  Not sure how I found it | My dissemination to other websites and the search engines was working. |
| 2. *Have you previously visited the Dissertation/Thesis Guide web site?* | 39 Yes<br>285 No | These were mainly new visitors. |
| 3. *Do you plan to bookmark (Have you already bookmarked) this web site so you can visit it again?* | 288 Yes<br>31 No | They planned to come back again. |
| 4. *What was the purpose for visiting the Dissertation/Thesis Guide web site?* | 12 No real purpose for my visit - just happened to stop by.<br>55 To get general INFORMATION about preparing a dissertation/thesis.<br>75 To better UNDERSTAND the process of preparing a dissertation/thesis.<br>162 To get ideas that I can PUT TO USE to actually complete my dissertation/thesis.<br>15 To help me to be able to ANALYZE/CRITIQUE the dissertations/theses of others. | This item was keyed to the cognitive domain of learning and it was apparent that the visitors were at the Application Level - they wanted to put the material to use. |
| 5. How much time did you spend at this web site? | 21 Just a minute or two (I briefly looked it over)<br>59 Approximately 5 minutes (I read some of the items)<br>109 5 – 10 minutes (I read a number of the items)<br>137 More than 10 minutes (I studied the information in detail) | They were not just cruising by - they were stopping and spending a fairly good amount of time reading the material. This was what I had hoped for! |

In addition, about 75 percent of the visitors were graduate students and the remaining 25 percent were faculty members and others who were responsible for advising students regarding their thesis or dissertation.  The visitors represented dozens of different disciplines from both the social sciences and natural sciences.  And, most interestingly, the average age of the visitor was 37.95 years – a lot older than I would have expected.  The complete survey results can be seen at <http://www.LearnerAssociates.net/dissthes/results.htm>.

## What the Users were Saying to Me

The "Comments" section of the survey was the especially good part.  Here there were lots of words of thanks.  But most importantly, a variety of very helpful comments that gave me not only more insight into who these visitors were but also some valuable advice on how to improve the website.

**Table 2**

**Selected Comments from Website Visitors**

| |
|---|
| "The topics introduced by you were most helpful but I was hoping for a "step-by-step" guide through all the Chapters in a Thesis - Chap. 1-5. I am at the final stage of my thesis, writing up Chapter 5...just don't know how to proceed,..." |
| "I have printed the guide, and hope it will be useful in writing my thesis. Just some advice on the website design, maybe you could have content menu always visible on the left side of the screen, to allow users to easily access the different sections, while still having an overview of the information in the guide." |
| "I think it would be most helpful to have a link to a well organized sample thesis. For many of us involved in distance education, it is difficult to access a sample product." |
| "I only have a couple of weeks before my dissertation has to be completed. I had hit a 'brick wall' and was having a mental black. Your site helped me considerably by giving me fresh ideas and by confirming that what I had done so far was on the right lines. THANK YOU!!" |
| "I have visited your site several times over the past six months. The first time was to get a general picture of what constitutes a well written proposal. The second time was to get practical tips for proposal writing, most specifically the literature review. This last time was to review your site before going to my first committee meeting." |

As a service to the visitors, I created a link on the website that would take them to a page with the complete results and comments of all participants in the study. I realized that the positive tone of the comments could provide additional encouragement to graduate students in the throes of working on their thesis or dissertation. I limited my online reactions only to answering direct questions that appeared in the comments. And I tried not to create any sort of defensive posture. After all, I was interested in their insights, not my rationalizations.

# Time to get Rich!

Once the website seemed to be moving along quite nicely on its own, I started wondering about the economic potential of such a device. It seemed that wherever I went on the web, I was faced with one banner ad after another. They popped up everywhere. And, although I seldom clicked on any of these ads, I assumed that someone must be and that someone else must be making a fortune from the people who were doing the clicking. I explored the different companies that managed the banner ads and found one that didn't seem to have very objectionable ads (e.g. fruit baskets, framed pieces of art, magazine subscriptions, and the like).

I was about to complete the simple sign-up sheet and install the coded information on the page when I realized that I was really moving away from my original intention of staying within an academic setting. What in the world did commercial ads have to do with a website that was designed to help graduate students navigate a successful dissertation? What were the trade-offs?

Clearly the trade-offs were not in favor of the graduate students. They had little enough money for schooling without my website trying to pry some of it away from them. However, I still had this urge to see if these ads really generated any viable income. So, I tried it. However, I promised myself I'd try it only on a very limited basis and would back away from the idea if it appeared not as viable as I had been led to believe. And in an attempt to create a bit of goodwill during this part of my experimenting, I agreed to give any earnings to our departmental Graduate Student Association and posted a notice to that effect on the webpage.

It took about 3 months before I was able to draw some very clear conclusions. First, the ads gave the webpage a very commercial feeling, which I didn't like. Second, the 300 or so hits that I was getting each day wasn't nearly enough exposure to generate many ad clickers. Consequently, the ads were earning the Graduate Student Association a dollar or two a month, which was hardly enough to warrant such commercialism. And third, the motivational emails I was receiving from the advertisers, encouraging me to push their products in bigger and better ways was downright annoying. My choice was obvious. I pulled the banner ads off of the website.

Not one to give up quickly, however, I still felt there must be some way to generate meaningful revenue from such a website and at the same time be seen by the website visitors as a service of some sort and not just an attempt to get them to buy something.. I was now committed to the Graduate Student Association and wanted to see if my website could indeed assist them. Finally, I thought that a page within the website that posted and reviewed books that dealt with the topic of completing a dissertation or thesis might be just the answer.

What a natural. Graduate students read lots of books. Why not make books the commercial aspect. The website visitor could visit the page, read the reviews, and purchase the book through the direct link to the bookseller that was provided. Or, more importantly, there was nothing in the way of users also reading the reviews and visiting their campus library and checking the books out. The choice was theirs. The website would now have the additional value of reviewing books on the topic and an easy click, if visitors wanted to purchase books.

It worked. The page of book reviews, with links to the bookseller, has now been up and running for two years. In that time the Graduate Student Association has earned about $650 in commissions – $300 from this single website. It certainly is not enough to get rich, but it is enough to assist a number of graduate students attending professional meetings.

**Table 3**

**Website Commissions from the Online Sale of Books (July 2001 - July 2003)**

| Total number of unique visits to the website: | Total number of books sold from the website: | Average number of visits per sale of a book | Total revenue from books sold: | Total commissions earned: | Commission as percent of total revenue: |
|---|---|---|---|---|---|
| 317,868 | 232 | 1370 | $4964.53 | $292.82 | 5.9% |

## Email as an Indication of Success

The website was now moving along quite well. Periodically I would check the counter to see how the webpage was doing or fix an undiscovered typo on the webpage. Most of my attention, however, was now focused on the emails that I was receiving, along with an occasional editing of the website. I decided at the beginning to provide substantive responses to those who took the time to email me. After a month or two that reality started to fade. There were way too many.

Emails seemed to fall into three categories. First there were those just wanting to say thanks.

> *"I found your website just in time. My defense is in two weeks and after reading your comments I feel prepared."*

> *"Great ideas - I've passed the address on to my friends."*

I would send back a short acknowledgment and a word or two of encouragement. Without a lot of effort, I was soon able to create a simple form letter or email to take care of those responses.

Then there were those emails that were looking for the sorts of very technical and individualized help that I really wasn't in a position to provide.

> *"Please send me some good research questions that could frame a study in the area of musicology."*

> *"What statistical test would be most appropriate to differentiate between..."*

> *"Could you send me an example of a dissertation in the area of thermal dynamics."*

For this type of email, I created a somewhat elaborate form letter that I was able to use. In essence, the response said that their question fell outside of my own area of expertise, adult learning, and I wasn't in a position to be very helpful. I included in my response some general encouragement and some very direct pointers about how to use the different search engines. Many of the technical questions could be answered well if the "advanced search" feature on certain search engines had been used.

The third type of email was the one that I found most compelling and tried to answer as fully as possible. These emails focused on the psychological or emotional side of completing a thesis or dissertation and were directly in line with the content of my webpage. The sender expressed some level of concern about his or her ability to finish the challenge successfully. I felt a commitment to provide a meaningful answer to each of these emails.

Concerns came through in these emails regarding the lack of professional encouragement that surrounded their graduate study, the anxiety they had regarding their defense, fears of trying to replace a committee member, or confusion over how to draw conclusions from their findings. Writing email responses to these inquiries was a time-consuming task, but it reminded me of the real purpose behind posting my webpage in the first place, that is, to provide some form of substantive help to graduate students. My webpage had taken me to the point that I had hoped I could achieve. To avoid this task would have been irresponsible.

## Widening the Net

With the webpage now running itself and my emailing time getting under control, I was ready to move to a new focus. It had been no surprise that most of the hits to my website came from North America and Europe. Next in line was Asia and then a very small group from Africa and Central or South America. In fact, the number of African hits was about the same as the number of Central and South

American hits.  How could this be?   Since graduate study in higher education was not a large field throughout the African continent, I had expected the African response to be small.  However, graduate study in higher education is well recognized in Central and South America and connectivity to the Internet was known to be good in Central and South America.  Why the low number of hits?

The answer was obvious.  It was the language.  More than likely those from Africa who were able to access my website were using English as their language of study.  But in Central and South America Spanish and Portuguese were the primary languages of instruction.  Unless I could find a way to translate my website into Spanish and Portuguese, I would not be able to effectively serve a rather sizeable population of graduate students.

I got on the web and in a few minutes found an online service that would automatically translate my website for free.  I copied and pasted my content into the form and in a few seconds I had a Spanish translation of my website.  I was very pleased and went to show it to one of our graduate students from Uruguay.  He took the pages in his hands, starred at them for a few minutes, and then started to laugh.  Yes, he admitted, it was Spanish.  However, the translation made a mess of everything.  Tense and gender didn't make sense, words with alternative meanings were substituted liberally, concepts associated with study in higher education were not used, and it was extremely difficult to be able to attend to the focus of the content.

Without a lot of persuasion, the Uruguayan graduate student agreed to do a meaningful translation, and within a month there was now a companion webpage in Spanish that could be easily clicked on.  We then went about the task of submitting sites to the Spanish language search engines and soon the hits from Central and South America began.  And recognizing my own limited Spanish ability, I credited the translator at the top of the webpage, complete with his own email address, so he could field the emails that would come in Spanish.

With Spanish now taken care of, I approached a colleague and friend from a Brazilian university.  He very graciously offered to do a Portuguese translation that would work well in Brazil.  Again, we followed up with the search engines to fully implement the process.

**Table 4**

**The Effect of Website Translations (Spanish & Portuguese) on Hits**

| Country | Average Hits | |
|---|---|---|
| | **Prior to** Translation | **Following** Translation |
| Mexico | 39/month | 233/month |
| Argentina | 17/month | 65/month |
| Chile | 5/month | 55/month |
| Venezuela | 5/month | 51/month |
| Peru | 8/month | 43/month |
| Columbia | 5/month | 39/month |
| Brazil | 40/month | 1663/month |

The increase in the number of hits as a result of the translations was immediate and substantial. This experience was a very powerful reminder of how internationally pervasive the worldwide web has become and how we sometimes forget about large segments of the world.

Visitors to the website have been identified from a total of 189 different countries. The United States represents the greatest number of visitors with over 170,000, but countries identified with over 5000 visits include the United Kingdom, Brazil, Canada, Australia, Malaysia, Mexico, Hong Kong, and the Philippines.


## Taking Home a Copy

Throughout the development and improvement of the website, many users let me know that they appreciated the material, had glanced at it on the web, and had printed a copy so that it could be read more carefully at a later time. Since it suggested that the material was valued enough to invest in the paper to print it, this information made me feel good. It also suggested that reading the material on the screen was not necessarily preferred by all the visitors.

One day I also printed a copy of the webpage, and it was only then that I realized that it didn't make nearly as much sense as a printed copy as it did as a webpage. This discrepancy became especially apparent in the section of hot links that were included on the webpage, the simple form for sending me feedback, and some other web-based devices I had included. On a webpage a clickable hot link is wonderful. On a printed page, however, a hot link has no real value. Certainly I didn't expect someone to sit with the paper in his or her hand and try to type a URL into his or her browser window.

Yet, creating a "take home copy" of the Guide demanded a bit of work. The Guide had not existed in print form since before the webpage development had been started. All development of the material in recent years had been done directly for the worldwide web. I proceeded to "copy" the entire Guide from the web and "paste" it into my word processor. I was careful to remove all indications of links and other web-based devices. I also added an introduction especially for the print version, told the reader that the Guide was available on the web, and included a short notification that gave the user permission to make copies of the print document for educational purposes.

After a bit of searching around the web, I found that the most popular way of posting printable documents was via Adobe Reader. I installed the Adobe Acrobat software on my computer, and it took only a few seconds to create and post the printable version of the webpage.

**Figure 4**

**The Website as a Portable Document Format (.pdf) Document**

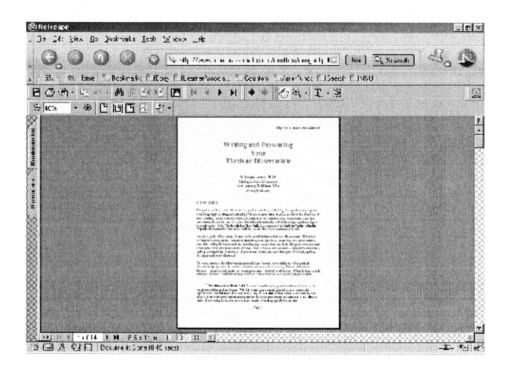

## Who could have Imagined?

Continuing to build the *Thesis/Dissertation Guide* as an educational resource has been a very enjoyable enterprise. Unlike documents stuck away in a file cabinet, this document has been out in the open and always easy to find. This very public aspect of a webpage, with the stream of emails that it has created, has been a constant reminder to continue to build the page, add and delete as needed, respond to those who need some help, and to always work to improve it. I would not have imagined that the creation of an educational resource could be such a dynamic process as this one has been.

When I first read Ivan Illich's (1971) <u>Deschooling Society</u> and his vision of *learning webs*, a major strategy for connecting people/learning while at the same time de-institutionalizing society, I had no idea that I would experience such a phenomena first hand in my lifetime. But the worldwide web has created just such an opportunity. With only a small investment, learners and teachers alike are empowered to share their knowledge with each other. The creation of a webpage as a viable educational resource has been, for me, an emerging project of significant proportions that has pushed and shoved me into a variety of teacher and learner roles. And it has been enjoyable throughout. I would never have suspected that I would have the opportunity to share my thinking with half a million people. Fortunately, it has happened.

**Reference**

Illich, I. (1971). *Deschooling society*. New York: Harper & Row.

# Chapter 21

# A Brazilian Agribusiness Distance Education Program

**Jose Chotguis**

## Introduction

In 2001 the Federal University of Parana at Curitiba, Brazil initiated a distance education program directed to agribusiness professionals. The Agribusiness Distance Education Program was made available to learners at 10 different sites in the State of Parana via a combination of 2-way interactive television, small group interaction and web-based instruction. The course was immediately successful, in terms of enrollments, with over 300 students enrolling from throughout the State of Parana in 2001 – compared to the 51 students who were enrolled on campus in the regular face-to-face course in the year 2000. However, a number of problems have developed during the first year of the program that suggests changes are needed.

Figure 1 shows the main page of the Agribusiness Distance Education Program (Curso de Pós Graduação em Agronegócio) website. (http://www.uep.org.br/)

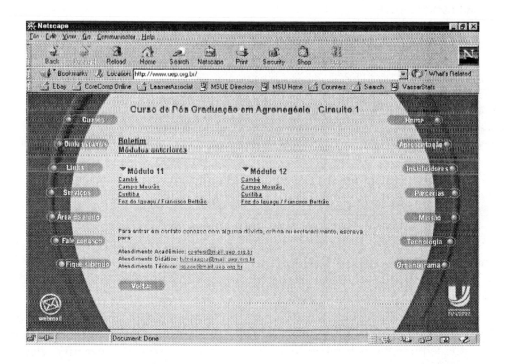

**Figure 1 – Home Page for the Agribusiness Distance Education Program**

## The External Context for the Program

Agribusiness, the focus for the distance education program, is Brazil's main business. This important sector is responsible for 37% of the exported products and 33% of the gross national product of Brazil. And most importantly, one third of the country's worker population have jobs that relate in some way to agribusiness.

In the last 15 years, as the government has opened the trade border with many countries, the agribusiness sector has been called upon to improve its products to more effectively compete with overseas competitors. There has been a very large demand, consequently, for knowledge and technological training. But, because the potential learners are spread about at considerable distance from each other, attending that demand and providing needed instruction has been a big challenge.

## The Internal Context for the Program

The Federal University of Parana was created in 1912. It is a public higher education institution, tuition is free, and the university operates primarily as a traditionally conventional education institution. During the last three years the university has been trying to implement a distance education center with very little success. A major factor in this lack of success is the faculty who is resistant to the idea of distance education and is slowing down the development of the program. Most of the professors argue that the required effort to redo the academic content to fit the new methodology extends beyond the low salary they earn.

However, the Department of Agricultural Economics and Rural Extension has developed a strategy with their faculty whereby their Agribusiness distance education program is offered as "continuing education" to non-academic students. This means that a fee can be charged for the instruction, either paid by the student or his/her company, which can then be used to supplement the faculty member's salary. This additional income has insured sufficient faculty for teaching the distance education program.

With the "solving" of the salary question, attention has turned to the actual teaching processes as the next major concern for the improvement of the effectiveness of the program.

## The Agribusiness Distance Education Program

The Agribusiness Distance Education Program includes an academic instruction portion consisting of 12 different courses that are taught by 10 different professors. This academic instruction portion is sequenced over a period of 13 months with the students spending a total of 360 contact hours. The 360 hours are divided into three different forms of instruction – two-way interactive television instruction (120 hours), group studies at each remote site (120 hours), and web-based instruction (120 hours). An additional 5 months, following the academic instruction portion, are required of each student to prepare a dissertation to complement his or her academic work. The time span for the entire program is 18 months. This information is presented in Table 1.

**Table 1 - The Agribusiness Distance Education Program: Contact Hours**

| Academic Instruction | | | |
|---|---|---|---|
| Two-way Interactive Television | 120 hours | | Instructor on campus, students at ten remote sites. Uses Intranet/email for communication between students and instructor. |
| Group Studies | 120 hours | | Students learn in groups at each site using material posted on the web. |
| Web Resources | 120 hours | | Students learn independently at their home/office/local learning center using resources posted on the web. |
| | 360 hours | 13 months | |

| Dissertation Preparation | | | |
|---|---|---|---|
| Independent study | 100 hours | 5 months | Students work independently with individual faculty member to prepare written dissertation |

| Totals | 460 hours | 18 months |
|---|---|---|

Figure 2 shows Module 11 from the website – including the General Objectives for the module, Specific Objectives, schedule of sessions, and information about the instructors.

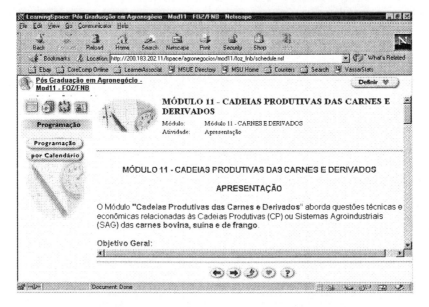

**Figure 2 – Module 11 on the Worldwide Web**

**Course Locations**  During the 13 month academic instruction portion of the program students attend the two-way interactive video classes at their local learning site during two different weekends each month.

This allows each instructor in the program to be working with two different cohorts of distance learners during each month.  Each cohort consists of 5 different groups of learners meeting at five different locations.  One cohort meets on the first and third weekends.  The other cohort meets on the second and fourth weekends.  This system of cohorts is shown in Table 2.

**Table 2 - Cohort Locations and Schedules**

|  | Locations | Schedule |
|---|---|---|
| **Cohort A** |  |  |
|  | Curitiba (A) | $1^{st}$ & $3^{rd}$ weekends |
|  | Francisco Beltrao (A) | $1^{st}$ & $3^{rd}$ weekends |
|  | Cambe | $1^{st}$ & $3^{rd}$ weekends |
|  | Toledo (A) | $1^{st}$ & $3^{rd}$ weekends |
|  | Campo Mourao | $1^{st}$ & $3^{rd}$ weekends |
|  |  |  |
| **Cohort B** |  |  |
|  | Curitiba (B) | $2^{nd}$ & $4^{th}$ weekends |
|  | Londrina | $2^{nd}$ & $4^{th}$ weekends |
|  | Francisco Beltrao (B) | $2^{nd}$ & $4^{th}$ weekends |
|  | Toledo (B) | $2^{nd}$ & $4^{th}$ weekends |
|  | Foz do Iguacu | $2^{nd}$ & $4^{th}$ weekends |

Each of the course locations is at a strategic point in Parana state. This provides for each learner to travel no more than 60 miles from his/her home location to attend the two-way interactive television sessions.

**Course Organization** The class activities for each learning group are divided into two separate sessions during a Saturday. The first session is in the morning and is four hours in length. This session uses the two-way interactive television system.

The professor, broadcasting from the main campus at Curitiba, provides information via a lecture, asks and answers questions, and helps the students understand the content for the session.

The second session, also four hours in length, is in the afternoon and uses an Intranet to electronically connect the students and professor in debate groups that are initiated by the professor. Students at each of the 5 locations work together as a team to respond to the situations presented by the professor.

The next class occurs in two weeks when the students again meet at the distance education location to be linked to the professor and the other four sites. During the two week interval between classes, the students access the course website and read learning materials that have been posted on the web, respond independently to assignments provided by the professor, and prepare for the next class session. The organization of the course is shown in Table 3.

Table 3 – Course Organization

| | Saturday Morning 8:00 am – 12 Noon | Saturday Afternoon 2:00 pm – 6:00 pm | Two week period between Saturday sessions |
|---|---|---|---|
| Learning Activities | Lecture, questions & answers, interactive | Group debates, practice | Individual Study |
| Interactive Technology | Two-way interactive television (synchronous) | Intranet, connected to professor and colleagues (synchronous) | Internet, connected to professor, tutors and colleagues (asynchronous) |
| Student Tools | Printed texts, session program, etc. | Class website, virtual library, web links, etc. | Class website, virtual library, web links, email, etc. |

Figure 3 shows the page from the website that is used as a discussion bulletin board for messages between faculty (Professor/Professora), tutor (Tutoria Agronegocio) and students.

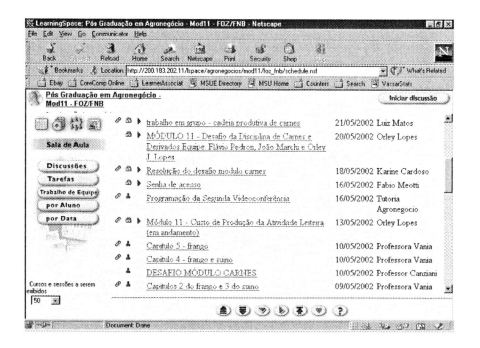

Figure 3 – Student-Faculty Discussion Bulletin Board

**The Learners** The students enrolled in the Agribusiness Distance Education Program are primarily professionals who have attained undergraduate degrees in areas such as agronomy, veterinary science, forestry, zoology, business administration, economics, and agricultural journalism. They are employed by enterprises that work with agribusiness such as agriculture cooperatives, banks, the rural extension service, government institutions, television stations, and newspapers.

These students/professionals voluntarily enroll themselves in the Agribusiness Distance Education Program, although they get partial scholarships from the companies for which they work. As most of the students are enrolled in continuing education, they are seeking to improve their knowledge so they might be able to find better jobs or receive a promotion to a higher position in their current employment.

Only two percent of the learners have previously been enrolled in a distance education course of any type. All of the learners have some familiarity with the computer where they work and 55% have their own computer at home.

## Major Concerns and Issues

As the Agribusiness Distance Education Program has been implemented a number of different concerns and issues have developed. These concerns/issues are best examined in terms of three different frameworks – concerns/issues as seen by the students, concerns/issues as seen by the faculty involved with the program, and concerns/issues as seen by the department offering the program.

**Concerns/Issues as Seen by the Students** During the first semester that the program was offered a total of 12% of the students dropped out. Though no specific study has yet to be undertaken to attempt to identify the specific reasons of those dropping out, it can be assumed that one or more of the following reasons is at work:

> **Content is too theoretical** – The faculty tend to teach at a very theoretical level without much attention to application and practice. Since the students involved in this program are only part-time students, not regularly enrolled as on-campus learners, they tend to have a strong application concern.

> **Little opportunity to interact with faculty** – Without the local presence and availability of faculty members there is no opportunity for the students to enter into live face-to-face exchange of information and ideas. In addition, the four hour time period for each two-way interactive television session provides very little question-answer opportunities due to the large number of students who are participating (150). And finally, questions that are emailed to the faculty tend not to be answered in a very timely manner. Such "human" interaction is essential to filling the interpersonal voids that can exist for students in a distance education program.

> **Boring television productions** – Though the major vehicle for communicating instructional content has been via the Internet and the worldwide web, the use of two-way television has been an important vehicle for reinforcing the information that is presented. Much of the material that is presented in this mode is taken directly from the face-to-face teaching done by the faculty member without concern for altering the presentation to better fit the uniqueness of

the medium. This has the potential affect of being very boring for the student – to be watching via television a lecture being delivered at another location.

**Lack of timely delivery of materials** – Study materials and assignments are often delivered to the students a few short days before assignments are due. Since the learners are very busy with the other aspects of their non-student life, it becomes very difficult at the last minute to schedule their time to allow appropriate preparation for class.

**Technology problems** – The newness of the technology creates a variety of problems that can further frustrate the learners. Such problems as technology breakdowns and poor audio/video quality are often experienced within the program.

**Appropriateness of local instructional space** – The program has attempted to use whatever space may be available at each local area. In some situations the instructional space is appropriate for both the two-way interactive television segments and the group interaction time. However, many of the locations use less-than-appropriate instructional space that the learners find uncomfortable and distracting.

**Concerns/Issues as Seen by the Faculty** Most of the faculty involved with this program can be considered very traditional faculty within the Brazilian higher education system.

**Adapting to the technology** – Many faculty do not desire to make the necessary changes to convert their typical face-to-face instruction to be viable within a distance education setting. This is brought about to a large extent by the large amount of time needed to prepare their instruction to accommodate the medium and the requirement to redesign their support materials and to add additional detail to better fit the needs of learners who are more diverse than typically found in the face-to-face classroom.

**Lack of face-to-face contact with learners** – Not being able to interact in a "normal" (face-to-face) manner with students can be particularly frustrating for the faculty member. The faculty member is not able to see the many non-verbal signs of when students are understanding/not understanding particular content, have questions they may be reluctant to ask, or when it is time to push ideas further.

**Uneasiness with technology** – Though it may be hard to believe, there are still a number of faculty who are involved with this program who have not fully accepted the use of email as a major vehicle for communicating with students. These faculty are often not comfortable with a computer or the technology enhanced procedures that are used for teaching in the program. And, in particular, two technology problems create extreme problems for many of the faculty. First, the audio/video link that connects all of the learning sites permits origination from only a single site at any particular time. This considerably reduces the feedback that is available to the instructor. The second technology problem that frustrates faculty is the audio/video delay that is experienced in the system when origination switches from faculty to student or back again. This delay, which can last as long as 10-20 seconds, hampers attempts to have any form of spontaneous two-way communication.

**Concerns/Issues as Seen by the Department** The Department of Agricultural Economics and Rural Extension is committed to providing agribusiness professionals, especially those who live at a distance from the University, access to their programs. This commitment has demanded a significant investment in two areas - technology and also faculty pay. These two areas have not traditionally had a lot of support. However, the collection of special fees from students participating in the

Agribusiness Distance Education Program has allowed the Department to procure the needed technology and to also augment the income of faculty members, thereby effectively improving their level of pay.

Interestingly, these two financial issues turned out to be the easiest to solve!  In fact, the issues that are now being faced by the Department are much more concerned with the disposition of the faculty rather than the financial situation in which they found themselves.  Improving the income of faculty members has had little effect on the ability of the Department to make appropriate demands regarding the attitude of the faculty and the spirit in which they approach teaching at a distance.  Though the Department continues to work to resolve the technical problems that exist in this distance education program, it can be expected that the program will not be substantively different until such time as the teaching philosophy, learning concepts, attitudes and behaviors of the faculty change – a set of problems that money alone can not solve.

**Chapter 22**

# The Open University of Venezuela:
# From Concept to Reality

Zobeida Ramos

## Introduction

The Universidad Nacional Abierta (UNA), the Open University of Venezuela, was first envisioned in 1977 by the Venezuelan Ministry of Education in an attempt to continue the "educational revolution" that was part of the Fifth National Plan for the economic and social development of the nation. UNA was viewed as a way to assist the development of a sector of students who could not enroll in traditional universities and needed an alternative system of education which did not require in-person attendance at classes. UNA was developed to deliver instruction through alternative means.

The purpose of this paper is twofold. First, to describe the principles and orientation of UNA as it was first proposed in 1977, drawing extensively on the very first project description. This historical perspective is presented in Part I of this paper. Part II then presents an examination and reflection on the first 25 years of operation of the university in its attempt to meet the learning needs of Venezuelans through a distance education-based higher education institution.

## Part I - The Original Concept of the Open University of Venezuela[1]

## Background

The Universidad Nacional Abierta (UNA) was created to promote an "educational revolution". It was built on three fundamental and major policies - Education for Democratization, Education for Innovation, and Education for Autonomous Development.

> **Education for Democratization** is seen as the basic building block for a democratic society. In addition to instruction in how to participate as a responsible citizen, the policy defined a minimum level of nine years of basic education for all citizens that would allow people to actively participate in a modern society that was undergoing rapid and accelerating change, to assist in the reduction of disadvantages that may be due to socio-cultural origin, and to actively participate in local community-based organizations.

> **Education for Innovation** challenged the educational system to develop a viable capacity for innovation that would promote a high level of academic quality. In order to accomplish this it

---

[1] Key ideas and concepts presented in Part I have been drawn from the initial project paper *The National Open University of Venezuela. Project.(1979)* Registro de Publicaciones de la Universidad Nacional Abierta. First English Edition, that was prepared in 1977 as a blueprint for the development of the Universidad Nacional Abierta

would be essential to a) transform the elite-oriented existing system of education to better fulfill the demands of mass education, b) incorporate into the educational process appropriate advances to support the theories, processes and technologies of contemporary education, and c) provide the student with a form of individualized education that would be relevant to his conditions, needs, and aspirations thereby stimulating his creative capacity and influencing the formation of meaningful values, motivations, attitudes, and conduct.

**Education for Autonomous Development** whereby the educational system must be seen as a coherent, articulated, and oriented whole which is primarily directed to satisfy the requirements of society, and its need for autonomous development.

These three policies clarified that Venezuelan education would not only meet learners' demands but it would also work to transform Venezuelan society through the development of a democratic foundation which could contribute significantly in the transformation of the existing economic, social, and cultural system.

## Major Goals

It was in this context that the Universidad Nacional Abierta was first conceptualized to assist in the fulfillment of these very essential policies. UNA was proposed as an innovative and imaginative solution that would effectively collaborate in resolving the problems of higher education by bringing the opportunity and influence of higher education to people throughout the nation for the development of the country.

UNA would embody these three major "educational revolution" policies by extending higher education, both geographically and socially, throughout the nation (Education for Democratization), creating a more educated populous that could serve as human resources for scientific and technological development and for the analysis of and search for solutions to national problems (Education for Autonomous Development), and use an innovative conceptualization of higher education - distance education - which would be carried out through the use of modern educational technology and oriented towards an individualized form of teaching/learning that is creative and promotes change (Education for Innovation). UNA was created to offer an efficient, novel, highly productive, and low cost way to attend to the growing demand for higher education - not only by Secondary School graduates, but also, and in each passing year, in greater proportion, by working adults, professionals and technicians who seek professional qualifications and to continue to improve their competencies.

To be successful, UNA would have to attend to certain **societal sectors** of the population, both young and adult, who work or, for reasons of geographical dispersion, cannot attend conventional institutions of education. Second, in terms of **economic efficiency**, UNA would have to offer the possibility of absorbing a growing student enrollment with only moderate operational costs in the first stages, and later decreasing these operational costs. This would allow for the maximization of the existing higher education physical infrastructure and academic resources, both of which are scarce and costly and thus must be used efficiently. And finally, in terms of the **social learning setting**, UNA would have to provide a highly motivating and significant teaching-learning situation for the student that would lead to the preparation of professionals with the capacity for rationale, critical thought, and creativity and who would be capable of working in multi-disciplinary teams in order to intelligently face the problems of development in a world situation of mutual dependence and multiple influences and alternatives.

# Objectives of UNA

With these major goals as a foundation, three groups of specific objectives were developed to guide the operation of UNA from inception.

### Institutional Objectives
-To form human resources for priority areas of socio-economic development at short, medium, and long range. Special emphasis to be given to the formation, professionalization, and up-grading of teachers.
-To prepare professionals who will act upon the social system as agents for the qualitative change demanded by the nation.
-To establish in the country a special sector of the instructional and administrative system of higher education, responding to a multi-sectorial approach. To encourage full participation of both public and private sectors in the planning and implementation of programs of UNA.
-To adjust the economic contribution of the State to UNA, to the fulfillment of national policies of human resource development, full employment, and optimization of the ability of Venezuelans to increase both production and productivity.
-To develop research for the solution of problems posed by the priority areas of development.
-To foster, through cultural action, the enrichment of the Venezuelan people with authentic values of a national culture, and the values of Latin American and world cultures

### Functional Objectives
-To develop, implement, and administer new strategies of teaching-learning, to heighten the economic efficiency, and to maximize the effectiveness of available resources.
-To carry out research, to evaluate experiences in the new fields of open and at-a-distance education, coordinating UNA's activities with actions being carried out by the Ministry of Education in the area of educational technology at other educational levels.
-To structure UNA's teaching-learning system as a modular system of learning, allowing the user to progress through the various stages of professionalization until reaching a high level of specialization.
-To produce a change of attitudes among users of UNA in order to reverse the relationship of responsibility existing in the traditional learning systems. UNA's user should take responsibility for his learning and the institution should do everything necessary to make this possible in terms of offering alternatives and resources which optimize the process of instruction.
-To organize the learning resources into strategies for the development of opportunities for permanent and recurrent education, making it possible to support professional development, the recycling of human resources, updating of abilities and knowledge, and cultural enrichment.

### Operational Objectives
-To optimize the efficiency of educational investment with the aim of lowering the costs per student and per program, through the application of the criterion of economy of scale.
-To cooperate in the rationalized expansion of the higher education system to permit the modification of the present distribution norms of post-secondary educational opportunities in the different socio-economic levels of the population.
-To cooperate with other higher education institutions so that they may increase in efficiency and effectiveness.

# Key Characteristics

A group of specific characteristics were identified to guide the actual offerings of the Universidad Nacional Abierta. These characteristics, inherent in the process of massive and distant education, served to strengthen the focus of the institution as an "open university." To begin, UNA would have **full national coverage to** ensure that there would be a close relationship between UNA and the different ecological, geo-economical, and social areas of the country. This would be accomplished through its local and regional centers and its students. A **diversification of programs** would provide the foundation for numerous careers, research, extension and the enhancement of a national culture. And, as **a social oriented Institution** it would include both a young and adult population that, due to labor, social, economic, geographic, or physical limitations, had not been able to enter or successfully continue in formal higher education. UNA would allow the student to remain in his geographical, social, and labor medium, thus allowing his direct and continued interaction with his surroundings and the reality with which he would continue to function.

One of the more essential characteristics was that UNA would be built around the use of a **self/independent learning system.** The student, with appropriate orientation, would set his own objectives in harmony with those suggested by the program and through each instructional module. The student, not having to attend classes on a regular/synchronous schedule, would be empowered to administer his own time, to study at his own rhythm, and to perform self evaluation. This would be accomplished through a **mediated interactive system of education** which would include the planned use of human and material resources designed to aid learning. Among these resources would be consultations, study groups, printed modules (the foundational media in the curriculum), television/radio programs and computer-delivered instruction, all of which would constitute the major channels of communication with the student.

And finally, UNA would work to **interact and cooperate with other educational systems** throughout the nation to conduct extension and investigation of learning processes within higher education for the purpose of not only improving its own programs but to also positively affect the programs of the rest of the sub-system of higher education and with the educational system as a whole.

# A Model for Curriculum Development

The curricular model of the Universidad Nacional Abierta was founded on the following considerations:

> **Reality** - The starting point for the personal and professional formation of the student would be constituted by the nature, characteristics, and necessities of the reality, the location of the individual within this reality and the possibility of introducing positive changes in that reality through the means of knowledge. Reality is the object of knowledge.
> **Student as an Adult Learner** - The student is an adult who is capable of contributing to his own development as well as that of the country. Through the increase in his capacity for formal, critical, and creative thought, the student will be able to confront reality, identify problems, and work towards their solution. The student is the subject and can also be the object of knowledge.
> **Science Is Subject to Change and Re-validation.** Through his formation, the student is able to apply scientific and technological knowledge to the solution of real problems and

collaborate in the development of science itself and its relationship to National Development. Science may be the media with which the knowledge of the reality is attained, and is at the same time the object of knowledge.

**Instruction Based on Application** - Instruction is conceived as the concrete existence of a set of opportunities/experiences which permit the subject to interact with the reality, and seek out solutions to its problems. Through this process, the student gains or increases his personal and professional formation.

**Interaction Between Theory and Practice** - Instruction, understood as the interaction between theory and practice and between knowledge and reality, encourages the interaction between teaching/learning and investigation. Instruction, in the special case of UNA, would also integrate teaching, investigation, and extension to fulfill the obligation of education to the community. The relationship between subject and object is brought about through the effective interaction between theory and practice.

**Education At-a-Distance** - UNA programs, fundamentally for adults learning at a distance, would artfully combine communications media as a key aspect of instruction which differentiates the progressive and formative educational plan from the more formal system.

The curriculum of UNA and the learning opportunities would permit the student, from his point of entry, to systematize his own experiences, increase his knowledge of reality, identify problems and the alternatives for their solution, participate in the solution of these problems through the application of science and technology, and contribute to the growth of certain areas of science itself. The curricular model presents the opportunity for the identification of the problems of the reality, the statement of solutions for the detected problems, and the expansion of science. The teaching-learning process permits the establishment of the relation between reality and knowledge; between theory and practice, and between teaching, investigation, and extension; using the store of experiences that the participant brings, as well as the new system of education-work relations which is characteristic of education at-a-distance.

## Key Aspects of the UNA Curriculum

There are a number of curricular elements that are integral to the operation of UNA.
**The Learning Module** Instruction in the Universidad Nacional Abierta would be provided through learning modules, a central element in the UNA curriculum, which are structured sets of self-instructional units that form part of a course and/or program of studies. The instructional design of the modules interprets the objectives established in the curricular designs of the programs of study that are offered by UNA.

The module, a key organizing element for both students and instructional designers, would contain print material, mass media presentations (broadcast via television and radio); support learning materials (audio-cassettes, video cassettes, bibliographic materials, etc.), individualized experimental equipment, practicums in industry and/or institutions, academic counseling and orientation, laboratory experiences in UNA and/or in other academic institutions, computer-based learning activities and social integration experiences. The programming model of the module is based, fundamentally, on the hypothesis that the lesser the degree of subjectivity in the determination of the content and processes of learning/teaching, the greater the probability of attaining a higher learning rate. In other words, technology is incorporated into the design in order to obtain a highly structured material which permits efficient self-instruction.

Modules would use the results of investigation and educational theories adapted to the Venezuelan situation, in order to guarantee the integral development of the student. The modules would take into account the student's adulthood and his potential for contributing to the qualitative social change that the Nation demands.

The structure of the module is very simple and is composed of the following components:

1. **Module title** and code identification
2. **A Listing of Related Modules** - that comprise an entire course of instruction.
3. **Module Introduction** - consisting of a brief explanation of the contents of the module, its importance, and its relation to the other modules in the course.
4. **A Listing of the Units Within the Module** - providing the student with a perspective of the time and effort needed for appropriate study of the module.
5. **Identification of Other Media That the Student Can Use** - this may include descriptions of educational counseling, group learning experiences, radio and television programs, bibliographic material, experimentation equipment, apprenticeships and other media to re-enforce the content of the printed units and to assist in the integration of objectives.
6. **The Timetable** - a basic instrument to show the student the distribution of the assigned tasks with regards to the time that will be needed in order to be successfully carried out. It is a vital instrument by which the student can be better oriented within the study process, showing him the necessary adjustments in his rhythm of learning and possibilities of recuperation of certain lags in the proposed program.
7. **The Units** - each unit to be preceded by a self-evaluation with its correction key and instructions for the student.
8. **An Introduction** - containing the presentations of the theme, motivation for the student, and the objectives (specified as a set of "behaviors") that the student is expected to attain by the end of the unit.
9. **The Contents** - presented through the units of information required for the achievement of the objectives.
10. **The Guide/Test** - a self-evaluation to provide the student the opportunity to perceive his basic knowledge, the most difficult objectives to attain, and the aspects that will be necessary to put emphasis upon in his learning process.
11. **The Development of the Contents** - the most extensive part of the Unit. It contains a full pedagogical development of the instruction with a close relationship to the objectives and with the utilization of teaching strategies established in the instructional design.
12. **The Final Test of the Unit** - permits the student to demonstrate his learning accomplishment with respect to the objectives.
13. **Remedial Instruction** - suggested activities that can be carried out by the student in order to resolve any learning deficiencies and/or to re-enforce the objectives of the Unit.
14. **The Final Test of the Module** - a summative evaluation of the module; it is applied as a face-to-face test by the University and contains all the elements considered necessary to judge the attainment of the objectives.

**Other Instructional Media** Besides the learning modules, UNA would offer other media to assist students in their learning experiences. Radio and TV programs would provide other learning elements not possible through the written materials, such as practice and demonstrations, as a re-enforcement of the existing instructional plan. It is not a simple structuring of classes by radio and/or television, but rather providing the student with other learning elements to attain the objectives more completely.

Radio and TV programs would be produced by "instructional design units", like the ones used for written materials. These units would include a content specialist, an instructional designer and an audiovisual expert who decide on the characteristics of the instructional material to be developed.

214

Radio programs, as well as television, are systematically broadcast. Before the broadcasts the student receives print materials related to the programs so that he may prepare himself and obtain greater benefit from the broadcasts.

These materials are also available to UNA students at Local Learning Resources Centers where the student is able to hear the radio recordings, complement them with visual material, or repeat the transmission recorded on video cassettes

**The Local Centers**  Local Centers are important elements in the delivery of the whole instructional process. Students attend Local Centers trying to solve a variety of problems and needs, which range from administrative to personal and instructional. Local Centers are found in each of the 22 states of Venezuela and, depending on the geographical size of the state, there may also be Support Units which link to the Center.

There are Learning Resources at every Local Center which provides a library service including books, reading guides, copies of special chapters (pointed out in the module and/or unit), complementary books, microfilms, etc. The student can also receive help in identifying audio-visual materials that exist in the Local Center that will specifically re-enforce his learning as well as other materials that can be used to sum up concepts or deepen knowledge.

In general, the Local Centers have the installations and comforts necessary to lend logistical support and counseling to the UNA student in each phase of his instruction. At the same time, the Local Center is where the student receives the media with which he will carry out activities that require the development of skills. Local Centers are administered by a Coordinator who acts according to institutional prescriptions.

**Group Learning Experiences**  An element which receives special attention in the instructional design of UNA is the necessity to interact, not only with instructional materials, but with faculty in the Local Centers as well other students. Among the means that assure the creation of situations that will be rich in possibilities for socialization and are most adequate for a distance education situation are group learning experiences. The group learning experiences give important benefits, as much from the student's point of view as from UNA's.

The principal advantages these group activities offer to the student are:

> -organized opportunities of great significance in the attainment of an integration of knowledge.
> - student support in their leaning process, so that he does not feel alone, a crucial problem in distance education, and develops a sense of belonging with the institution and fellow students.
> - an increased probability of remaining in the system and within a learning rhythm because of the external influence of collaboration on the task of acquiring knowledge and systematic work habits. This substitutes for the continuous re-enforcement the student receives in a formal face-to-face education setting.
> - a defined and set contact with a Local Center for receiving information about the University, clarification of doubts, and knowledge of the facilities available to him.

From the point of view of UNA, the existence of the group learning experiences provide for the ongoing supervision of the development of learning, and eventually, the opportune application of corrective measures. They also significantly increases the opportunity for student socialization and for his interaction with the Institution.

## Part II - The Reality and the Challenges of the Open University of Venezuela[2]

## After the First Twenty-Five Years

The Universidad Nacional Abierta started in 1978 with seventeen thousand of students. By 1985 it was growing at a rate of 8% per year (Chacon, 1990). Today, UNA has approximately forty thousand students.

UNA had a number of problems right from the very beginning. Romero (1994) describes these as serious implementation problems. First, there was a rush to get the University up and functioning as quickly as possible. UNA immediately started registering students rather than providing enough time for the appropriate development and reproduction of most instructional materials, In addition, the instructional design model was incomplete and not fully designed.

At that time, UNA had to work hard for its credibility among the other Venezuelan higher education institutions. This was primarily due to UNA's unique approach to education whereby teaching was conducted through alternative means and without the need for face-to-face interaction. The other universities and potential employers questioned the quality of the human resources that would be used and their ability for providing a high quality of education.

However, the target population of learners was excited with the opportunity to study at an institution where they could enroll and complete their studies without the typical constraints found at traditional universities.

## Major Policies, Goals and Objectives

UNA's major policies, goals and objectives have remained as they were originally envisioned in the initial Project Paper. These original policies, goals and objectives continue to influence most all of the institutional decisions - education has been guided by open access for all people, the curriculum has been open to all types of educational innovation, and the experiences of UNA are now recognized by the other Venezuelan higher education institutions and often copied by other universities. And most importantly, UNA actions are lead by societal needs.

### Economics

One particularly difficult area for UNA has been economics. The dream of lowered costs as a result of an efficient and effective system of mass education has yet to be realized (Barrios, 1999). This has been partly a function of the general economic situation of Venezuela and also the relative value that the government places on UNA when compared to other institutions of higher education. UNA's current student enrollment, forty thousand students, is ten times the size of the next largest national

---

[2] It should be noted that the critical reflections and analysis that are presented in this section are based on the author's own experience and do not represent any official position of the Universidad Nacional Abierta.

university, Yet, the UNA budget is but a tenth of the amount of that institution. When viewed another way, we find that the UNA budget has only increased ten percent from that which was first appropriated.

This situation has led to the extremely careful administration of resources which at times forces a sacrifice of quality instruction. As a consequence, UNA's instructional system cannot be as updated as desired, more modern means of communication - essential for an open university - are slow to be adopted, and the number of faculty, currently about 900, is insufficient to serve the large number of students.

## Commitment to Students

Consistent with the original plan, UNA is committed to guaranteeing nationwide higher education opportunity. UNA still has its twenty Local Centers, and support units have been created to reach those students located in places far away from the Centers. The curricular offering still remains as originally conceived with students able to obtain degrees in Education (Pre-school, Learning Disabilities, Math, and Basic Education), Engineering (Systems and Industrial Engineering), Administration and Accounting, and Math (Analysis and Probabilistic). And, agreements have been made with other higher education institutions so that it is possible for students to transfer credits and complete their studies at UNA.

Though UNA was originally planned to serve mainly adult/non-traditional students, Tugues (1998) reports that the number of students who are working at a job while taking classes at UNA has decreased. Though the median age of the student body remains high, 31 years, the number of young non-working students has continued to increase. Leal (2000) studied the characteristics of UNA students and found that they are most likely to have cognitive limitations, are lacking in abilities to successfully participate in independent study, have low motivation to remain at UNA and complete their studies, lack appropriate time for studying, have difficulty in being self-directed learners, exhibit interaction problems, have feelings of isolation, and instructional problems.

Research on the assertiveness of UNA students shows that those who obtain better grades tend to remain in the system. And, those who do not obtain good grades tend to quit (Chacón, 1990). It is also evident that an essential course for most students, one that strongly relates to later student success at UNA, is the Introductory Course. This course serves to help students learn to effectively plan their academic program and the amount of time that must be devoted to studying.

Completion rates at UNA, as can be expected, are low. Currently about 14% of those who begin their professional studies at UNA actually complete their degree (Contasti, 2000). The greatest percentage of students at UNA are majoring in the field of education, followed by administration and then engineering, with math being the smallest major. Completion rates follow a similar pattern with education being the highest.

## Systems Approach

An important characteristic of UNA is the organization and operation of the institution as a systems approach whereby communication is the key element in the system. This demands viable communication between the various elements of the system that support the development and delivery of the curriculum.

Planning, instructional design, production, distribution, tutoring and evaluation are all components of the distance education system and must function in a coordinated manner. In actual practice, it has been very difficult to balance all aspects of the system so that the various components operate in harmony and are mutually supportive of each other. The processes do not flow as they should. Chacón's (1990) research suggests that the lack of a coordinated systems approach to support distance education is not a problem unique to the curriculum of UNA but exists in other locations. Most Latin American distance education universities do not have such coordinated systems; those who write courses rarely teach them, tutors rarely participate in the elaboration of a course or instructional media, and the author of a course neither corrects exams, nor helps students with their difficulties.

Communication among program deans, the faculty who organize the instruction (all of whom are located in Caracas), the faculty at the Local Centers (who are spread all over the nation), between students and faculty at the national level, and among students does not flow easily. Even in today's world of high speed electronic communication the communication process within UNA relies mainly on written communication and respect for traditional organizational channels must be maintained. This greatly contributes to a process which is complicated and extremely bureaucratic (Barrios, 1999).

## Curriculum Implementation

Further curriculum problems in the early years of UNA included the long time period needed for the development of instructional materials. At the beginning, self-instructional texts were designed and only 30% had audiovisual materials to complement them. State broadcasting systems became difficult, asystematic, and in some cases the coverage of the broadcasting system was not wide enough. Computer-based instruction was scarce at UNA's beginning. Today it is implemented mainly due to of the interest of the tutor and not as an institutional activity planned in the curriculum. Thus, administering learning processes in times of rapid changes and growth of knowledge is not easy for an institution that works on scarce resources.

The learning-evaluation process has always been a great challenge at UNA. Most courses use tests and assignments to measure outcomes and this is done through written tests which students must take in face-to-face situations, like traditional education. Questions continue to be raised regarding the validity and reliability of these means. Further, the ability of UNA to produce, reproduce and distribute tests to effectively measure student learning is not well functioning. Yet, and just like other distance education institutions, no alternative procedure has been found to evaluate learning.

## Faculty

The tasks of tutoring at a distance have been studied by Bermúdez (in Chacón 1990). Bermúdez describes four main functions performed by the teacher/tutor as 1) clearing learner doubts, 2) guiding students in the use of complementary media, 3) correcting exams and assignments, and 4) counseling. If we look at the day-to-day experience of UNA it is easy to observe that tutors do not receive any systematic training to perform these tasks. The need to have effective tutor training programs for these four functions is paramount especially when considered in terms of the unique skills needed when teaching at a different location than that of the learners and working with a heterogeneous nationwide population.

Studies that have examined the relationship between teaching effectiveness and the number of students

218

per tutor show that in distance education, as well as in traditional systems, learning results improve if the teacher-student ratio is low (Chacón, 1990). However, data from UNA's Programming Office reveals that the number of students per professor was and still is extremely high. This problem became apparent when UNA's student population started to grow yet the number of faculty remained static. In addition, the average professor at UNA is responsible for teaching and evaluating from five to eight courses, all of them related to their professional background but with different content.

## Major Challenges Yet To Be Faced

It is obvious that UNA requires a revision of its organizational model, using a less bureaucratized model, led by technological alliances with other institutions which can serve to empower UNA's action.

UNA's curricular model must be analyzed in terms of a new educational paradigm for teaching at a distance. There must be more attention paid to moving from self-instruction to collaborative learning (Tancredi, 2001). Instructional materials must be improved to better serve the diverse needs of a heterogeneous population. Updating these systems is a challenge, especially at this time when knowledge becomes so vast and changes emerge faster than actions designed to adjust to them. New technologies must be used to reach students in different and more efficient ways that are clearly reflective of the societal context.

It has become very clear that there exists an important and essential role for systematic research of all educational processes at UNA. Systematic research is needed to better identify student characteristics, needs, and instructional problems; the quality and efficiency of the many instructional processes; a profile of the type of professor best suited to serve UNA and its students; follow-up on the value of the UNA experience to UNA's alumni; and market and societal needs.

UNA must not compromise the quality of the teaching that is provided. An aggressive process for teacher development must be implemented so that needed tutor/teacher skills are developed and updated constantly. More efficient ways to deliver instruction must be found in order to increase the probability that the mass education offered by UNA is of the highest quality.

An intranet system should be developed to facilitate communications among Local Centers, integrate the faculty who are dispersed so widely, empower the use of existing resources and develop new media. It has also become evident that UNA must become more capable of linking to a global system of communication.

Curricular designs must be revised to make them more flexible so that UNA may respond more immediately and efficiently to emerging market needs. Extension education and continuing education programs must be developed as a major vehicle for offering flexible programming.

After twenty-five years of experience it has become clear that there exists many problems that must continue to be dealt with. However, UNA reaches out further each year and continues to gain strength and appears very capable of reaching its goals. Each year there is less and less doubt in people's minds regarding the potential of distance education systems. With the advent of new instructional technologies the idea of distance education as a viable form of learning, as opposed to face-to-face instruction, becomes more apparent. The potential for professors and students to substantively interact, even when separated in location and time, has been greatly enhanced as the availability of new technology improves. The power of those who control "information" and the "means" for delivering the information has decreased to the point where it is now becoming possible for a learner to go as far as he wants.

UNA should be proud of its achievements which have been accomplished under the most difficult of conditions. It is never easy to be one of the first to move into uncharted new areas. This has been the challenge for UNA and it has succeeded far more than could have been expected with the constraints that have existed throughout the first twenty-five years. UNA is poised today to meet the new challenges that lie ahead and to work to improve the pioneering system that it has established.

It has become apparent that the first twenty-five years have been used by UNA to establish a distance education presence for Venezuela. The challenge during the next period of time will be one of transition and the emergence of different perspectives. It will be essential that new initiatives be mounted, that new ideas be tried and that it all be accomplished with the speed that is demanded in today's world.

## References

Barrios, H. (1999). *El aporte posible de la mediática a la educación a distancia: El caso de la Universidad Nacional Abierta.* Informe de Investigaciones Educativas. Volumen 1 y 2, pp. 85-101.

Chacón, F. (1990). *Universidades Latinoamericanas a distancia: Una comparación de procesos y resultados.* International Council for Distance Education. Fondo Editorial Universidad Nacional Abierta, 134-140.

Contasti, M. (2000). *Evaluación Institucional. Rendimiento graduacional de las cohortes anuales de la UNA (1979-1998).* Informe de Investigaciones Educativas. Dirección de Investigaciones y Postgrado de la Universidad Nacional Abierta. Volumen XIV, N° 1 y 2, pp.11-23 .

Leal, N. (2000). *El mundo interior del estudiante UNA (aportes para la comprensión del marco fenoménico del estudiante a distancia, sus percepciones, expectativas y dificultades).* UNA Documenta. Universidad Nacional Abierta. Año 14. Volumen 1, pp.49-65.

Romero, Y. M. (1994). *La Instrucción como Unica Esperanza.* UNA Opinión. Volumen 13. N° 1, pp.62-67.

Tancredi, B. (2001). *Retos y posibilidades de la UNA en tiempos de transición.* UNA Documenta. Universidad Nacional Abierta. Volumen 1-2, Caracas, enero-diciembre.

*The National Open University of Venezuela. Project.(1979)* Registro de Publicaciones de la Universidad Nacional Abierta. First English Edition

Tugues de T, J. (1998). *El Perfil del Estudiante de Pregrado en la UNA.* UNA Opinión. Volumen 14, pp.21-25.

# Chapter 23

# The Challenges Facing Distance Education in Southern Africa

## Stanley Mpofu

## Introduction

Distance education has hit the developing nations with a vengeance. The advent of political independence in Africa has been associated with greater educational opportunities for the majority of the people: people who were denied these opportunities before. There is tremendous pressure on governments to provide education to all who want it. However, there is not enough room in educational institutions to accommodate all who clamor for educational opportunities. Distance education is seen as the means to accommodate the ever-increasing demand for education. The last ten years has witnessed a rush for distance education by most African societies. However, in most cases the rush for distance education has been headlong. Large numbers of students have been enrolled before the procurement of the necessary resources.

This chapter examines the challenges facing the provision of distance education in selected African institutions and the implications thereof.

## The Inevitable Push Toward Quantity of Education and Not Quality of Education

Education is considered a very valuable commodity in Africa. One of the major reasons for the rise of African nationalism that led to the many liberation wars was that colonial education systems favored the European minority. In many cases the African took up arms in an attempt to correct that injustice.

Political independence in Africa became synonymous with education. Politicians from all corners promised more and more education. No politician would live to see a single day in office if he/she did not promise more educational facilities - particularly schools for children. Suddenly each and every child was at school, something that was simply not possible before independence.

Unfortunately, the opening of the flood gates has been, to a large extent, the reason for the downfall of the education system in a number of African countries. Standards have been compromised in the name of quantity. The necessary resources, both human and material, have been in short supply. The pre-independence educational systems were not ready for the overnight influx of students. Although the Ministry of Education in most African nations receives a larger portion of the budget than any other Ministry, the amount still falls short of what is required to run a viable educational system. There was very little planning prior to the opening up of education to all and sundry.

Quality education continues to be a prerogative of the rich and the educated. The children of the elite do not go to public schools that allow all to enter. Instead, they go to private schools that offer quality education at a price that the poor cannot afford. In other words "real education" remains in the hands of those who can afford it. Children of the elite do not attend just any university. They go to better places like Cape Town, Stellenbosch, Witwatersrand, Rhodes in South Africa, and Oxford and Cambridge in the United Kingdom. This puts the children of the poor at a serious disadvantage when they compete for limited job opportunities.

The poor masses of Africa remain the most significant group in African politics. Without the unqualified support of the poor, the current crop of African leaders would have long been voted out of power. To reward the poor for their undying love and thus be seen to be responding to their ever-increasing demand for education, African governments have made education a political issue. Hence education remains the biggest business in all African countries.

## Distance Education As a Viable Alternative to Formal Education

Despite the high demand for formal education, African societies cannot afford it. Apart from the fact that formal education is, to a very large extent, a misfit to the needs of the continent, with thousands remaining unemployed after "completing" it, it is very expensive per person. It has slowly dawned on most African governments that there is a need for an affordable alternative. Distance education offers African societies an opportunity to bring education to all at an affordable price. Accordingly, distance education initiatives have sprung up all over Africa.

Three generations of distance education can be discerned in Southern Africa (Mpofu, 2003). The first generation has been correspondence teaching via a single media where there is no face-to-face interface between the tutor and the students. The second generation of distance education features multi-media, predominantly print, broadcasting and cassettes for teaching. In addition, it features occasional face-to-face tutorials, largely for student support purposes rather than for instructional purposes. Lastly, the third generation features advanced technologies such as telecommunications, computer networking, and audio and video conferencing. Tutorials, particularly through video and computer conferencing, are regular features of the third generation of distance education.

## Three Generations of Distance Education

| First Generation | Correspondence Teaching using Single Media |
|---|---|
| Second Generation | Multi-media Teaching using Print, Broadcasting and Cassettes |
| Third Generation | Advanced Technological Teaching using Telecommunications, Computer Networking & Audio/Video Conferencing |

The practice of distance education in Southern Africa has barely entered the second generation of distance education (Mpofu, 2003). In this regard, distance education institutions are no more than large correspondence colleges. Students are provided with a set of readings and assignments. Using the readings, and very little else, students do the assignments and submit them for marking. Tutors mark the assignments and return them to the students. There is very little human interface between the tutors and the learners.

Four distinct categories of distance education institutions can be distinguished in Southern Africa. Each category represents a different approach to distance education and reflects the organization and history of the institution in which it is practiced.

**Categories of Distance Education Institutions**

| Category 1 | Programs Available Only Via Distance Education | University of South Africa (UNISA) |
|---|---|---|
| Category 2 | Distance Education As An Extension of A Conventional University | Center for Continuing Education - University of Botswana |
| Category 3 | Public Correspondence Schools | Namibia College of Open Learning (NAMCOL) |
| Category 4 | Private Colleges Offering Distance Education Programs For Specific Audiences | Central Africa Correspondence College (CACC) |

Firstly, there is the university whose programs are available only through distance education. A notable example is the University of South Africa (UNISA), which has never been anything else but a distance education institution. Founded in 1946, UNISA offers, through distance education, virtually all the programs that you would find in a conventional university. With more than 150,000 distance education students all over Africa (University of South Africa, 2003), UNISA is perhaps the largest correspondence school in Africa. Secondly, there is the distance education unit that is an extension of a conventional university. The task of this unit is to externalize the conventional university's programs. In other words, the unit offers, through distance education, programs that are already available on a face-to-face basis. Notable examples include the Center for Continuing Education at the University of Botswana and the Center for External Studies at the University of Namibia. These two units offer, through distance education, some of the programs that are offered on a full-time basis by their respective universities. The contents of a particular degree program are the same irrespective of the mode of delivery. For example, the Department of Adult and Non-formal Education (DANFE) at the University of Namibia offers a full-time Diploma in Adult Education and Community Development with a current enrolment of 330 students (University of Namibia, 2003). In addition, DANFE offers, through the Center for External Studies (CES), the same Diploma to about 500 students, through distance education. The teachers of the full-time program are the same "teachers" for the distance education program. For the majority of courses, the full-time tutors are the ones who wrote the modules that are used by the distance education students. They are the ones who meet with the distance education students twice a year for a week in each case for face-to-face "instruction". And, of course, they are also the same tutors who set and mark assignments, tests, and examinations.

In terms of student numbers, the distance education units of conventional universities are just as big as the conventional universities they are appended to. For example, the University of Namibia has a current enrolment of about 8000 students, about half of whom are enrolled through the CES. The third category of distance education institutions consists of public correspondence schools whose major purpose is to enable formal school dropouts to complete high school. The Namibia College of Open Learning (NAMCOL) and the Botswana College of Distance and Open Leaning (BOCODOL) are notable examples of government initiatives that offer "failures" of the school system an opportunity to complete high school through distance education. With an enrollment of over 20,000[3] students nationwide, these initiatives serve to keep alive the dreams of many school dropouts who would otherwise be condemned to a life of poverty.

---

[3] This figure has been estimated from the reports presented by NAMCOL and BOCODOL to the DEASA meeting held at UNISA, Pretoria, South Africa on October 5, 2003.

Lastly, the fourth category of distance education institutions is made up of private colleges that offer distance education programs at any level of study to whoever is interested. The Central Africa Correspondence College (CACC), the International Correspondence Schools (ICS) and the Damelin Group of Colleges are notable examples in this regard.

Together with UNISA, this fourth category of distance education institutions have been providing correspondence education for several decades. As such, they cannot be seen in the same light as the newcomers, the Category 2 institutions, which have come into being in recent years in direct response to the public demand for learning spaces. The way these latter day correspondence colleges, particularly universities, have jumped onto the distance education bandwagon has led to extreme frustration for both students and tutors. Most of these programs have been implemented without adequate preparation. And, many are destined to collapse before long due to the fact that they came into being for the wrong reasons such as financial pressure.

## A Creative Use of Distance Education to Meet Contemporary Problems of Southern Africa

A recent study conducted under the auspices of the Ministry of Health and Social Services in Namibia suggests that in some regions the majority of schools may grind to a halt due to the loss of teachers to HIV/AIDS (National Aids Coordination Program, 2002). The Ministry is considering several strategies that could ensure that this does not happen. One such strategy will involve shortening the period of teacher training so that teachers can be deployed sooner than is the case now. Alternatively, teachers can be trained through distance education.

One of the schemes under consideration is similar to what occurred in Zimbabwe in the early eighties. At that time Zimbabwe adopted a distance education teacher-training scheme. The scheme was entitled Zimbabwe Integrated Teacher Education College (ZINTEC) and recruited school leavers for teacher training. Recruits spent the first term, 3 months, of their three-year training program at a teacher college. After that they were immediately deployed as trainee teachers in various parts of the country. While working as trainee teachers they continued their studies with their respective teacher college through distance education. They did assignments and tests at their places of work, and their progress was monitored by their tutors who visited them at their respective schools. They came back to the college for the last 3-month term.

The ZINTEC scheme was designed to address the shortage of teachers that occurred immediately after independence due to the expansion of the education system. The ZINTEC colleges have now been converted into conventional teacher training colleges, because the teacher shortage no longer exists. However, the effects of HIV/AIDS may see the return of the ZINTEC scheme. A scheme like this allows for the placement of trainee teachers in actual classroom settings where they are able to provide service while, at the same time, they are working toward the development of further competencies. The ZINTEC distance education program ensured that schools were adequately staffed at all times.

Something like the ZINTEC scheme could go a long way in mitigating the teacher shortages due to HIV/AIDS in schools in Southern Africa where the effects of the epidemic have reached alarming proportions. The technology used by the ZINTEC scheme was very simple. Printed material and occasional visits by tutors were very effective in preparing teachers for their profession.

# The Dilemma of Distance Education

Distance education has become the buzzword in educational circles in Southern Africa. However, the rhetoric has **not** been accompanied by the allocation of the necessary resources. Distance education has become a way of increasing enrollment at conventional institutions that simply do not have space to accommodate everyone who would like or need a university education.

In a number of instances distance education came into being due to the need to increase enrollment in higher education. Most universities, for example, need to enroll a certain number of students per year to qualify for government grants. Without the distance education units, most universities would simply not be able to qualify for the grants. Distance education has become a way of meeting that requirement. However, there has been very little preparation for distance education. Distance education continues to be an appendage at most conventional universities. Despite the even split in student enrollment between the conventional and the distance education sections, the latter plays a secondary role to the former in respect to resource allocation. Distance education programs do not receive an appropriate percentage of the available funds.

The push toward distance education in Southern Africa has been guided by a philosophy of "enroll them now, and teach them later." It has been too easy to enroll students at a distance since there is not an immediate need for classrooms, tutors or reading materials. As such, hundreds of students have been enrolled without the necessary resources to support an appropriate learning experience. The attitude seems to be, "We will cross that bridge when the students come for face-to-face instruction, later in the semester." This approach has been disastrous. Lecture rooms are not big enough to accommodate the large numbers that eventually come to campus for distance education programs. Lecturers, most of whom are part-timers, are not always available to tutor during the university vacation - the primary times during which distance education students are invited for face-to-face instruction. Course modules are simply not available when the students report for the "vacation school", as it is referred to.

On average, it takes 18 months to produce a single distance education instructional module. Three instructional modules are required for each course. The academic year for distance education programs is 18 months long. This means that distance education students who are enrolled for a course before a writer has been engaged for that course, and there are many such instances, can finish the course before the first of three modules is produced. This has indeed been the case for a number of courses at the University of Namibia (UNAM) (Center for External Studies, 2003). This immediately brings forward the question, "How then does teaching occur in distance education?" Tutors are forced by circumstance to teach distance education students, in two weeks, what they teach conventional students in a year.

At UNAM the vacation school happens during the April and August short vacations when full-time students are on holiday. These meetings are meant to enable the tutor to clarify issues that students do not understand in the distance education instructional module. However, in practice, the tutor is often required to teach as much content as possible since the distance education module, in most cases, was not available. Even in cases where the module exists, the tutor is expected to go through the module if he/she can. Anything else is considered unsatisfactory. Students have often complained about those tutors who do not use their allotted time slots to teach.

In cases where the module is non-existent, the teacher is forced to make available to distance education students, in one way or another, the notes that are available to the conventional students.

The result is the wholesale photocopying of large amounts of material from books. In some cases the students are also given recorded lectures from the tutors. In this way distance education students get on tape or CD what the conventional students get face-to-face.

## Distance Education Techniques

To make up for the obvious shortfall in face-to-face instruction, several techniques have been put in place for distance education students.  These techniques include the study group, telephone and video conferencing.

**Techniques to Help Support**
**Distance Education Students**

| | |
|---|---|
| Study Group | Face-to-face student meetings on a regional basis – facilitated by a local tutor |
| Telephone Conferencing | Group meetings at local university center connected to main campus via speaker phone – facilitated by tutor on main campus |
| Video Conferencing | Two way interactive video links at satellite campuses – facilitated by tutor on main campus |

The study group is a very important feature of distance education in Southern Africa. Students who live in one region or district are encouraged to meet occasionally at a central place. The study group meeting is normally facilitated by a local tutor who has been hired for that purpose. This could be a local school teacher or some other local professional who holds a college degree. Naturally, it is not always easy to match the expertise of the tutor with the subject at hand. In most cases there is a single tutor for all courses. Due to the mismatch between the expertise of the tutor and the subject matter, the study group phenomenon can be a source of frustration for both tutors and students. Several study groups have dissolved when  students, who view them as a  waste of time and resources, stop attending.

Telephone conferencing is a useful distance education delivery tool in the Southern African region. Occasionally, learners who reside in a particular district are asked to assemble at a local university center, operated by a major university, to participate via speakerphone.  The tutor, located at the main campus, interacts with them on the speakerphone. Though the purpose of telephone conferencing is usually to answer students' questions, in practice, the students usually agree on a topic and then ask the tutor to explain that topic.

Video conferencing is slowly becoming a major feature of distance education in the region. Universities operate satellite campuses/stations at a number of distant locations.   For example, UNAM has a satellite campus nearly 800 kilometers away. The student, instead of automatically coming to the main campus for the vacation school, reports to whichever campus is nearer to where he/she lives  - the main campus or a satellite campus. The tutor then teaches the students in front of him/her at the main campus and at the same time, through the use of video conferencing also teaches those at the other campuses. Of course, this arrangement is not as smooth as it sounds.  Since most students have not had access to any reading material prior to the video conference, it is difficult to get consensus on what to talk about in the given two hour period. The current trend seems to be to separate the two groups – those on campus and those at the satellite center – and to meet separately with each group.

## The Paradox of Technology in Distance Education

Although advanced technology is slowly becoming an important feature of distance education in Africa, it remains the single most significant handicap of distance education in the continent. Today's distance education thrives on high technology. However, a number of things mitigate against the use of high technology in the provision of distance education in Africa. First, developing nations, which includes all African countries, are significantly lacking in "high technology". That seems most logical since the historic view of the difference between nations of the "first world" and "third world" is based on technology. Developing countries were called third world countries because they were using old or backward technology. And, of course, most still do.

A second block to the use of advanced technology in Southern Africa is that most "high technology" runs on electrical power - a rare commodity among the people who need distance education the most. Thirdly, computer technology, which is undoubtedly the key to the future provision of distance education worldwide, is still in its infancy in the developing world. It goes without saying that there is a gross shortage of personal computers for students at most African universities. For example, the last time I counted there were about 20 personal computers in the UNAM Library for the 8000 students, and half of them were not working. In order for a student to use a computer it must be booked in advance and often a student may have to wait a week or more to use one. The majority, simply do not bother booking them. If they have to use a computer they seek the services of people who work with computers, such as secretaries, and pay a fee for the service. If this is the situation for full-time students at a modern university in the capital city, you can imagine the situation for distance education students, the majority of whom reside in the rural areas.

And finally, high technology is still a novelty to many. For this reason, most high-tech media devices are likely to be distractions to teaching and learning. The technology is so powerful that it, not the content of the instruction, demands the attention of the student. As Marshal McLuhan (1967) so aptly put it, "the medium is the message". It will be some time before the technology is taken for granted as a necessary means for teaching and learning in distance education. When the technology is the object of appreciation it ceases to become the means to an end. Instead, it becomes the end itself. For example, video conferencing is relatively new in Africa. And, for most it is the object of appreciation and hence a distraction to teaching and learning. At UNAM we use video conferencing to link on-campus students with distance education students at the Northern campus. It takes many weeks before the medium of instruction becomes a normal part of the class and the perplexity which is written all over the faces of the students in front of us and those on the screen begin to relax.

## The Challenge of Distance Education in Southern Africa – Balancing the Use of High and Low Technology

Given the importance of technology in distance education, what then is the way forward for the provision of distance education in African institutions of higher learning? It would be folly to suggest that African countries must continue with or revert to basic technology. It would be equally wrong to suggest that they must discard the old technology, which has stood the test of time, and substitute it with new gadgets that they are not quite ready for widespread use. Developing nations must use what they have available and at the same time begin to appropriately invest in suitable high technology. Where basic technology such as the printed word and the audiotape apply, they must move ahead and use it to its full worth. And where high technology such as computer networking is called for they must invest heavily in it.

Most developing nations find themselves in a cleft in respect to technology. They have discarded "third world" technology before fully understanding how the "first world" technology works. Most do not have the means to acquire first world technology. And those who have the means to acquire it lack the capabilities to maintain and thus sustain it. Julius Nyerere, the first president of Tanzania, once remarked, "we should not get rid of the little corner store, before we build the supermarket". In respect of technology, most African countries destroyed the little corner store before they were prepared to even start building the supermarket. In short, "third world" countries have tried to run before they can walk. In most cases, it is too late to go back to "third world" technology that worked perfectly well and was sustainable.

Earlier this year, I needed a typewriter and was told there was none on campus. When the word processor came into being, typewriters were discarded. The campus is full of broken down computers. And, due to the frequency of breakdowns in the computer system, secretaries spend many days twiddling their thumbs because they have nothing to do. The simple solution is that there should be a match between the adoption of new gadgets and the training of people who will maintain them. Otherwise, the old basic technology that is easy to maintain should not be discarded.

The contention that computers are not suitable for developing nations is a fallacy. To say computers are unsuitable for Africa, for example, is tantamount to suggesting that all these gadgets such as motorcars, guns, and airplanes, all of which seem to be doing very well, are unsuitable for Africa. The computer can do well if there is adequate political will to invest in it. Like the many other gadgets that did not originate from Africa, the computer has been adapted for particular environments. The breakdowns of computer systems and networks have nothing to do with their suitability for Africa. They have more to do with the lack of knowledge and relevant skills on the part of the users and those who have to maintain them. Plus, the shortage of parts and the necessary software is largely due to the lack of the political will on the part of governments to invest in computer technology just as much as they have invested in other things such as military ware.

The major reason why developing societies lack the necessary technology is that they have not become dependent enough on certain technologies to invest in them. In other words, computers are rare commodities in Africa because we have not become dependent enough on computers to invest in them. When we reach that stage we will make sure that there are enough computers and they run perfectly. Until then computers are just a novelty. Without any doubt, simple computer applications like email and PowerPoint, will eventually bring computers to the center of African life. Of course, many of these technologies are addictive. Email makes corresponding so easy. Once you become hooked, it is very difficult to stay away from it. PowerPoint is slowly becoming a necessity to most of us. Few academics would now use an overhead projector for a presentation at an international conference. PowerPoint has become the "in" thing when it comes to presenting at such important gatherings. Anything else looks very shabby. The pressure is on for every one to use PowerPoint. Even those who have yet to adopt the use of computers in their professional life find themselves under pressure to use PowerPoint for their presentations. The need for survival in the academic world has forced many to invest in laptops and other such niceties. Africa will get there, slowly.

Would the availability of computers alleviate problems of distance education arising from the scarcity of high technology? I do not think that technology alone would be a solution without a certain level of sustainability. In places where computers have become a way of life the sudden availability of computers would certainly be a welcome addition to the sustainability of distance education programs. It would, without any doubt, solve some immediate problems. For example, if all the staff members at UNAM would have personal computers in their offices, something that is still a dream here, there would be much greater opportunity for tutors to produce quality modules for distance education.

When I joined the University of Botswana in 1995, there was one common area in the entire university with six personal computers for the use of all University staff. When I left in 1999, my own department had a room set up with computers available for staff use. It is hard to imagine that only four years ago personal computers were not available to all staff members in their offices at the University of Botswana. Today, the University of Botswana has installed a computer in each staff member's office.

Giving personal computers to staff members does not in itself guarantee utilization. Computer phobia is still very much in place in Africa. The gadget is still new to many. The Faculty of Education at UNAM has a policy that gives preference to senior academics when it comes to the distribution of equipment. Accordingly, professors have computers in their offices while junior lecturers have to make the long walk to the Computer Center. Meanwhile, many professors do not know how to use the computers that they have in their offices. They come from the old school where computers did not exist. They simply keep them in their offices as status symbols. And, the juniors who were trained recently in institutions where the computer is a way of life are sitting idle without computers in their offices.

Since computer technology is relatively new in Africa, it will take several decades before distance education can benefit from it. Sophisticated media such as the web and electronic mail are still many generations away in most parts of Africa. For the foreseeable future, distance education in Africa will be dominated by basic technology. However, this is no reason to despair. Distance education must go on with whatever is at our disposal. Computers will eventually become commonplace in Africa, and this will certainly foster a new way of life in Africa. Governments will be forced to invest in them just as they have invested in the other necessities such as the motorcar. Meanwhile, *Aluta Continua*[4] in distance education with printed material, audio tape recorders, and the telephone.

## References

Center for External Studies (2003). *Minutes of the meeting of the board of studies held on April 2, 2003.* Windhoek: Center for External Studies, University of Namibia.

McLuhan, M. & Fiore, Q. (1967). T*he medium is the message: An inventory of effects.* New York: Bantam.

Mpofu, S. (2003). What is wrong with lecturing? A case for - and against lecturing. *DEASA Occasional Papers: An Occasional Journal of the Distance Education Association of Southern Africa,* 1(1).

National Aids Coordination Program (2002). *HIV/AIDS: A sentinel survey.* Windhoek: National Aids Coordination Program, Ministry of Health and Social Services.

---

[4] *Aluta Continua* is Swahili for "the struggle continues".

University of Namibia (2003). *Student's records.* Windhoek: University of Namibia.

University of South Africa (2003). *UNISA Online – Statistics* [Electronic version]. Retrieved October 11, 2003, from http://www.unisa.ac.za/Default.asp?Cmd=ViewContent&ContentID=38

**George H. Axinn** is Professor Emeritus at Michigan State University in the area of International Rural Development. He has directed major institutional development projects in Nepal and Nigeria, served as Executive Director of the Midwest Universities Consortium for International Activities (MUCIA) and headed the Food and Agricultural Organization's (FAO) Nepal program for several years, and later the Regional Office for India and Bhutan. Over the years he has taught many different classes on agricultural extension, on non-formal education, and on International Development. He resides in Arizona and regularly teaches a graduate seminar in Michigan via distance education (especially when there is snow in Michigan!). He is also heavily involved in the care and feeding of homeless people in the Tucson area.

**Tim Brannan** is Assistant Professor, Department of Teacher Education & Professional Development, Central Michigan University, Mt. Pleasant, Michigan. Previously he has held positions as Director, Instructional Technology and Distance Education at Lansing Community College (Michigan) and Director of Staff Training for Michigan State University Extension. His academic and research background is in distance education and online professional development. Tim has been awarded several grants to explore the integration of technology in K-12 curriculum from the Michigan Department of Education.

**Jose Chotguis** is Professor in the Department of Rural Economics and Extension at the Federal University of Parana (Brazil). Prior to joining the university he served as a rural extension agent. Currently he offers classes in agricultural extension to undergraduate and graduate students and serves as Director of the Continuing Education Program that includes distance education graduate courses in Agribusiness, Forest Management, Regional Development, and Natural Resources Management. His distance education program provides a major learning opportunity for both alumni and professionals throughout Brazil, Argentina, Uruguay, Paraguay and Bolivia.

**Marguerite Cotto** is Vice President for Lifelong and Professional Learning at Northwestern Michigan College in Traverse City, Michigan. Previously she directed NMC's University Center - a unique partnership between Northwestern Michigan College and senior universities located throughout Michigan.

**Steve Evans** is Senior Television Producer-Director, Communication and Technology Services, College of Agriculture and Natural Resources at Michigan State University. In addition he is Director of LearnNet - a web-based video on-demand delivery network from Michigan State University Extension.

**Diane Golzynski** in a member of the staff of the Michigan Department of Community Health and a key contributor to the Michigan Nutrition Network, a multidisciplinary, community-based, public-private collaboration to build and strengthen alliances focused on nutrition and physical activity. She has been an academic faculty member at Michigan State University (Dept of Food Science and Human Nutrition) and California State University, Fresno (Dept of Food Science and Nutrition). Her *Food Service 2000* distance education program has become an industry standard for the training of food service employees throughout the United States.

**Kathleen Guy** is a nationally known consultant in the areas of strategic planning and fundraising counsel for nonprofit organizations. She is Executive Director of College Relations and the Foundation at Northwestern Michigan College in Traverse City, Michigan, Past President of the Washington, D.C.-based Council for Resource Development and Founding Partner of the Eaton Cummings Group. In her current role as chair of the National Philanthropy Initiative, she is involved in training community college presidents to increase philanthropy to their colleges. Her academic and research background is in the area of higher education leadership. Having driven the 360-mile weekly round trip from Traverse City to East Lansing, Michigan for six years as a graduate student, she experienced "old school" distance learning and has a special appreciation for the advantages of "new school" distance learning.

**Bernard Gwekwerere** is a Doctoral candidate in the Department of Educational Administration at Michigan State University. Previously he served as an Agricultural Extension Specialist and Training Manager in Zimbabwe. His research interests focus on issues of persistence among online learners. He combines his experience working with adult learners in the developing world and his studies in online learning to research issues of integrating technology and lifelong learning.

**Rory Hoipkemeier** is Director of Life Justice for the Catholic Diocese of Lansing, where she attempts to communicate all the Social Teachings of the Church throughout 95 parishes in the state of Michigan. She is a graduate of Michigan State University in Extension Education, Special and Elementary Education as well as Social Studies. She examined community-based radio stations and their role in providing nonformal education for her Master's thesis. Her educational interests have led her to teaching in Indonesia and Thailand and homeschooling her own children.

**Simone Jonaitis** Simone Jonaitis is the Executive Director for Continuing Education at Grand Valley State University (Michigan). She has spent most of her academic career in the field of Adult and Continuing Education and has taught and directed programs for adult learners both in the States and in Latin America. She is the past president for the Council for Continuing and Higher Education and has been recognized as an Outstanding Continuing Educator by the University Continuing Education Association. Her main interest is enhancing access to higher education and promoting the success of non-traditional learners.

**S. Joseph Levine** is Professor Emeritus of Adult Education/Extension Education at Michigan State University. His academic and research background is in the area of adult learning and he enjoys combining that with his long time interest in radio and technology. He has degrees in music education, guidance and counseling, and curriculum research. His strong interest in distance education was initiated in 1966 when he received a grant from the Library of Congress to develop the *Recorded Aid for Braille Music* – a complete learn-at-home recorded method to assist blind learners in playing a musical instrument. When not designing distance education programs he is usually speaking around the world as an amateur radio operator (W8JRK).

**Stephen D. Lowe** is Professor of Christian Education and Associate Dean of Distributive Learning at Erskine Theological Seminary in South Carolina. He has served in theological distance education for the last ten years both as a faculty member and as an administrator. His interests are in the application of adult learning theory to distance education and spiritual formation in seminary distance education communities.

**Stanley Mpofu** is Professor and Director of the Centre for Continuing Education of the National University of Science and

Technology (Zimbabwe). He has published extensively on many aspects of adult and continuing education, including open and lifelong learning. His professional career began as a faculty member in the Department of Adult Education at the University of Zimbabwe in 1987. He has also worked in the adult education departments of the University of Botswana and the University of Namibia, where he served as head of department from 2001 to 2003. He serves on the "Series Editorial Board" of the Institute for International Cooperation of the German Adult Education Association (IIZ/DVV) which produces books with a strong emphasis on African perspectives of adult education and training.

**Zobeida Ramos** is Professor and head of the Department of Faculty Development at the National Open University (Universidad Nacional Abierta – UNA) of Venezuela. She has a bachelor and graduate degrees in education, and has developed wide experience as a teacher in secondary and higher education in Venezuela, as well as in the design and administration of distance education programs offered by UNA. She has served as Cluster Coordinator for the Instructional Technology & Distance Education (ITDE) Graduate Program in the Fischler Graduate School of Education and Human Services at Nova Southeastern University. Her research interests are in the areas of adult and continuing education, faculty development and curricular and instructional design, especially applied to distance education.

**Diane Sams** has been involved in distance education both as a student and a facilitator. She earned her degree in Human Development from Washington State University's Distance Degree Program, becoming interested in the process as well as the content of the distance education program. Her graduate studies include the online Master of Distance Education program at the University of Maryland University College (UMUC), with an emphasis on student support and motivation. She is an exam administrator for UMUC distance education exams and a volunteer member of the family readiness team at a US Air Force family support center.

**Ryan Shaltry** has been involved with many areas that support the technical side of distance education and online communities. He is an experienced Internet developer, systems administrator, and technology aficionado. Currently he is a systems engineer for a major communications company. Ryan also independently operates a successful online community, allMSU.com, which is specifically designed for Michigan State University students and serves over 65% of the MSU student population.

**Lyn Smith** is an Educational Designer/Senior Lecturer for the Faculty of Education, University of Auckland. Since 1995 Lyn has been involved in the development of distance Teacher Education programs in New Zealand and her passion for high quality interaction in e-learning has stemmed from this work. A 2004/5 fellowship allowed her to travel in New Zealand and overseas to study issues related to the design and evaluation of e-learning environments. Some consultancy projects have grown out of this work, including advisory work with Australasian organizations and tertiary institutions, and the further development of national e-learning professional networks.

**Gary Teja** has been involved in leadership development at-a-distance in the U.S. and Latin America for the past 30 years, most recently through Christian Reformed Home Missions, Grand Rapids, Michigan. He also is director of an online Master's program at Calvin Seminary and adjunct professor at Reformed Bible College. His hobbies (and therapy) are antiquing and restoring a turn-of-the-century Victorian home in downtown Holland, Michigan.

**Laura Trombley** is the Extended Education Representative for the Southwest Region of Michigan State University Extension. Her graduate studies have been conducted at a distance from Athabasca Univerity - Canada's leading distance-education and online university - with a focus on instructional design. Her interest in becoming an online student was initially sparked by participation in one of MSU's first distance education courses, conducted via e-mail in 1996.

**Neil VanderVeen** is a Senior Instructional Systems Developer with the Camber Corporation and consults with governmental agencies in the areas of program planning and evaluation with particular emphasis on leadership training. He has previously held positions in training and organization development with The University of Toledo and the State of Michigan in addition to a wide range of consulting clients in the manufacturing sector.

** *** **

Have a comment or a question for an author? Please address your email to the specific author and send it to:

**author@LearnerAssociates.net**

# Index

## A

acceptance, 83, 102, 183
accountable, 31, 80, 91-92, 97
action-reflection, 5
Adobe Acrobat, 197
agenda, 4-6, 9, 67, 69, 70, 129
Albertelli, G., 120
allMSU, 113, 115-119, 121-122
alumni, 31, 35, 180, 219
analysis, 109, 170, 176, 210
Anderson, S., 24, 54, 70, 168, 170
andragogy, 11, 14, 16, 38, 64-66, 70, 87
application, 11, 51, 78, 80, 164, 166, 169, 174, 205, 211, 213, 215
Aslanian, C., 86
assessment, 12, 14, 25-26, 29-30, 34, 43, 45-46, 48, 51, 75, 78, 101, 110, 113, 153, 171, 177
assumptions, 11, 21, 37-38, 63-66, 68, 70, 81, 155
asynchronous, 8, 11, 14, 16, 28, 40, 69, 90, 95-96, 99, 101, 108, 113, 118, 124, 144-146, 173, 204
Atchley, R. C., 68, 70
attitudes, 27, 53, 146, 207, 210-211
attrition, 73-75, 79, 85-87, 129
audio, 6, 12, 40, 124, 157-158, 160, 206, 213, 215, 222, 229

## B

bandwidth, 158, 160, 165, 169
banner ads, 193-194
barriers, 5-6, 18, 79, 153
Barrios, H., 216, 218, 220
Batelle Institute, 153
Beck, E., 74, 86
behaviorism, 11
behaviors, 66, 207, 214
Bell, A. G., 3-4
benchmarks, 26, 28-29, 36
Beyer, H., 162, 170
Biederman, L., 150, 153
Blackboard, 28, 175-177
Blanchard, K. H., 78-79, 86
blended training, 169
Bloom, B., 38, 42, 100-111, 176
bookmark, 175, 192
Botswana College of Distance and Open Leaning, 223
Brickell, H. M., 86
broadcasting, 6, 203, 218, 222
bulletin board, 8, 14, 39, 50, 118, 129, 174, 204
Bunker, E. L., 17, 24

## C

Caffarella, R. S., 9-10
California Virtual University, 26
campaign, 29-32, 34-35, 151
campaign chair, 32
Carnevale, D., 26, 36
Carr, S., 73, 86
Case, P. S., 32, 34, 75, 86
CD, 40-41, 129, 171, 178, 226
Central Africa Correspondence College, 223-224
Chacón, F., 217-218, 220
challenges, 4-5, 25, 70, 76, 162, 166- 167, 183, 220-221
chat, 11, 83, 94, 99, 101, 108, 145, 163, 165, 167-168, 174
class hours, 145
CODEC, 27-28, 41, 51, 157
cognitive domain, 38-39, 192
cohort, 202
collaborative, 39, 79, 110, 116, 219
collaborative learning, 11, 219
colleagues, 143, 175, 187-188, 204
commitment to learning, 124, 133
communication, 4, 6, 11-15, 28, 41, 49, 84, 92, 101, 123, 129, 144, 150-151, 155-156, 160, 163, 165, 176, 178, 190, 201, 206, 212, 217-219
communication skills and preferences, 123
community, 5, 13, 26-27, 30-31, 40, 44, 48-49, 51, 53-54, 65-66, 74, 83, 90, 99-102, 110-111, 116, 118-120, 149, 151, 153, 162-163, 171-172, 174, 180, 209, 213
community college, 149, 151, 171 172, 180
*communiversity*, 153
completion rates, 74, 217
complexity, 4, 8, 28, 37, 68
comprehensive marketing survey, 27
comprehensive needs assessment, 27
computer, 4, 6, 11-12, 14-15, 17, 27-28, 45, 51, 64, 75, 86, 94, 101, 113-114, 126, 129, 130, 133-134, 136, 143, 145, 147, 152, 156-158, 163, 169, 171, 182-185, 188, 197, 205-206, 212-213, 222, 227-229
computer networking, 171, 222, 228
Computer-Assisted Personalized Approach (CAPA), 113, 115-117, 182-184
computer-based, 45, 163, 183-184, 213
computer-delivered instruction, 212
conferencing, 16, 23, 86, 124, 156, 222, 226-227
constructivism, 11
Contasti, M., 217, 220
content-centered, 161
continuing education, 9, 185, 200, 205, 219
Cookson, P., 12, 15, 86
cooperative learning, 163-164, 166-167
copyright, 176
correspondence, 3, 6, 12, 45, 74, 87, 99, 127, 179, 222-224

correspondence education, 12, 224
correspondence schools, 223
correspondence teaching, 222
cost, 5, 27-29, 79, 119, 139, 150-151, 155-159, 161, 169, 188, 210
course management system, 171, 173, 177
course materials, 4, 80, 83, 174
course website, 8, 178, 203
courseware, 28, 34, 168
Covington, B., 28, 36
critical reflection, 5
curriculum, 12, 15, 18, 26, 55, 65, 161, 165, 181-182, 184-186, 212-213, 216-218
curriculum designer, 161
customers, 18

# D

debate groups, 203
delivery medium, 12
delivery of information, 18
democratic society, 209
dependent learner, 38, 81
desktop video conferencing, 156, 158-159
development, 3-4, 6, 14, 18, 26-28, 34-35, 37, 43, 54, 58, 63, 66, 68-69, 76-78, 83-84, 86-87, 89, 99, 102, 105-106, 110, 113, 116, 149, 151-153, 161-163, 165, 169-170, 173, 183-186, 197, 200, 209-219, 224
development officer, 34-35
developmental tasks, 11, 69
dialogue, 8, 13, 23, 39, 40, 50, 90, 96, 106, 117-118, 145
directive, 13, 105
Dirr, P. J., 5, 9
discussion, 14-15, 19, 23, 29, 39, 40-41, 80, 92, 100-101, 103-110, 113-117, 123, 126, 131, 136, 145-147, 168, 171, 173, 204
discussion board, 39, 41, 92, 113-115, 117, 173
distance education, 1, 4-10, 12-13, 15, 17-19, 22-29, 31, 33-41, 43-46, 48-54, 63-70, 73-83, 85-86, 89-91, 94-95, 97, 99-100, 123-133, 135, 137-139, 141, 149-150, 155, 161-172, 176, 178, 186, 193, 199-200, 203, 205-207, 209-211, 215, 217-227, 229
distance education center, 200
distance education program, 12, 15, 20, 22-23, 25-29, 31, 33-35, 37-41, 43-44, 46, 48-54, 67-70, 73-75, 85, 91, 100, 127, 129, 135, 139, 155, 162, 164, 199-200, 205, 207, 223-225, 229
distance education technology, 24, 165, 171
distance learning, 4, 6, 10, 12, 26, 36, 86, 124
distance-bridging technology, 17, 24, 172
Driscoll, M., 70
dropout, 73-74, 129
DVC, 141, 155-158, 160
DVD, 40-41, 56, 126

# E

Eastmond, D. V., 74, 86
economics, 205, 216
educational delivery, 25-26, 34
educational initiative, 5
educational material, 187- 188

educational measurement, 44
educational resource, 52, 187, 198
educational revolution, 209-210
effective distance education, 25, 40
effectiveness, 15, 64, 200, 211, 218
electronic campus, 171, 174
elite, 210, 221
Elliott, B., 75, 86
email, 14, 20, 27, 41, 50, 58, 103, 109, 127-128, 136, 144, 177-178, 188-189, 194-196, 201, 204, 206, 228
emancipatory learning, 67
emoticon, 13
empower, 1, 22, 76, 219
empowering evaluation, 49-50
endowment, 151
Enniskillen Agricultural College, 158
enrollment, 26-27, 73, 76, 81, 87, 154, 172, 178-179, 210, 216, 223, 225
equity of control, 6
Erikson, E., 68, 69, 70
evaluation, 12, 23, 34, 43-55, 68, 146, 163, 168, 176, 212, 214, 217-218
Evans, T., 9
expenses, 28
external funding, 25, 27, 33

# F

face-to-face, 7-8, 13, 17, 18-19, 22, 39, 40, 45-46, 54, 67, 70, 91-93, 96, 99, 103, 113, 125, 127-129, 156, 162-166, 169, 171, 173-174, 177, 179, 199, 205-206, 214-216, 218-219, 222-223, 225-226
face-to-face instruction, 19, 45, 113, 163, 173, 206, 219, 225-226
facilitate, 4-5, 13, 19, 22, 26, 51, 52, 76, 78, 85, 103, 110, 113, 150, 157, 160, 185, 219
facilitating learning, 9
facilitation, 13, 153
facsimile, 3-4
faculty change, 207
faculty pay, 206
faculty training, 27, 176, 179
family relationships, 165
feasibility, 30-31, 159
feasibility study, 30-31
Federal University of Parana, 199-200
feedback, 3, 23, 39, 41, 45, 50, 56, 58, 67, 83, 93, 99-100, 102-104, 109-110, 113-114, 128, 136-137, 144, 159, 164-166, 178, 181-182, 184-185, 188, 197, 206
financial issues, 207
financially supported, 9
firmware, 28
Fjortoft, N. F., 75, 86
flexibility, 45, 69, 95, 139, 144-145, 176
flexible, 14, 33, 67, 95, 97, 153, 171, 219
flexible schedule, 97
formative evaluation, 47-48, 168
Foundation Center, 33
Freire, P., 67, 70, 75, 82, 86
functional, 9, 22
fund raising, 29-31, 34-35
funding, 25, 27, 29, 31, 33, 36, 45, 47, 51, 164, 170, 183

# G

Gagne, R., 55, 69, 70
Garrison, D. R. 49, 54, 63, 70
Gibson, C., 17, 24, 74, 75, 80, 86
Gordon, E., 165, 170
Gould, R. L., 68, 70
graduate student, 143, 182, 187-188, 191-196
grants, 29, 33, 225
Greenfield, J. M., 34, 36
Grobman, H., 47, 55
group discussion, 19, 50, 106, 136
group learning, 214-215
group project, 178
Grow, G. O., 78, 86

# H

Harasim, L., 86
helping adults learn, 16, 64
Hersey, P., 78, 79, 86
hits, 155, 189-191, 194-197
Holtzblatt, K., 162, 170
Holubek, E., 163, 170
home location, 203
home page, 176
home study, 12
homework assignments, 113, 115, 117, 163, 174
Horgan, B., 26, 36
Horton, M., 67, 70
hotlink, 13, 117
Houle, C., 66-67, 70
HTML, 13, 15-16, 87, 120, 176, 187-188
humanism, 13
humanistic psychology, 13
Hülsmann, T., 14, 16
hybrid, 171-173, 175-176, 179
hybrid classes, 171
hyperlink, 13
hypermedia, 13

# I

Illich, I., 198
impacts, 44, 82, 158
implementation, 25, 29, 43, 53, 68, 162, 174, 179, 184, 211, 216
implementation of distance education, 25
independent learner, 77, 93, 101
independent study, 12
infrastructure, 27-29, 36, 150, 156, 174, 210
innovation, 36, 209, 216
inputs, 44, 52, 144-146
Institute for Higher Education Policy, 28, 36
instruction, 5-8, 12-13, 17-22, 27, 37, 41, 68, 70, 75, 79, 87, 94, 103, 124, 143, 160-165, 167, 171, 173, 175-177, 181, 184-185, 196, 199, 200, 202, 206, 209, 211-215, 217-219, 223, 225-227
instructional design, 27-28, 37, 43, 51, 76, 167, 175, 183, 213-217
instructional designer, 28, 37, 43, 51, 175, 213-214
instructional materials, 18, 163, 166, 168, 184, 215-216, 218
instructional media, 160, 218
instructional module, 212, 225
instructional objectives, 157
instructional space, 206
instructional strategies, 5, 8, 66, 168
instructional support, 75, 83, 177
instrumental motives, 66-67
intellectual property, 115
interact with faculty, 205
interacting, 23, 101, 165
interaction, 12, 20-23, 28, 39, 40, 50-51, 64, 67, 76, 79, 91-93, 99-101, 103, 109, 110-111, 124-126, 136, 158, 163, 166-169, 185, 199, 205-206, 212-213, 215-217, 219
interactive, 13, 23, 24, 28, 41, 50-51, 67, 94, 124, 150-153, 155-157, 160, 162, 170, 199-200, 202-206, 212, 226
interactive media, 162
interactive video, 202, 226
International Correspondence Schools, 224
International Council for Correspondence Education (ICCE), 6
Internet, 11-14, 27-29, 41, 75, 124, 126, 134, 141, 143-147, 152, 156-158, 165, 175, 184-187, 190, 196, 204-205
Internet etiquette, 14
Internet Scout Report, 190
Intranet, 201, 203-204
intrinsic motives, 66, 70
ISDN, 28, 156-157
issues, 9-10, 22, 28, 54, 75, 79, 86, 103, 107-108, 115, 162-163, 168-169, 176, 188, 205, 207, 225
Iuppa, N., 162, 170

# J

Johnson D., 163, 170
Johnson T., 163, 170

# K

K-12 schools, 29
Kashy, D. A., 116, 120
Kashy, E., 116, 120
Kasworm, C. E., 78, 79, 86
Kaufman, R., 51-53, 55
Kearsley, G., 12-16
Kellogg Foundation, 150
Kember, D., 74, 78-80, 82-84, 86
Kerka, S., 73, 86
King, A., 163, 170
Knowles, M. S., 11, 38, 42, 64-66, 70-71, 75, 78, 86
Koble, M. A., 17, 24
Kortemeyer, G., 116, 120
Krebs, A., 33, 36

# L

language skills, 144, 146
Lansing Community College, 171-180
Leal, N., 217, 220